16.

→YY

0333 304454 1002

D0120998

MASTERING

COMMERCE

MACMILLAN MASTER SERIES

OTHER BOOKS BY THE SAME AUTHOR

MASTERING

COMMERCE

R. R. PITFIELD
A.C.I.S., M.B.I.M.

MACMILLAN

BASIC

© R. R. Pitfield 1982
© Text-figure illustrations:
The Macmillan Press Ltd 1982

All rights reserved. No reproduction, copy or transmission
of this publication may be made without written permission.

No paragraph of this publication may be reproduced, copied
or transmitted save with written permission or in accordance
with the provisions of the Copyright Act 1956 (as amended),
or under the terms of any licence permitting limited copying
issued by the Copyright Licensing Agency, 33 – 4 Alfred Place,
London WC1E 7DP.

Any person who does any unauthorised act in relation to
this publication may be liable to criminal prosecution and
civil claims for damages.

First edition 1982
Reprinted 1982 (twice), 1983 (3 times), 1985 (twice with
revisions), 1986, 1987, 1988

Published by
MACMILLAN EDUCATION LTD
Houndmills, Basingstoke, Hampshire RG21 2XS
and London
Companies and representatives
throughout the world

Typeset by
Reproduction Drawings Ltd
Sutton, Surrey

Printed in Hong Kong

ISBN 0-333-31288-0 (hard cover)
ISBN 0-333-30445-4 (paper cover — home edition)
ISBN 0-333-31065-9 (paper cover — export edition)

This book is also available under the title
Basic Commerce
published by Macmillan Education.

LEABHARLANNA ATHA CLIATH
CHARLEVILLE MALL LIBRARY
ACC. NO.   0333 304454
COPY NO.   MM 1002
INV. NO.   1394
PRICE IR£   5.52
CLASS   380

CONTENTS

CONTENTS

CONTENTS

CONTENTS

CONTENTS

CONTENTS

ILLUSTRATIONS

ILLUSTRATIONS

PREFACE

This book is written for those who are embarking on a study of commerce. It has particular relevance to basic examinations in the subject, taken in schools and colleges and also offers a knowledge of the structure and function of commerce to those students requiring this for the examinations of professional bodies.

The student of commerce is faced with a somewhat formidable task because of the wide range of the subject. One object of this book is to help the reader by grouping the various aspects in a logical sequence and by providing a 'link' at the beginning of each chapter. Because commerce affects the daily lives of us all, it has been possible to illustrate the subject with practical examples. It is considered that the introduction of some reality into the reading should help the student by making it more interesting.

The exercises at the end of each chapter can be used by the reader to test his assimilation of the text and it can also be used as a form of revision. Many of the exercises require the student to think beyond the strict confines of examination questions so that his understanding and his interest in the subject will be increased.

My thanks are due to those companies and authorities who kindly gave permission to use material which appears in some of the illustrations.

Ronald R. Pedfeld

ACKNOWLEDGEMENTS

The author and publishers wish to thank the companies and organisations for their help and co-operation in granting permission to reproduce copyright work and trademarks.

THE DIVISIONS
OF PRODUCTION

This chapter explains the scope of the book and provides a framework ,for later studies.

Everyone requires a wide range of things in life. Each person who works helps to provide those things. We therefore begin by seeing how human wants are satisfied and, in particular, the part which is played by commerce. You should therefore first look at Figure 1.1 and refer to it again as you read through the chapter.

1.1 PRODUCTION

Production relates to the activities which are necessary in order to satisfy the wants of mankind. These wants are for:
(a) *goods* - that is, tangible things such as food and motor cars: and
(b) *services* - that is, intangibles such as entertainment and medical care.

All goods must begin as gifts of nature because man cannot *create* anything. What he does is to take those things which are provided by nature and *convert* them. For example, man cannot create animals (although he can ·assist nature by scientific breeding). He can, however, convert animals into saleable products such as meat, wool, hides, etc.

We can therefore trace any good back to a natural source. Thus trees provide the source of wooden articles; the many things made of plastic derive from coal and oil; glass comes from sand; steel objects start as iron ore.

The journey from natural product to the completed good is usually a long one and involves the efforts of a considerable number of people. All these are engaged in what is known as *production*: that is, they participate in making goods available. They include those who do not actually

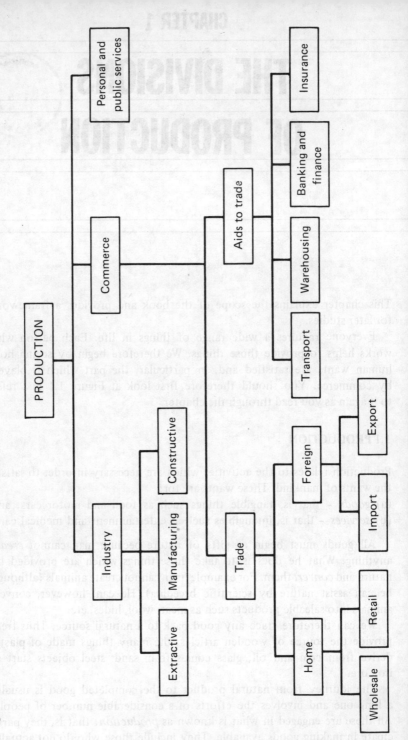

Fig 1.1 *the divisions of production*

make goods but who make production possible. We can therefore analyse production into divisions as shown in Figure 1.1. Before considering the divisions in detail they can first be summarised as follows:

Industry. This relates to *obtaining* natural materials and *converting* them.

Commerce. This relates to all the other activities which are necessary for particular products to reach the buyers in a usable condition.

Personal and public services. These are those activities which make production *in general* possible by providing a social structure in which it can operate.

The relationships of these divisions can be explained if we consider some of those people who are involved before woollen coats can be purchased in English shops. Figure 1.2 gives only a very broad outline of this because there are far more people concerned than can possibly be shown in an illustration.

1.2 INDUSTRY

The coat starts life on the backs on sheep in, say, Australia. A farmer shears the sheep and sends the fleece to an exporter in, say, Sydney. The exporter then sends the fleece from this and other sheep farmers to an importer in England.

Several stages would next be involved because the fleece must be cleaned, combed and spun into yarn. This would then be sold to woollen mill owners, who would weave it into lengths of cloth. The cloth would then be sold to clothing manufacturers, who would make coats from it. These would be sold to wholesalers, who, in turn, would sell them to retailers. So, after a lengthy journey and the efforts of many people, the coats would appear in the shops.

Many of the people involved in the total operation would have been concerned with the *physical* aspects of production: that is, the actual *making* of the coats. *Such people are said to be engaged in industry.* As shown in Figure 1.1, industries are divided into three categories.

The sheep farmer, because he deals with the natural product, is said to be in an *extractive* industry.

Those engaged in converting natural products are either in *manufacturing* industries (such as those in the second illustration) or in *constructive* industries.

Examples of extractive industries: fishing, agriculture, mining, fur-trapping, forestry.

Examples of manufacturing industries: engineering, chemicals, textiles, steel, oil-refining.

Examples of constructive industries: builders of roads, houses, bridges.

Fig 1.2 *the divisions of production in the making of woollen coats*

Sheep farmer		Extractive industry	Primary
Exporter		Commerce	Tertiary
Importer		Commerce	Tertiary
Sundry processing		Manufacturing industry	Secondary
Woollen mill		Manufacturing industry	Secondary
Clothing manufacturer		Manufacturing industry	Secondary
Wholesaler		Commerce	Tertiary
Retailer		Commerce	Tertiary

1.3 COMMERCE

Production, however, requires the services of others than those who actually *make* goods. We have already seen that exporters, importers, wholesalers and retailers were involved in producing the coats but none of those people changed the *physical* aspect of the product. Nevertheless, their services were essential because the coats would never have reached the shops without them.

The same can be said for a considerable number of other people. Thus transport was involved at every stage, starting with the sheep farmer moving his fleece to Sydney. Banks would play a part throughout in providing finance and sundry services. Insurance companies would give cover for all sorts of risks.

All these people would be engaged in *commerce* because they *assist* in the making of the coats. Commerce, then, is a division of production and includes *all those activities which help to bring goods from the makers to the consumers.*

1.4 PERSONAL AND PUBLIC SERVICES

All the functions mentioned above are necessary so that *particular* goods reach the consumers. Other services are also needed, even though they are not specific to any one product. They are required so that production *generally* is possible.

As production takes place within an organised society, it is necessary to ensure that that society is not disrupted. Accordingly, it is necessary to have a legal system and for there to be policemen, firemen and armed forces. There must be a civil service and local government organisations. Similarly, the health of the people must be protected, which means that medical services are required. The provision of recreation and relaxation is also essential, so that professional sportspeople and entertainers of all kinds can be said to play their part in production.

1.5 PRIMARY, SECONDARY AND TERTIARY PRODUCTION

Having considered the divisions of production we can now arrange them in a sequence:

(a) *Primary production* relates to the *extractive* industries: that is, those concerned with obtaining the direct products of nature.
(b) *Secondary production* relates to the industries which convert natural products: that is, the *manufacturing and constructive industries.*
(c) *Tertiary production* relates to *commerce* and *personal* and *public* services.

(See Figure 1.2 for how these divisions relate to the manufacture of coats.)

1.6 THE SCOPE OF COMMERCE

In this book our main concern is with the branches of commerce as they are shown in Figure 1.1. *'Trade' relates to the buying and selling of goods.* The other branches ('aids to trade') refer to supporting services which make trading possible. At this stage the following points must be considered. They serve as a summary of the various aspects of commerce. These are discussed in more detail later in out studies.

(a) The importance of assessing demand

The demand for any good depends upon a number of factors. Unless account is taken of those factors a person intending to sell goods may find he is unable to do so because he has miscalculated the extent of the demand. This may be explained as follows.

A good must be able to satisfy the needs of possible buyers. It is pointless to produce something which no one requires. It is also pointless to produce something when an existing product can satisfy the need more effectively or more cheaply.

The price of the product must be one which those who want it are able to pay. A poor community may have sufficient money to buy only the bare necessities of life, so that no matter how useful the article could be to them they will not be able to afford it. For example, washing up is easier if detergents are used, but those who cannot afford detergents must continue to use less efficient methods. The farther away an article is from being a necessity, the more things there are which have prior claims on a person's money. Those who can afford only necessities or near-necessities cannot buy other goods.

The tastes and habits of consumers sometimes influence demand. Some people will not use certain goods because to do so would be against their religious beliefs or the traditions in which they have been brought up. For example, some races suffer from malnutrition because there is a shortage of the kinds of food they have always eaten but they refuse to eat other foods which are available which would be at least as good for them.

A producer must therefore do all possible to ensure that what he intends to sell at a certain price will be bought by sufficient people to give him a profit. This means he must carry out market research in order to measure the demand accurately. He may also have to *create* demand by advertising.

(b) The part played by wholesalers and retailers

Most goods are produced in large quantities because this reduces the cost of making each item. On the other hand, most purchases are in very small amounts. The clothing manufacturer may make a batch of several hundred coats but they would be purchased as individual items. There must therefore be a point where someone has to reduce the bulk to saleable quantities. Accordingly, there is a need for wholesalers and retailers to come between the producer and the ultimate buyer.

(c) The importance of efficient transport

At various stages of production, goods have to be transferred to points which are convenient for carrying out subsequent operations. The fleece has to be moved from Australia to England because that is where it can be processed. It then has to be transferred to the mills, after which there will be several movements until the coats eventually reach the retail shops, which may be spread across the country. Transport is therefore an essential element.

(d) Each stage must receive its reward

People engage in commerce in order to make a profit or to receive a wage or a fee. Each of the many persons involved in production makes a contribution to its effectiveness and expects to be rewarded for doing so. As the Australian exporter finds a market for the fleece and arranges for its shipment, he hopes to sell to the importer at a price above what he paid the farmer plus his costs. Those who helped by providing professional services (such as accountants, lawyers and advertising agents) would be paid fees. When selling to the next stage each manufacturer would expect to make a profit. Transporters would levy charges. Each of the many employees would be paid a wage.

The price at which the product is sold to the ultimate buyer must therefore include all those rewards.

(e) Production is fuelled by finance

Every stage of production has to be undertaken before the reward due to that stage is received. During that period all the costs of production have to be met, so that the producer has to spend money which he hopes to recoup later. The sheep farmer, for instance, has to bear all the expenses of rearing his sheep, besides having to pay other costs. The same problem exists for the exporter, the clothing manufacturer, the retailer and all those who provide services. There must therefore be facilities whereby finance is available to bridge the gap. This may be provided by investors who put money into a business on the understanding they share in any profits or it may be lent in return for a promise to repay it with interest.

(f) The services provided by banking and insurance

Every business operates with the assistance of banks and insurance companies. The banks help by providing safe custody for cash. The cheque system and other forms of transfer makes it unnecessary to move notes and coin from place to place when receiving or paying money. Banks also provide loans.

The risks of loss by fire, burglary, theft and many other hazards are reduced by taking out insurance. The premiums which are paid for this facility ensure that, remote though the possibility may be, any loss will be met by the insurer. The sheep farmer may insure against a disease killing some of his sheep; the exporter will insure against loss of his shipment at sea; and all the offices and factories will be insured against loss by fire.

1.7 SPECIALISATION OF OCCUPATIONS

We have seen that in order to produce anything the services of a considerable number of people are usually required. It will also be obvious that each person plays a comparatively small part in the total operation. This is because each person specialises in what he does. Perhaps the sheep farmer *could* find his own market for his fleece, but even if that were possible he could not do so efficiently. Instead, he concentrates on what he knows best – raising sheep. The task of finding a market belongs to the exporter – and he does nothing else.

The needs of man are many and varied. It would be impossible for a person to have all the things he requires unless he had the co-operation of others. This can be demonstrated by considering the position of a man who *has* to be entirely self-sufficient. If he is alone on an island, he will have to build a shelter, catch and kill animals, grow and cook food and make clothes. This may be possible if he has the ability to do all those things but, even so, he would certainly work very long hours just to stay alive. If, however, he were joined by other people, his problems would be very much less. The work would be divided so that each person did a different *type* of work, contributing to the total needs of everyone. The result would be that, although more people had to be fed, clothed and sheltered, the personal work-loads would be reduced.

An illustration of this is given in Figure 1.3. The objective is to provide what are essentials in any community – food, shelter and clothing. The aim is to divide the work so that each person does those things for which he is best fitted. The labourer does the heavy work of clearing the ground for the farmer and providing timber for the builder and the toolmaker. The latter provides tools and implements for each of the others specialists. The herdsman and the farmer produce food to be cooked by another specialist. The herdsman also provides wool and skins to make clothes with.

All these processes must be planned and co-ordinated so that the right supplies are available at appropriate times, that some produce is stored and that priorities of work are decided on. This is carried out by the leader of the group, who may therefore be said to be engaged in 'management'.

1.8 THE BENEFITS OF SPECIALISATION

Specialisation of occupation is practised by all forms of society. The benefits of doing so in a primitive community, such as the one discussed above, are the same as those which apply in the most sophisticated of societies. They are as follows.

Fig 1.3 *specialisation of occupation in a small primitive community*

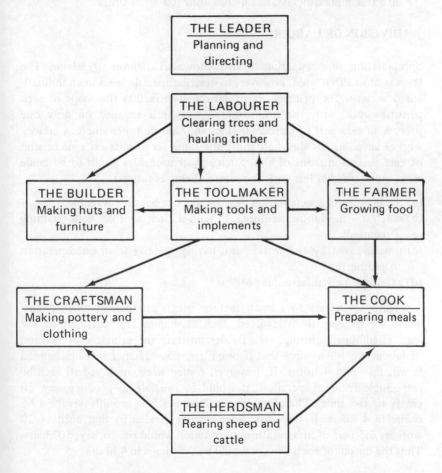

(a) *Each person does that for which he has the most aptitude.* Some people have naturally inventive minds; for others their superiority is in physical strength; some are 'born leaders' and have the ability to organise; others are 'good with their hands'. A person performs best when doing those things at which he is naturally most proficient. For example, the mathematically minded person *likes* figures and is most likely to work in that field.

(b) *Each person concentrates on a narrow range of activity.* Because specialisation focuses a person's activities on a comparatively small area he becomes more expert. The least efficient person is the 'Jack of all trades'. The lone castaway would not be efficient in all the tasks he has to do because he could not concentrate on any one of them.

(c) *Repetition increases efficiency.* Even an inexpert person will usually do a task more quickly after he has done it a lot of times.

1.9 DIVISION OF LABOUR

Specialisation of occupation is also known as *division of labour.* The term is most often, however, used to describe specialisation in an industrialised society. The principle is to narrow even further the scope of each person's work, with the result that a worker is engaged on only one process, or even part of a process. This can result in, for example, a factory worker spending his day tightening the same set of nuts on a succession of cars passing in front of him. Such a system enables goods to be made more quickly and at less cost, the reasons being as follows:

(a) the benefits of specialisation described above become available;

(b) much of the labour required is semi-skilled, so that little training is required;

(c) time is saved by the worker not having to move from one operation to another; and

(d) extensive mechanisation is possible.

Figure 1.4 relates to a small factory which produces wooden chairs. There are six operations involved, such as shaping the seat, turning the legs, assembling, painting, etc. To demonstrate the principle of division of labour we will assume that if one man makes each chair singlehanded it will take him 4 hours. If, however, 6 men were employed to each be responsible for one operation, it would be possible to produce, say, 10 chairs in the time. Therefore, the output per man would average 1.66 chairs in 4 hours. If the work were further divided so that each of 20 workers did *part* of an operation, production would rise to, say, 50 chairs. Thus the output of each worker would be 2.5 chairs in 4 hours.

Fig 1.4 *division of labour in a furniture factory*

SOLE WORKER
DOING ALL
OPERATIONS

PRODUCES 1 CHAIR
IN 4 HOURS

6 WORKERS
DOING 6 SEPARATE
OPERATIONS

PRODUCE 10 CHAIRS
IN 4 HOURS

= 1.66 CHAIRS PER WORKER

20 WORKERS
DOING 20 SEPARATE SUB-OPERATIONS

PRODUCE 50 CHAIRS
IN 4 HOURS

= 2.5 CHAIRS PER WORKER

1.10 MASS PRODUCTION

The circumstances in which division of labour is carried to extremes are those where mass production operates. This is a system aiming to produce an enormous output of goods by using the least possible number of workers. It is achieved by reducing the scope of each worker's activities to the minimum and by the extensive use of machinery.

When motor-cars first became popular it was necessary to produce a huge quantity of them as quickly and as cheaply as possible. Henry Ford developed the 'assembly-line' system whereby the work flowed on a belt from one end of the factory to the other. On the journey each worker performed simple operations, making his contribution to the total, so that at the end of the line finished cars were driven away.

Today the trend is for mechanisation to be extended by *automation*. Instead of people operating machines, many of the machines are electronically controlled to carry out complex operations automatically.

1.11 COMMERCE IS CONCERNED WITH SURPLUSES

In every society each producer creates more than he personally needs. In our study of a primitive community it can be seen that the cook would prepare more meals than he required for himself, the *surplus* meals being those needed by his fellows. In turn, he would enjoy the surpluses provided by the others. In such a society there is no buying and selling, but in more advanced communities the surplus output of one person is *traded* for the surplus output of others. As we have seen, many people do not produce goods at all but provide *services*. Again, these are given in exchange for the surplus production of others.

As a society becomes more sophisticated, so the efficiency of its production increases. For example, fertilisers increase crop yields, and improved mechanisation results in higher output by factories. If a society's surpluses increase, it can afford more and better services, so that the more efficient a society is the higher its standard of living. Because fewer people are required to produce goods when production is highly efficient there are more people available to provide services, e.g. doctors, entertainers, scientists, writers, etc.

Commerce therefore relates to the exchange of surpluses. As the surpluses increases, so will more commercial services be required to exchange and distribute them. It is obviously pointless to produce a large amount of goods unless they can be sold at a profit. As production increases it therefore becomes necessary to seek out new markets and to promote sales by advertising. As markets expand, more and more commercial services are required in order to dispose of the goods. More people are required for moving the goods; more clerical workers are needed; additional specialist services are necessary. It therefore follows that increased commercial activity goes hand in hand with increased production.

EXERCISES

1 Explain the connections between primary production and secondary production in the making of upholstered chairs.

2 List some of the people involved before a tin of sardines reaches the consumer.

3 Tea is grown in Sri Lanka and drunk in England. Why do the tea planters take no part in exporting what they grow?

4 What types are each of the following industries: (a) oil-drilling; (b) pottery; (c) shoe-making; (d) whaling; (e) carpentry; (f) road-building?

5 In respect of each of the following, state if they are engaged in primary, secondary or tertiary production: (a) tailor; (b) pearl diver; (c) shopkeeper; (d) accountant; (e) industrial chemist; (f) fruit farmer; (g) fruit-canner; (h) professional footballer; (i) ships radio officer; (j) shepherd.

6 Distinguish between trade and the other branches of commerce.

7 There could be enough food to feed everyone, yet millions starve. Why?

8 In a supermarket, what sort of people are likely to be: (a) the manager; (b) shelf-fillers; (c) cashiers; (d) store detectives; (e) maintenance staff?

9 Refer to Figure 1.3. Trace the people involved in providing food, show the part played by each one and explain why their efforts must be co-ordinated.

10 Refer to Figure 1.4. Can you identify any disadvantages which may follow the dividing of the work between 20 people?

11 Why does the cost of a house include: (a) wages for the men who dig the foundations; (b) the interest the builder has to pay on money borrowed to pay his expenses during building; (c) the salary of the typist to the man who installed the electricity; (d) petrol for the builder's lorry?

12 Describe briefly what you consider to be the purposes of commerce and indicate how (a) an accounts clerk in a wholesale warehouse, (b) a butcher's assistant, and (c) a cinema attendant, help in the attainment of those purposes.

13 What do the following people contribute to the production of a diamond ring: (a) assayer; (b) jewellery designer; (c) diamond cutter; (d) doctor to a gold-mining company; (e) jewellery shop assistant; (f) security guard to a gold importer; (g) policemen?

CHAPTER 2

SOLE TRADERS AND PARTNERSHIPS

This and the next two chapters are about the *forms* in which private business is carried on. (Private businesses are those which are not publicly owned by central or local government.)

In this chapter we will consider *sole traders* and *partnerships*. These are said to be 'non-corporate' concerns. This means that such firms are not recognised by law as being separate from those who own them.

A *limited company*, however, is a 'corporate' body, entirely separate from those who own it. This special type of organisation is dealt with in Chapter 3.

In Chapter 4 we consider private business units *generally*. To do so we include a study of two types of business which differ entirely from the others – *co-operative societies* and *building societies*.

2.1 CHOOSING THE FORM OF A BUSINESS

In establishing a business one has the choice of working alone (in which case one is a *sole trader*) or of joining with other people to form a *partnership* or a *limited company*. In making the choice one must bear in mind that there are different consequences of trading as a sole trader, as a partnership or as a company. These are discussed in this and the two following chapters but the most important of them can first be summarised in the form of the following questions:

(a) *Who actually owns the business?*
(b) *Who controls the business?*
(c) *What financial risks do the owners take?*
(d) *How are profits distributed?*

2.2 VENTURING INTO BUSINESS

Whatever form a business is to take, certain principles always apply. To illustrate these we will assume that a Mr Mark Zebedee wishes to have his own business. At present he is employed as an electronics engineer and he has invented a piece of electronic equipment. He could sell his invention to a manufacturer but, instead, he decides to set up his own firm to make and sell the apparatus. Before giving up the security of a regular salary as an employee he must satisfy himself on a number of points, including the following:

(a) Will the product sell at a profit?
Obviously he is convinced that the equipment is sound *technically*, but will it *sell*? Will there be enough people who agree it is useful? Would they be willing to buy it at a price which will give Zebedee a profit? If the item is to be a component, he must be sure that manufacturers will incorporate it in their products. If it is to be sold to the public, retailers must be confident it will sell. Zebedee must therefore be sure there is a *profitable market* for his product.

(b) Has he enough money of his own?
Starting almost any business can be very costly. The amount of money put into a business is known as its *capital* and it is very difficult to judge just how much will be required. The financing of business is discussed in Chapter 19 but we can make one important point here. Zebedee will require to have enough money to keep the business going until he reaches the stage where it makes a profit. To have enough to *start* the business (to buy machines and materials, for instance) is insufficient. Building up a business is a slow process, and for some time Zebedee will have to pay his expenses with little or no money coming in.

(c) Can he manage alone?
Zebedee knows he will have to work hard. He may be able to employ people, but will he need to have someone to join him in the business to help him manage it? He may have to share the business with someone who can provide some specialist knowledge which Zebedee does not possess. If he does not have enough money, he may have to bring in someone who can provide the extra capital.

As a business grows, its form often changes. To understand this we will later look at how Zebedee's business alters in its form as it develops.

2.3 THE REALITIES OF BEING A SOLE TRADER

A sole trader is an individual who owns and controls a business and who receives all its profits or bears all its losses:

(a) A sole trader *owns* the business. This applies even if someone has lent him some of his capital, because a lender is not a member of the firm but a *creditor*.

(b) He *controls* the business because he has sole responsibility for all decisions. This applies even if he has managers, because they would be *employees* and not members of the firm.

(c) He does not have to share his profits with anyone but if the business fails he has no one to share the loss with.

A sole trader operates what may be truly called a 'one-man business'.

2.4 THE ADVANTAGES OF BEING A SOLE TRADER

These may be summarised as follows:

(a) The business is a very personal one

The way the business is conducted will reflect the personality and character of the owner. Zebedee would have personal contact with those he does business with, so that anyone dealing with the firm would be dealing with *him*. Therefore, the reputation of the firm will be a reflection of his own reputation. He will have close contact with his employees and will be well placed to get their loyalty.

(b) The owner makes all the decisions

Zebedee would not have to consult anyone about decisions which have to be made. They will therefore be made more quickly and most positively.

(c) No formality is required to establish the business

Forming a sole trader business does not bring into existence another 'legal person'. There is therefore no necessity to 'register a birth'.

(d) No details of the business have to be published

Information about the business must be given (particularly to the Inland Revenue) but it does not have to be made available to the public.

2.5 THE DISADVANTAGES OF BEING A SOLE TRADER

These can be considerable and include the following:

(a) The owner's liability is unlimited

If Zebedee's business failed, he could be made bankrupt. If there were insufficient money to pay the creditors after the firm's assets had been sold, then Zebedee would be liable to the extent of his personal possessions. Thus everything he had may have to be sold to provide cash for the firm's debts. A sole trader is therefore said to have *unlimited liability*. This is because the law says that the business and its owner are one and the same: that a *sole trader has no separate 'legal entity'*. (As we shall see in the next chapter, this does not apply to companies because they are 'limited-liability' companies.)

(b) The owner has personal burdens

As control of the business is in the hands of one person, he cannot share his responsibilities. Zebedee has to take all the worry of the business onto himself; there is no one he can discuss problems with. He has to work long hours and has the constant fear of the business being neglected if he becomes ill.

(c) Expansion may be limited by insufficiency of capital

If the business progresses well, Zebedee may wish to expand it. This will usually require more capital, and unless he has some spare money outside the business the only way to get the extra capital may be to 'plough back' some of the profits. This means he must give up some of his profit and put it back into the business, but he may not be able to afford to do this. He *may* be able to borrow the money but this would mean spending some of his profit to pay the interest and to 'save up' to repay the lump sum. Almost certainly he would have to give some security for the loan. In any case, lenders are generally reluctant to lend to small businesses, particularly when there is only one owner. Someone may offer to provide the extra capital if he is allowed to become a joint owner of the business, but Zebedee may not be willing to give up his independence.

(d) Some essential expertise may be lacking

As a sole trader Zebedee has within the business only the technical knowledge *he* possesses. He may be a poor manager; he may have little knowledge of accounting; he may know nothing about marketing. If he could afford it, he could employ such experts, of course, but they could only *advise* him. He would still have to take the decisions himself.

(e) The business dies with the owner

As we have seen, Zebedee and the business are one and the same. If Zebedee dies, then the business comes to an end, so that there is *no continuity*. The business would be part of Zebedee's estate and may have to be sold to pay death duties.

2.6 WHY SOLE TRADERS SURVIVE

We have seen that there are many risks in running a one-man business; indeed, the failure rate is very high. The fact is, however, that a considerable number of businesses *do* flourish as sole traders. The main reason for this is the *nature* of any such business, as the following examples will show:

(a) The amount of trade may be small and the business may be very local. A small grocery shop, for example, may survive because it can offer an adequate service to the nearby community.
(b) The business may be a very personal one. An accountant will have close contact with his clients and therefore could well operate as a one-man business.
(c) A business may be one in which account has to be taken of the individual requirements of its customers or clients. For example, an interior decorator must allow for the very personal likes and dislikes of those for whom he does work.

It is for these reasons (among others) why most sole-trader businesses are small. This is not invariably the case, however. There are examples of fairly large businesses which are solely owned, but this is possible only if the owner appoints efficient executives to share the responsibilities of management. In fact, a sole trader may have to *prevent* his business from growing too large. There are limits to what one man can control, so that to avoid having to share his business with others an owner may deliberately restrict his business to a size he can manage himself.

Many small business, however, are vulnerable. Unless it is the sort of business which can succeed *only* if it is small (such as a painter-artist), it will face competition from larger units. This may result in the small business failing or being 'taken over' by a more powerful one. As we will see in Chapter 4, the tendency is for businesses to increase in size. Any small business is costly to run if one relates total expenses to total sales. There may therefore be a point where the only way to reduce costs and improve efficiency is to expand. This would call for more capital and additional expertise. It would be at that point that the form of the business may change. It may become a company, and the implications of that are discussed in the next chapter. Alternatively, it may become a partnership.

2.7 PARTNERSHIPS

In law, a partnership is regarded as being *an association of individuals engaged in business*. In England (but not in Scotland) *a partnership is not a legal entity*. This has the following consequences:

(a) Each partner (like a sole trader) has *unlimited liability* for the debts of the business.
(b) A partnership cannot sue or be sued in its own name. Anyone claiming against the firm must take action against any or all of the partners as individuals.
(c) A contract cannot be entered into in the name of the firm. Contracts must be in the names of the partners.
(d) If any partner dies, withdraws from the firm or becomes bankrupt, the partnership is dissolved. There is therefore *no continuity*.
(e) The business is *owned* by the partners.
(f) *Control* is shared by the partners.
(g) No account of the firm's activities has to be published.

2.8 FORMATION OF A PARTNERSHIP

Except in certain circumstances, a firm may not have more than 20 partners.

There are no registration formalities for the same reason as applies to sole trader businesses.

As between themselves, it is necessary the partners have some written agreement. This takes the form of a *partnership deed*, setting out the rights and obligations of the partners. The following points would have to be specified:

(a) How much capital each partner would put into the business.
(b) How the profits would be divided. Usually, the proportion paid to each partner is the same as the proportion of the firm's capital he contributes.
(c) What part each partner will play in the day-to-day running of the business. A partner may have *no* management duties, in which case he is known as a 'sleeping partner'. It may be necessary to decide how decisions are to be made, so that some method of voting would have to be agreed upon.
(d) Partners working in the business may be paid a salary besides being entitled to a share of the profits. There may be, say, two partners who work full time, while the others work part time. Therefore, the amount of salaries must be decided.

2.9 TAKING A PARTNER

Let us assume that Zebedee's business is now well established and that he takes a Mr Joseph Baxter as a partner. What could be his reasons for doing so?

(a) Perhaps Zebedee needed more capital in his business. He may have wished to expand but had been unable to 'plough back' enough of his profits to provide the extra finance. Perhaps Baxter was willing to contribute capital and play no part in running the business, in which case Zebedee could do things his own way as he did before.

(b) It may be, however, he *wanted* Baxter's help. Perhaps Baxter is also an electronics engineer who has some expert knowledge he can bring into the firm. Alternatively, he may be able to provide some expertise Zebedee does not have. Perhaps Zebedee realised he had made mistakes in the past because he is a poor manager or he has little knowledge of accounting or finance. Baxter may be able to provide the necessary experience, leaving Zebedee to concentrate on the technical side.

(c) Zebedee may have been feeling the strain of running the business alone. If he has help, this will reduce his burden and even allow him to take holidays.

Taking a partner can provide disadvantages, however:

(a) Unless Baxter is a sleeping partner, he must now be consulted about important decisions. Zebedee is no longer 'king', able to do as he wishes. For example, if Baxter is the accountant he may well disapprove of some of Zebedee's ideas as a scientist! The possibility of conflict therefore exists.

(b) A partnership can be dissolved at any time. If Baxter decides to leave and take his capital with him, it will probably present Zebedee with considerable problems.

(c) As contracts can be made by individual partners on behalf of the firm, it is possible that, unknown to Zebedee, Baxter may enter into an unfortunate agreement and put the business into difficulties.

In general, therefore, a partnership will be successful only if there is a good relationship between the partners. If they are not 'in tune' they will be pulling in different directions and the business will suffer.

EXERCISES

1   A man decides to set up business to repair domestic electrical appliances. What estimates should he first make?

2   How does ownership and control differ as between a sole-trader business and a partnership?

3 Look around your area and name firms which prosper as sole traders. In each case explain why the business flourishes.

4 A sole trader is 'king of his own castle'. Is this an advantage or not?

5 Sole traders and partners have 'unlimited liability'. What does this mean, and why is it important?

6 There is no 'continuity' in a sole-trader business or in a partnership. What dangers does this present?

7 Compare Zebedee's position as a sole trader with that of being a partner.

8 Assume that Zebedee had invested £10 000 in his business when it was formed and that Baxter contributed £5000 when he became a partner. The firm then borrowed £5000 with interest at 10 per cent per annum. The capital sum has to be repaid after 5 years, so the partners set aside an equal amount of the profits each year towards the repayment. Each partner draws a salary of £5000 per annum. If the business made a profit of £13 000 in a year *before* payment of salaries and interest, how much of the profit could each partner draw from the business?

9 After the partnership was formed, Zebedee was anxious to improve his invention and increase its sales. Baxter had become a partner because he, too, had an invention and wished to market it through the business. Give examples of the conflicts between them which could be caused as a consequence.

10 What terms are usually contained in a partnership deed? Why is it advisable to have such an agreement?

11 Mr Jones is an accountant and for some years has been in business on his own, dealing with the accounts of local traders. Mr. Smith is employed by a company as its taxation expert. What advantages would each get if Mr. Jones admitted Mr Smith as a partner?

12 What are the possible advantages and disadvantages of a man, his brother and his two sons running a business as a partnership?

CHAPTER 3

LIMITED COMPANIES

A very high proportion of private businesses trade in the form of limited companies. This is because to do so provides considerable advantages over being in business as a sole trader or in a partnership. The advantages of running a very small business as a limited company are in many respects the same as apply to companies with capital amounting to millions of pounds. In fact, most companies are not large.

3.1 THE SPECIAL FEATURES OF LIMITED COMPANIES

Limited companies differ from sole traders and partnerships in the following respects:

(a) A company is a 'legal entity'

It is an incorporated body entirely separate from the people owning it. This can be explained if we assumed that Mr Zebedee started in business trading as a limited company instead of as a sole trader. If he started with £10 000 as his capital, he would have it in the form of shares; say, 10 000 shares of £1 each. There must be more than one shareholder in a company so he could name his wife as the second shareholder. If he wanted to, Mr Zebedee could have 9999 shares registered in his name and his wife could own the other share. This may appear to make it a 'one-man business' and in practice it is. In law, however, there are now *three* 'legal persons' – Mr Zebedee, Mrs Zebedee and the company. This means that Zebedee can enter into contracts with the company, though this may seem as though he is contracting with himself! All agreements made by the firm will be in the name of the company and not in the name of Zebedee, though it would be he who decided to make the contracts.

(b) Shareholders have limited liability

In the previous chapter we saw that if the firm were unable to pay its debts, Zebedee would be personally liable for the difference, either as a sole trader or as a partner. If he traded as a company, however, the most he could lose would be the amount he paid for his shares. If, therefore, the business failed, Zebedee would lose his £10 000 but no one could make him sell his personal possessions.

These two factors explain why so many companies are formed. A man can set up a very small business, knowing that in law he and the business are separate and that if things go wrong he cannot lose any more money than he put into it. Some companies are very small indeed. In theory, at least, a company could be formed with a share capital of two pence, there being two members each holding a penny share!

(c) Public disclosure must be made

Unlike sole traders and partnerships, companies must publish information about themselves, including their accounts. As a sole trader or a partner Zebedee would not have to do this, but if he trades as a company any member of the public, on payment of a small fee, can see the accounts and other information about the business.

(d) Continuity is assured

Over a period the membership of a company may change completely but the company as a legal person will continue to exist. For example, the Hudson's Bay Company was formed about 300 years ago. Since then the membership of the company has changed repeatedly but the *company* remains. A company never dies (although it can be 'killed' by being wound up), because if someone is to sell his shares someone else must buy them.

3.2 PRIVATE COMPANIES AND PUBLIC COMPANIES

British law prescribes as follows:

(a) Any limited company (private or public) must have at least two share-holders.
(b) Only a *public* company may invite the public to provide it with finance.
(c) A *public* company must have the 'authorised minimum of allotted share capital' (currently fixed at £50,000).
(d) The name of a *public* company must end with the words 'public limited company' or 'plc'.

3.3 FORMATION OF A PRIVATE COMPANY

Let us now assume that Zebedee and his partner have developed their business so that it is a prosperous concern. They wish to expand and therefore require more capital than they themselves can provide. We saw that in the early days of a business it would be unlikely that anyone would put money into it, but now that Zebedde's business is making good profits people would be willing to invest so that they may share in those profits. The two partners therefore find a few people to join them and provide the extra capital. Probably they can arrange to be the only directors so that they can continue to manage the business as previously.

They therefore plan to form a private company and to sell the business to it. (Remember, the company is a 'legal person', so that the partners, as 'persons', would be selling their assets to another 'person'.) The price they would receive would be in the form of shares in the company.

Having reached an agreement with the newcomers, Zebedee and his partner must then establish the legal status of the company by registering it.

3.4 REGISTRATION OF A COMPANY

Before a company (whether it is a private one or a public one) can be registered the following documents must be lodged with the Registrar of Companies:

(a) The *Memorandum of Association* (see below).
(b) The *Articles of Association* (see Section 3.6).
(c) A statement of the share capital which is to be raised (on which duty it payable).
(d) Personal details of the directors and the secretary. Each of them must sign a statement expressing his willingness to accept office.
(e) A statement of the address of the company's registered office.

If the documents are in order, the Registrar will issue a *Certificate of Incorporation*, establishing the business as a limited company. At that stage a *private* company may commence trading. As we will see later, a public company must complete further formalities before it can operate as a business.

The procedure for registering a company is illustrated in Figure 3.1.

Fig 3.1 *forming a private company*

(1) Zebedee and Baxter invite two others to
join them as shareholders

Zebedee   Baxter   Johnstone   Evans

(2) Johnstone agrees to be the company secretary

(3) The following documents are lodged with the Registrar of Companies:

   (a) The *Memorandum of Association* and the *Articles of Association*
(signed by all four)

   (b) A statement of the share capital and a declaration that the law has
been complied with (signed by Johnstone as secretary)

   (c) Particulars of the directors and the secretary (each signing
a consent to act)

(4) Registrar issues *Certificate of Incorporation* establishing the
business as a limited company

(5) New members pay the agreed amounts, share certificates are
issued and the Register of Members is written up

3.5 THE MEMORANDUM OF ASSOCIATION

This is a company's 'charter'. It establishes the company's relationships
with the outside world. The one relevant to the company formed to take
over Zebedee's business could appear as shown in Figure 3.2.

Fig 3.2 *a Memorandum of Association*

MEMORANDUM OF ASSOCIATION

1. The name of the company is Zebedee Electronics Limited

2. The registered office of the company will be situated in England

3. The objects for which the company is established are 'to develop, manufacture and market electronic equipment as components and complete articles and to do all such other things as are incidental or conducive to the attainment of such objects'

4. The liability of the members is limited

5. The share capital of the company is one hundred thousand pounds divided into one hundred thousand shares of one pound each

We, the several persons whose names and addresses are subscribed, are desirous of being formed into a company in pursuance of this Memorandum of Association and we respectively agree to take the number of shares in the capital of the company set opposite our respective names.

Names, addresses and descriptions of subscribers		Number of shares taken by each subscriber	Signatures
1. Mark Zebedee of	Electronics engineer	30 000	
2. Joseph Baxter of	Electronics engineer	15 000	
3. David Johnstone of	Accountant	10 000	
4. William Evans of	Bank manager	10 000	
Total shares taken		65 000	

Dated the third day of March 19 . .

Witness to the above signatures
John Smith
15 Broad Street
Blanktown

The items may be explained as follows:

1. The name of the company must include an indication that it is a limited company. A name may not be chosen which could be confused with that of another company.

2. The registered office will be in either England (and Wales) or Scotland.

3. A company may not do anything which is beyond its *objects*. A person putting money into the company will know what sort of business it can engage in, so that there is no possibility of the company doing something which the investor would disapprove of. It could otherwise happen that the company would do something which may be riskier than the investor would like.

4. This establishes the limited liability of the members.

5. This fixes the amount of share capital the company *may* raise. (It will be seen that at this stage only £65 000 is being subscribed.)

3.6 THE ARTICLES OF ASSOCIATION

These set out the *internal rules* for governing the company, rather like the regulations of a club. It establishes the relationships between the company and the shareholders. It includes such matters as voting rights at meetings, the powers of the directors, the amount the company may borrow without having to seek the consent of the shareholders, and so on. The members may change any of the Articles by voting.

On joining a company a shareholder agrees to be bound by the Articles, in the same way that a person joining a club agrees to abide by the rules as they then are.

3.7 INCORPORATION OF A PUBLIC COMPANY

A public company may start life in that form but the more usual procedure is for it to be converted from a private company. This is known as 'going public'.

As the public is to be invited to take up shares and thereby provide the company with capital, a *prospectus* is issued. This is a form of advertisement and, because of the possibility of fraud by those issuing it, its contents are very strictly prescribed by law. Obviously, people must be given all the facts so that they clearly understand what sort of business they are being invited to put money into. The prospectus is therefore a long and detailed document, giving a history of the business, those who are to run it, what it intends to do, the profits it expects to make, etc.

People are reluctant to subscribe for shares unless they know they can, if necessary, sell them on the Stock Exchange. The importance of being able to do so is explained in Chapter 19 but it can be said here that there is no automatic right to use the Stock Exchange for buying and selling particular shares. The Stock Exchange must give its permission before this can be done. The promoters of the company must therefore ask for that permission before they issue the prospectus. This is known as *seeking admission to listing*. Before giving its approval the Stock Exchange will carry out an exhaustive investigation of the company and all those connected with it. It will examine the prospectus even more thoroughly than the law will. This is part of the Stock Exchange's responsibility for protecting investors.

Those asking for shares in response to a prospectus will do so on *application forms*, enclosing a cheque for the number applied for. The directors will then issue *allotment letters* to those people whose applications they accept. Usually, an issue is 'over-subscribed', so that the shares have to be rationed. A person allotted fewer shares than he applied for will, of course, be sent a cheque for the overpayment.

Unlike a private company, a public company cannot commence trading immediately it is incorporated. It must first show that the public issue has been a success. If the minimum capital (which is the amount the directors have stated in the prospectus as being the sum which must be raised before the company can start operations) is not received, then all the money subscribed must be refunded. If the sum *was* raised, the company will inform the Registrar accordingly and also confirm that the directors have paid for their shares. The Registrar will then *issue a Certificate of Trading,* allowing the company to commerce business (see Figure 3.3).

Fig 3.3   *Zebedee Electronics Ltd 'goes public'*

(1) The directors consult with their financial and legal advisers and

   (a)   work out their financial plans
   (b)   draft a prospectus
   (c)   apply to the Stock Exchange for admission to listing

(2) The Stock Exchange carries out an investigation and gives its permission

(3) A prospectus is published

> PROSPECTUS
> ZEBEDEE
> ELECTRONICS
> LIMITED

(4) The public applies for shares

> APPLICATION
> FORM
> FOR 500 SHARES
> BY J. SMITH

(5) The company 'rations' the shares

> ALLOTMENT
> LETTER
> FOR 400 SHARES
> TO J. SMITH

Cheque to refund overpayment

> J. SMITH   £....

(6) The company informs the Registrar and the Stock Exchange that the issue was successful. The Registrar issues the *Trading Certificate*

> ZEBEDEE
> ELECTRONICS
> LIMITED
>
> CERTIFICATE
> TO COMMENCE
> TRADING

(7) Share certificates are issued and the Register of Members is written up

> ZEBEDEE ELECTRONICS
> LIMITED
> J. SMITH 400 SHARES

> J. SMITH
> £400

3.8 SAFEGUARDING A PUBLIC ISSUE

There is always the possibility that a public issue of shares will be a 'flop': that is, the total amount required will not be received.

For most issues a prospectus is *not*, in fact, published, Instead, a merchant bank buys all the shares from the company and then invites the public to apply for them. This is done by issuing an advertisement called an *Offer for Sale* which must contain the same information that a prospectus has to. The bank is therefore a 'retailer' of the shares, relieving the company of the risk of an under-subscription.

A public issue is also usually insured. *Underwriters* (large financial concerns) agree, for a fee, to buy any shares the public fails to take up.

3.9 CONTROL OF A COMPANY

A company is managed by a board of directors. They run the business on a day-to-day basis and take all the major decisions. The law prescribes only a few matters which require the consent of the shareholders. The shareholders' powers are even less than they may appear because any decisions taken by them be by voting. Not all shareholders necessarily have votes, and those who do usually have one vote per share. Directors cannot be removed or new ones appointed unless over 50 per cent of the votes are in favour. This means, of course, that if the directors and their supporters hold the majority of voting shares they cannot be removed. Looking at the *Memorandum of Association* of Zebedee Electronics Ltd it will be seen that so long as Zebedee and Baxter stand together the other shareholders have no power to interface.

We can therefore say that a company is

(a) *owned* by its shareholders;
(b) *managed* by its directors; and
(c) *controlled* by those holding a majority of the voting shares.

Voting members are invited to attend annual meetings called by the directors. With the notice of the meeting are sent the annual accounts and a report on the activities of the year. The accounts are formally presented at the meeting and any new directors and auditors appointed. In practice, few members attend public company meetings. This probably indicates that shareholders of large companies recognise that they have little influence in the running of their company.

3.10 COMPANY CAPITAL

A company's capital is broadly in two forms:

(a) Debentures
These are *loans*. A person lending money to a company is not a *member*; he is a *creditor*. Therefore, he is not an owner. Unlike a shareholder, he *must* be paid the interest on his investment and the capital sum must be repaid on the due date. These payments must be made whether or not the company is making profits. If the payments are not made the debenture-

holders can force the company to be wound up. Loans are usually secured on assets of the company but sometimes they are unsecured.

(b) Shares

These are issued to people who thereby become *members* of the company. They share in the profits and what they receive are called *dividends*. If a company makes no profits or insufficient profits, the shareholders receive nothing because dividends are payable only from profits. The amount of any dividend is effectively decided by the directors because shareholders cannot vote to pay a larger rate than that recommended by the directors.

There are two main types of shares:

1 Ordinary shares

The holders of these are known as 'the true risk-bearers' because they are paid last. They share in the profits remaining after everyone else has received their dividends. Because this surplus cannot be estimated *ordinary shares carry no fixed rate of dividend*. If profits are low, dividends will be low or nil. If profits are high, then dividends will be high. A person buying ordinary shares therefore runs the risk of receiving a small dividend (or none), but he is prepared to accept this because he will do exceptionally well if the company makes high profits. Such shares are therefore 'speculative'.

Ordinary shareholders usually have votes but this is not always the case. Ordinary shares are sometimes referred to as 'equities'.

2 Preference shares

As the word indicates, these are paid *before* the ordinary shares. The dividend rate is fixed. The rate is not *guaranteed* because, as stated above, no dividend can be paid on any share if there are no profits. If any preference dividend is not paid, then the arrears must be paid off when the company can afford it before anything is paid to the ordinary shareholders. A *redeemable preference share* is repayable on a specified date.

Under normal circumstances preference shareholders have no votes.

A person buying shares is given a *share certificate* as evidence of ownership. That held by Baxter after the private company was formed could be as shown in Figure 3.4.

Fig. 3.4 *a share certificate*

Certificate No. 2   15 000 shares

ZEBEDEE ELECTRONICS PLC
(Incorporated under the *Companies Act 1948*)

This is to certify that Joseph Baxter of 2 Tower Road Blanktown is the
registered holder of 15 000 ordinary shares of one pound each, fully paid,
in the above company, subject to the *Memorandum* and *Articles of Association* of the company

Given under the Common Seal of the company on   . . . 19 . .

No transfer of these shares or any portion thereof can be registered until this certificate has been deposited at the registered
office of the company

3.11 HOLDING COMPANIES

A company can amalgamate with another company by holding all or a
majority of the voting shares of that company. If Zebedee Electronics
wanted to sell some of its products direct to the public, it could buy the
controlling shares in a chain of stores. The result would be that it would be
sure of getting its goods into the shops and it could also keep out competitive products if it wished to do so. Also, of course, it would share in the
profits made by the stores because that company would declare dividends
which would be paid to Zebedee Electronics as the shareholder.

Figure 3.5 illustrates what the situation would be if Zebedee Electronics
plc held 60 per cent of the voting shares in a chain called *XYZ* Supplies
plc. We have already seen that anyone holding over 50 per cent of the
voting shares in a company effectively controls that company because he
can decide who will be its directors. Zebedee Electronics could therefore
determine the policies of *XYZ* Supplies, particularly as the illustration
shows that Zebedee and Baxter were made directors of *XYZ* Supplies.

A company which controls another in this way is known as a *holding
company*. The company which is controlled is called a *subsidiary company*.

The process can extend to sub-subsidiaries. The illustration shows that
XYZ Supplies plc. already held all the shares in a company called Hitone
plc. The consequences of this for Zebedee Electronics are shown at the
bottom of the illustration.

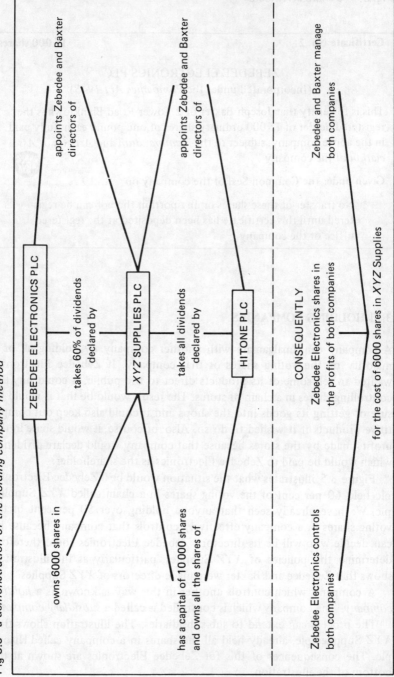

Fig 3.5 *a demonstration of the holding company method*

3.12 WHY PEOPLE BUY SHARES

We have seen that if a company is formed it can attract money from those outside the business. We must therefore consider *why* people are willing to invest in company shares:

(a) Liability is limited
If a person has, say, £10 000 to spare, he could set up his own business. If he did so, however, he would run the risk of losing all his possessions if the business failed. As a shareholder, the most he could lose would be £10 000.

(b) There are no management worries
If the investor had his own business he would have to work in it and shoulder all the worries and responsibilities which go with it. He assumes the directors of the company are good managers so he leaves them to run the business which he partly owns as a shareholder. Meanwhile, he can carry on his normal life as an employee or a retired person.

(c) A capital profit is possible
If the company does well, the value of the shares will increase. If he wished, he could sell them to give himself a capital profit.

(d) He is protected by law
The law will not 'protect a fool from himself', so it will not be sympathetic if a man loses money investing in a company which obviously had no hope of success. The law will, however, ensure that all he needs to know about the company is published, that he will receive protection if the directors act unfairly towards him and that action will be taken if there is fraud.

EXERCISES

1 Mr Oak and Mr Ash own between them all the shares in Timber Ltd. What is the effect of there being three 'legal persons' here?

2 What effect would it have had on the business if Zebedee died when (a) he was a sole trader; (b) he was a partner with Baxter; (c) he was a director of Zebedee Electronics Ltd?

3 *AB* Ltd has a capital of £100 000 in ordinary shares. Mr *X* has 30 000 shares and Mr *Z* has 35 000 shares. Neither is a director. To what extent could they influence the policies of the company?

4 List the differences between private companies and public companies. Why should a private company wish to 'go public'?

5 Distinguish between a *Memorandum of Association* and *Articles of Association.*

6 In connection with a public issue of shares, define: (a) a prospectus; (b) an offer for sale; (c) application and allotment; (d) underwriting; (e) admission to listing.

7 Who controlled Zebedee Electronics Ltd when it was formed as a private company? Could Zebedee be sure he could always get his own way in running the business?

8 'Shareholders are members of a company; debenture-holders are creditors.' Explain this statement.

9 Why are ordinary shareholders the 'true risk-bearers'? To what extent is such shareholding speculative?

10 What rights have shareholders to receive dividends? What determines how much they receive?

11 A limited company has issued 200 000 ordinary shares of 50p each and 50 000 £1 preference shares paying a dividend of 10 percent. Its net profit for the year was £20 000. It is decided that a quarter of this sum would be placed to reserve. How much will the holder of 1000 ordinary shares receive as a dividend?

12 If a company was formed to run the first airline between some remote islands, would you prefer to: (a) buy ordinary shares; (b) buy preference shares; or (c) take up debentures in it? Give reasons for your answer.

13 What constitutes a *holding company*? What control has such a company over its subsidiaries?

CHAPTER 4

PRIVATE BUSINESS UNITS GENERALLY

We have studied the main forms of private business and you may now find it useful to revise by referring to the features which are summarised in Figure 4.1. We have also seen how the forms tend to alter with the growth of a business. (However, although we have traced the development of Zebedee's business from sole trader to a large company, it must be remembered that a business can start in any form the owners wish it to have.) In this chapter we consider the reasons why businesses grow, the methods of doing so and the problems which growth often brings. We also look at two other types of business which differ widely from those we have studied so far.

4.1 WHY BUSINESSES GROW

In Chapter 2 we saw that some firms are small because of what they do. There are no advantages for such businesses to grow beyond a certain size and, indeed, they may be unable to operate if they *did* grow. In general, however, businesses tend to get larger. We have seen how Zebedee's firm grew to become a large public company. Some of the huge corporations which exist today started in a very small way. For example, the gigantic group of oil companies which trade under the name of Shell began with a man exporting shells from the tropics for Victorian ladies to use as ornaments.

Why, then, is there this constant tendency to every-increasing size? Here are some of the reasons:

(a) To meet an increasing demand
If more and more people want the product or service which the business provides, then the business must expand to meet that demand. If it is a manufacturer, it follows that it then requires more space, machines, labour and capital. Consequently, the business must become larger. If the market

Fig 4.1 *a comparison of private business units*

	Sole trader	Partnership	Private limited company	Public limited company
Formation formalities	None	Partnership deed	Registration with the Registrar of Companies	
Legal status	None; firm inseparable from owner(s)		A 'legal person' separate from owners	
Ownership	The trader	The partners	The shareholders	
Change of ownership	By sale of the business assets	By sale of partner's part with consent of others	By transfer of shares with consent of all members	By transfer of shares (unrestricted)
Control	By the trader	Shared by partners	By the holders of the majority of voting shares	
Management	By the trader	Shared by partners as agreed	By the directors	
Number of members	1	Up to 20	Minimum 2. There is no maximum	
Owners' liability in event of insolvency	Unlimited	Jointly and severally unlimited	Limited to amount of capital contributed	
Owners' entitlement to profits	The total	The total, divided as agreed	Dividends as declared by directors; preference shareholders paid first	
Termination of the business	At will, on death or on insolvency	On insolvency, by agreement of partners, on death or bankruptcy of a partner	By compulsory or voluntary winding up	

grows, the business must grow too. If it does not meet the demand, then another business will fill the gap. The electronics industry is a fairly new one and is expanding rapidly, so that businesses such as Zebedee's must grow with it. Businesses in other industries which are declining will not grow.

(b) To obtain the benefits of large-scale production
Figure 1.4 showed that if production is well organised, the cost of making each chair falls with every increase in the number of chairs made. Mass production in a car factory enables the cost of a car to be reduced considerably, provided enough cars are made. This is because, in general, the higher the output the lower will be the cost of each item produced. There are several reasons for this. For example, if you double the size of a factory so as to hold twice as many machines, the cost of lighting, heating, rates, office supplies, etc., will increase but it will not *double*. You may need more clerks but you will not require twice as many. Also, you would be buying more materials, and the more you buy the lower the price you have to pay.

(c) To afford additional facilities
A large business can pay for extra facilities which a small firm cannot afford. As his business grew, Zebedee would have been able to pay for efficient managers, to spend more on machines and to buy more sophisticated equipment. Increased size therefore reduces costs even more.

(d) To reduce risks
A business with a lot of money in it can get through difficult times more easily. A 'slump' always produces bankruptcies in small firms, while larger concerns can 'weather the storm'. Also, if a firm is large enough to dominate an industry it has no fear of competition. Until it reaches that size it has to compete against others.

4.2 HOW BUSINESSES GROW

For a business to expand beyond a certain size it must use the limited company system so that it can employ one or more of the following methods. These can be broadly divided into (a) increasing the finance available, and (b) merging with another company.

4.3 EXPANSION BY INCREASING FINANCE

The methods available for increasing a company's finances are as follows:

(a) By issuing more shares
As we saw in the previous chapter, investors will always be willing to buy

shares in a company which is making good profits and which wants to grow and make yet *more* profits. A public company therefore has a source of finance available to it. At various stages in its growth Zebedee Electronics asked the public for more money and, because it was prospering, it received it.

(b) By borrowing

Some investors prefer to take no risks, so they take up debentures instead of shares. The company has the disadvantage that it *must* pay the interest on loans but this is rarely a problem because loans usually are only a small part of the capital. Companies also borrow from banks and finance houses.

(c) By ploughing back profits

A company may obtain additional finance by retaining a fairly large part of its profits. This, of course, would mean that ordinary share dividends would be lower than would otherwise be the case. The company, however, would have extra capital on which it pays no interest or dividends.

This method of expanding is known as 'internal growth'.

4.4 EXPANSION BY MERGING

One company can merge with another by buying its shares. An example of this was given in the previous chapter when holding and subsidiary companies were discussed. A company can, of course, only buy shares from those who already hold them. To gain control of a company it is therefore necessary to offer the holders enough to persuade them to sell. If the offer is made to *all* the shareholders at the same time and at the same price it is known as a *takeover bid*.

Mergers (which are sometimes referred to as *amalgamations*) take the following forms:

(a) Horizontal merger

This can happen when two companies are engaged in the same stage of production. For example, if two companies have shops serving the same market, one could take over the other and so eliminate the competition. The more usual reason, however, is to combine the two businesses to make a more efficient one. This means bringing together the best features of each company and removing those which duplicate each other. This is known as *rationalisation*. Zebedee Electronics could merge with another company doing much the same type of work. Perhaps the other company has experts on its staff and technical facilities which Zebedee Electronics has not; this would be one way of 'buying' them. Possibly the other company would also benefit for similar reasons. Many such mergers are therefore sensible ways of helping both companies.

(b) Vertical merger

This is possible when two companies are at *different* stages of production in the same industry. If a car-manufacturing company takes over a company which makes headlamps it is then assured of those supplies. A clothing manufacturer may merge with a company owning a chain of shops and thereby be certain of having sales outlets.

(c) Diversification

It is quite common for large companies to take over businesses with which they have nothing in common. The intention is to spread the risk so that if one part of the total suffers a fall in profits at least some of the others will prosper. In other words, it avoids the dangers of having 'all the eggs in one basket'. For example, one company owns most of the English shoe-shop chains, a famous London store, garages, a motor manufacturer, an engineering company and betting shops! Combinations of this sort are known as *conglomerates*.

An illustration of these methods is given in Figure 4.2

4.5 THE PROBLEMS OF GROWTH

Although businesses grow because larger firms can be run more economically, there can be a point where inefficiency shows itself. As a business gets larger, management of it becomes more difficult. There are more people to manage and the organisation becomes increasingly complex. It becomes more difficult to make decisions because more people have to be consulted. Even the most ambitious realise that a business cannot expand indefinitely.

There can also be social disadvantages. If a company is so large that it has the major part of the market, it can keep prices unnecessarily high. This is one of the evils of *monopoly*. Fortunately, there is some protection against this. If a firm or combination of firms controls more than one-quarter of a market, the Monopolies Commission can recommend that the monopoly be broken. If a proposed merger would result in a monopoly then the Government can forbid it.

However, some monopolies charge high prices simply because they are not efficient enough. As they have little competition, they do not try so hard to reduce costs as they would otherwise do.

There is also the fact that if a large company collapses the consequences are particularly severe. If a large car-manufacturing company fails, a lot of people will become unemployed and many investors will lose money. Also, a large number of other companies which have been suppliers to the manufacturer will be in difficulties, so there will be further unemployment and financial losses.

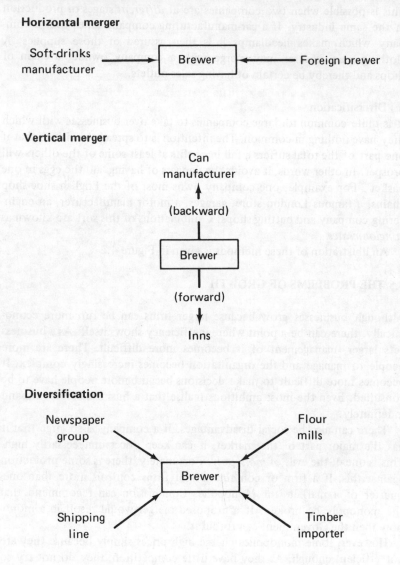

Fig 4.2 *types of merger*

Horizontal merger

Soft-drinks manufacturer → Brewer ← Foreign brewer

Vertical merger

Can manufacturer

(backward) ↑

Brewer

(forward) ↓

Inns

Diversification

Newspaper group → Brewer ← Flour mills

Shipping line → Brewer ← Timber importer

4.6 MULTINATIONALS

There are very large companies which operate in several parts of the world. Although production and marketing takes place in different countries, direction remains at the centre. Each part may be merely a branch of the company but frequently there is a subsidiary company and a local board of directors in each country. Examples of such companies are the Ford Motor Company and Unilever. Such a system enables products to be made which are directly suitable for local markets, it reduces transport costs and it may make it possible to produce goods where labour costs are lowest.

Multinational companies are not always popular. A country which has in it a large foreign company may resent the outflow of profits, particularly if the company shows little understanding of the country's problems. If an English manufacturer makes goods in another country, there will be resentment about the loss of jobs at home. The directors will always have a 'global view' of the business, so that they may make decisions which affect people in distant countries. For example, it may appear sensible to the directors to move production from one country to another. This would benefit the company but it could mean hardship in the country which lost the factory.

4.7 NON-PROFIT-MAKING BUSINESSES

The object of almost all private businesses is to make profits and distribute them to the owners. There are exceptions, however, such as clubs and societies which provide their members with benefits in the form of discounts on purchases, financial help in the event of illness or death, etc. Such organisations do not operate at a loss, of course, but what would otherwise be referred to as profit is regarded as being a 'surplus'. It is from this surplus that the members obtain their benefits. The principle in any such concern is merely to balance income against the outgoings.

It is somewhat remarkable that two non-profit-making types of organisation are very large indeed and operate in competition with big 'capitalist' concerns. The co-operative societies are major units in the retail trade. Building societies handle enormous funds and dominate one particular section of the financial world.

4.8 THE CO-OPERATIVE MOVEMENT

The co-operative societies which can be seen operating in most British shopping areas are *owned by their members*. Membership of a retail society can be obtained on payment of a nominal sum (usually a pound) for a 'share'. The 'profits' of the society are distributed to the members but, unlike other businesses, the 'dividend' is not based on the amount invested. Instead, it is based on the amount spent on purchases. In effect, therefore, members buy their goods at a discount. (For many years the profit 'share-out' was made half-yearly but the practice today is to give dividend stamps for each purchase. These can be cashed or used to pay for further purchases.)

This method of distributing 'profits' is based on the fundamental principle of the movement and goes back to 1844 when the first society (at Rochdale) was formed. At that time 28 weavers joined together as a socialist body so that they would no longer be exploited by 'capitalist' shopkeepers. They bought food at wholesale prices and sold it to the members at fair retail prices, the profits later being distributed to each member according to the amount he or she had spent.

The membership now amounts to several millions but the original principles remain largely unaltered. The societies set high standards of working conditions in the days when shopworkers were badly treated. Part of their income has always been used for educational, welfare and social activities.

The movement consists of a number of local societies. Each society elects a management committee, which in turn appoints executives to run the business. The members of the society, who have one vote each, appoint the management committee. Therefore, *control rests with the members.*

In 1862 the Co-operative Wholesale Society was formed to supply the retail societies. It also acts as a manufacturer, owning factories and tea plantations. Its profits are distributed to the retail societies according to the amount of their purchases in the same way that retail society profits go to their members.

(The part played by co-operative societies in the retail trade is discussed in the next chapter.)

4.9 BUILDING SOCIETIES

Another type of business which is non-profit-making and which started as a working-class 'self-help' movement is the *building society*. In the nineteenth century a group of people combined in order to buy their own houses. Each person paid in a sum of money every week until there was enough in the 'pool' to buy one house. A lottery was then held and the winner was given the money to purchase his house. The process was repeated until all the members had their own houses.

The disadvantages of the system are obvious. The last person whose name was drawn would have paid for his house before he owned it. There were also problems when a member wished to withdraw from the scheme. Nevertheless, the system was the foundation of the building societies as we know them today.

Building societies overcame the disadvantages of the early method by having two types of people involved. There are those who put money *into* a society (known as the *investors*), and those who draw money *from* the society (known as the *borrowers*). One part of a society is a savings bank which pays interest to those who deposit money with it. From this fund of money the society lends to those who wish to buy their own homes and who pay interest. The society does not make 'profits' in the usual sense of the word because there is no one to whom profits are paid. It has to balance the income from investors and the repayments of the borrowers against the sums lent to borrowers and the amounts withdrawn by investors. In so doing it must take account of the interest it pays and the interest it receives.

Thus a society satisfies two different demands – of those who want a safe, convenient way of saving, and of those who require mortgages to buy their own homes.

4.10 AGRICULTURE CO-OPERATIVES

This is another form of non-profit-making business which exists in many countries. Such a system enables small farmers to obtain some of the benefits of trading on a large scale. The co-operative may be in the area of purchasing so that the members can buy seed, fertilisers, etc., at wholesale prices. Co-operation can also take place in marketing so that produce is packed and sold by a central body.

4.11 THE CHAIN OF DISTRIBUTION

So far, we have grouped businesses into *forms*. We have seen that there are differences between them as regards ownership, control, the liabilities of the owners, legal status and the methods of sharing profits and losses. We now have to group them *according to their functions in getting goods to the consumers*. As we saw at the beginning of our studies, this is the scope of 'commerce'.

After they have been produced, most goods pass through several hands before they reach the ultimate buyer. Each of the firms involved plays a part in the whole process, so we have another example of *specialisation*. Each firm is a 'link' in the 'chain of distribution'. In the three following chapters we will consider the features of each link but first we need to have an over-all picture of the possible routes from manufacturer to consumer (sometimes referred to as the 'channels of distribution'). This is given in Figure 4.3:

(a) It will be seen that some manufacturers sell direct to the consumers, ignoring all the other links. For example, it is possible to post orders for footwear, blankets, books, etc., to the manufacturers, who will then deliver them direct. Direct selling also applies when something is made specially for a customer, such as a suit.

Fig 4.3 *the channels of distribution*

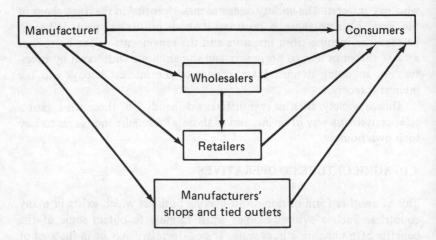

(b) Alternatively, the manufacturer may send all his goods to a wholesaler. The wholesaler may then sell the goods in smaller amounts to retailers (that is, shops), who in turn will sell them to the public. The wholesaler may, however, sell direct to the consumers.

(c) A further method would be for the manufacturer to bypass the wholesalers and sell to the retailers direct. Most large stores buy direct. In many cases the retail shops are owned by the manufacturers, examples being the sale of footwear and medicines. The retailers may be 'tied' to the manufacturer. For example, petrol stations sell only one make of petrol; the beer sold in most public houses come from whichever brewer owns the inn.

EXERCISES

1 Would Zebedee Electronics Ltd increase its efficiency as it grew larger? Give reasons for your answer.

2 Why has the limited company system resulted in the growth of businesses?

3 What sort of mergers are each of the following: (a) a cinema chain and a flour mill; (b) a chocolate manufacturer and a cocoa plantation; (d) a company making domestic electrical appliances and one making telephone switchgear?

4 If the electronics industry is booming, what dangers does Zebedee Electronics Ltd face if it is short of capital?

5 A London property company also owns a newspaper, a shipping line and a travel agency. What is the purpose of such a structure?

6 A company can accumulate capital by building up its reserves. What are the advantages and disadvantages of doing so?

7 Name a foreign multinational company which operates in your country. What arguments can you put for and against the presence of that company?

8 What are the dangers of a company becoming so large that it dominates an industry?

9 Explain the socialist principles of the co-operative movement. Who controls a co-operative society?

10 In your own area: (a) where could you buy goods direct from the manufacturer; (b) which retailers stock the products of only one manufacturer; and (c) which shops get their goods from wholesalers?

11 Suggest different ways in which a shirt manufacturer could distribute his products to consumers.

CHAPTER 5

THE RETAIL TRADE

Retailing is carried on by those businesses which sell goods to the final consumer. The obvious example is provided by the shops we all know and deal with. The retailing stage, therefore, is the one where goods reach the end of their journey from the manufacturer. At the close of the previous chapter we saw that some goods are sold to the consumer by the manufacturers or the wholesalers. This does not mean that in those instances there is *no* retailing. The manufacturer or wholesaler who sells direct to the consumer is *acting* as a retailer; he adds retailing to his other activities. Whatever channel of distribution is used, the retailing *function* always exists.

In the past almost all retailers confined their activities to retailing; they did not combine it with other activities. These we can call 'traditional' retailers. The principles of retailing, however, are much the same whoever does it.

5.1 THE FUNCTIONS OF THE RETAILER

A retailer provides services to those to whom he *sells* and to those from whom he *buys*. These can be shown when we see what the functions of traditional retailers are:

(a) They break bulk into saleable portions
'To retail' originally meant 'to cut again'. A retailer is therefore a person who buys goods in large quantities and then reduces them to quantities of a size acceptable to the consumers. A retail grocer may buy a tonne of sugar but his customers will want to buy sugar in 1 kg packets. This is not only a convenience to the shopper but also to whoever the retailer bought the sugar from. This is because the supplier will want to dispose of the sugar in large quantities. In terms of labour and clerical costs it costs him no more to sell a tonne of sugar in 1 kg packets than it does

to sell one packet. In fact, if he had to serve the public with small packets, his administration costs would by *higher*.

(b) They put the goods in a saleable condition

Consider what happens if you want to buy a chop for your lunch. You would not get it from the man who kills the animals. You must go to a retail butcher because he buys whole carcases and cuts them up in the ways his customers want the meat. He therefore not only reduces the bulk but he also serves his customers by presenting the goods in an acceptable form. Again, there is also a service to the supplier of the meat.

(c) They make goods immediately available to consumers

Many of the things we buy in grocery shops come from all over the world. Even most of the goods produced in our own country are unlikely to be made locally. If we wish to buy a radio set made in Taiwan or a shawl made in India, we expect to be able to go to nearby shops to get them. Even if the article is made only fifty miles away, we do not expect to have to buy it there. Retailers provide goods where their customers want them. Consequently, shops are in centres of population; the goods are taken to the consumers.

This also provides a service to the manufacturer. All his goods will be *made* in one place but they will be *required* in innumerable other places. Retailers set up business where the demand is high; the manufacturer will produce where it is most convenient for *him*. Fruit will be canned near orchards and it is for the retailers to see that the tins are available where people are waiting to buy them.

(d) They measure consumer preferences

A retailer is in constant contact with the buyers of goods, but the makers of those goods are not. Unless the retailer studies the likes and dislikes of his customers, he will find he is stocking some goods he cannot sell. For example, a shopkeeper may notice that the sales of a particular type of tinned food are falling rapidly. Because he knows his customers personally, he discovers that, for example, the food is too highly seasoned for most of them. Without the retailer's help the manufacturer would not know why the sales are falling. If a firm is considering making a new product, it frequently first asks retailers if they think it will sell well.

Differences often exist between different parts of a country. For example, within Britain far more white bread is eaten in Scotland than is eaten in most of England. By using the local knowledge of retailers: (a) customers will get what they require; (b) manufacturers will make what they can sell.

5.2 POSSIBLE PERSONAL SERVICES OF A RETAILER

The functions listed above are those applicable to any retailer because of the *nature* of retailing. Some retailers also provide services of a personal nature to their customers:

(a) Because of the type of goods they sell some retailers provide *advice and information*. For example, if one were contemplating buying a tennis racket, one would expect to receive some expert guidance in a sports shop. It is normal to ask the advice of chemists about medicines; a good paint retailer will give helpful answers to questions from a person thinking about decorating his own home.

(b) A *delivery service* must be provided by some retailers. Obviously, this is necessary when selling heavy goods such as furniture, refrigerators, television sets, etc. Others provide it where it is not essential, and this is done as an extra services.

(c) In some retailing it is usual to provide an *after-sales service*. This may be an undertaking which has almost invariably to be given by a retailer to repair any faults which occur within a certain time in such goods as motor-cars, domestic electrical appliances, etc. (Such an undertaking is known as a *warranty*.) In other cases a retailer may promise to service an article he has sold: that is, to check its efficiency from time to time.

(d) Some retailers provide *credit facilities* for their customers.

5.3 TYPES OF RETAILER

Retailers may be distinguished between:

(a) those who sell in shops and those who use other methods;
(b) small units and large units;
(c) those who are solely retailers ('traditional retailers') and those who combine retailing with manufacturing and/or wholesaling.

5.4 STREET-MARKET TRADERS

These retailers operate in open markets which are usually controlled by the local council. A rent is payable to the council, which imposes regulations about cleanliness, noise, traffic congestion, etc. Many of these market-places have been in existence for centuries. Fruit and vegetables are commonly sold in such markets and there are also long-established markets for such goods as textiles, china, etc. Some of the traders also produce the goods they sell, such as vegetables and flowers. Others buy from manufacturers and wholesalers, or, in the case of second-hand goods, from previous owners.

Prices are usually below those in shops because of the street traders' low overhead costs.

5.5 INDEPENDENT RETAILERS

These usually own single shops. As we saw earlier, some businesses must be small because of the nature of the service they provide. Many, however, are in direct competition with large retail units. Every town has some small grocers, though, because of the high rents charged, few will be found in the main streets.

Like most forms of business, it is more costly, relative to size, to run a small shop than a large one. A small retailer cannot get the advantage of the lower prices which are available for large purchases from suppliers and his overheads are greater when measured against the amount of his sales. Consequently, his prices are almost invariably higher than those charged by the large shops.

Why, then, do they survive? It must first be said that many of them *do not*. For many years there has been a steep decline in the number of independent shopkeepers, and this seems likely to continue. Those who survive do so because they provide services which the large shops do not. The 'little corner shop' still exists because it is close to its customers. If one needs one or a few items in a hurry, it is reasonable to go to the nearest place to get them. Few people, however, do their *main* shopping in such places. The weekly trip for groceries will usually be to a larger shop where the prices are lower and the choice of goods available larger.

The small shop will often be open during hours when the large ones are not. Again, the small shopkeeper scores on the grounds of convenience.

In the past many small shops had an advantage because they gave credit and the large shops did not. The position is now reversed. Small shopkeepers cannot afford to sell on credit because it is costly and risky. On the other hand, many large shops are now more ready to give credit and, indeed, are *anxious* to do so.

5.6 MULTIPLE SHOPS

These are always operated by large companies and the distinguishing feature is that they have numerous branches. They usually all trade under the same name and are decorated in the same style. This makes them easily recognisable, so that a Woolworth store, for example, in one town will be similar to one in any other town. (Some large companies, however, trade under a variety of names. For example, footwear is sold in England in shops carrying different names but most of them are owned by the same company. It is not uncommon for what appears to be several different shops, but which in fact are part of the same firm, to be trading near one another.)

All the branches are directed from the centre. Although each branch has a manager, all the buying is done at the head office (giving the advantages of bulk buying) and policies are imposed from there on such matters as staff wages, selling prices, advertising, etc.

Some sell only a particular type of good and these are known as *specialist multiples*. The shoe shops already mentioned provide one example. Others sell only suits, dresses, motor accessories, furniture, etc. Mothercare Ltd, for example, concentrates on selling goods suitable for babies and young children.

Other shops sell a variety of goods and they are known as *variety chain stores*. The most well known of these is probably F. W. Woolworth & Co. Ltd. Such shops contain what is really a lot of other shops, perhaps supplying goods ranging from confectionery and haberdashery to electrical supplies and furniture.

In recent years specialist multiples have tended to become variety chain stores. Marks & Spencer Ltd no longer confines itself to clothing but also sells food, wine, cosmetics, etc. Boots the Chemists Ltd originally sold only pharmaceutical products but now it also deals in records and discs, books, domestic cleaning materials, cameras and a multitude of other goods.

5.7 DEPARTMENT STORES

These are stores which contain a large number of different shops. To the extent that they offer a wide range of goods, they are similar to variety chain stores, but department stores always occupy very large premises and have a distinctive 'atmosphere'. Probably the most famous department store is Selfridges.

The nature of department stores has changed since they first became popular in the early part of the century. They then catered for the more prosperous classes and were most successful in the West End of London. They offered to those who could afford it the opportunity of doing all their shopping under one roof, probably spending much of the day in the store. The surroundings were luxurious and there was an emphasis on personal attention. Probably only Harrods is able to maintain these standards today. The stores also provided services in the form of restaurants, hairdressing salons, children's nurseries, etc.

The prosperity of such stores declined when wealth became more evenly distributed between the social classes. Eventually they had to change in order to survive. The atmosphere of 'exclusiveness' was removed so that more customers could be attracted. In other words, the stores had to have a more 'popular appeal'. Department managers no longer had sole control but, as in the chain stores, had to abide by decisions made at head office.

Although their character changed, a few remained as single shops, but others, such as Debenhams and Army & Navy Stores, became chains.

5.8 CO-OPERATIVE RETAIL SOCIETIES

The constitution of co-operative societies was discussed in the previous chapter. As retailers they are variety chain stores because they sell a wide range of products and they are controlled from head offices. They also provide services which are not available in other chains, such as banking, a funeral service and delivery of coal, milk and bread.

The societies were started as a working-class movement, but with changing social conditions they lost much in competition with the other large stores. This was not only because the large retailers were expanding rapidly but also because the societies held on to principles which were no longer practical. For example, the management today is in the hands of experienced and well-paid executives, whereas for many years the business was run by ordinary members. Although they were firm believers in the philosophy of the movement, they were not practical businessmen.

The societies have reduced their prices to the level of their competitors, whereas previously they did not do so because they considered that price-cutting was morally wrong. They had found that their customers were not prepared to pay higher prices in spite of their ideals. By increasing their efficiency the societies found that prices could be reduced without causing hardship to their staff.

To get more of the benefits of large-scale retailing the number of societies has been reduced by a series of amalgamations. In 1967 there were 625 regional societies and the movement is now well on its way of reaching its target of 50 societies.

Although retail societies are linked to the Co-operative Wholesale Society (CWS), they are not controlled by it. Each society makes its own policies and fixes its own prices. All the goods are no longer bought from the CWS because in order to satisfy customer demands it is necessary to also buy from other sources.

5.9 SUPERMARKETS AND HYPERMARKETS

The distinctive features of these stores are as follows:

(a) Size
They are always large. A supermarket has over 186 square metres of floor space; a hypermarket is one with more than 2500 square metres.

(b) Quick turnover

Only goods which sell readily are stocked. Sophisticated stock-keeping methods ensure that only the minimum amount is in stock at any one time and yet supplies rarely run short. This provides a saving in storage space and ensures that perishable goods are always fresh.

(c) Small work-force

Customers serve themselves and pay at check-out points. This results in a considerable saving in wages.

(d) Low prices

Prices generally are very competitive. This is because purchases are on a vast scale and operating costs are reduced to the minimum.

(e) Range of goods

A wide variety of goods is stocked to encourage 'one-stop shopping'. If a person buys groceries in the store, he or she will, because he or she is already in the shop, probably buy meat, wine, etc., as well.

Hypermarkets differ from supermarkets in other respects apart from size. They aim to attract the shopper who is a motorist. The stores are situated outside large towns and provide extensive parking space. The principle is that the time and money spent in travelling to the store will be more than offset by the savings enjoyed in buying a large amount of goods at low prices.

5.10 VOLUNTARY RETAIL CHAINS

Small firms in the grocery trade have suffered heavily in competiton with the large retailers. One of their problems has been that because of the size of their trade they bought only small amounts from wholesalers. Large firms which can give big orders for their goods get them at very much lower prices. The retailers' answer has been to form themselves into groups under an agreement with wholesalers. All the orders by the retailers go to the wholesalers in the group so that the latter can place large orders with the manufacturers at very much lower prices. Thus the wholesalers are certain of a flow of orders from the retailers and the retailers get the benefit of substantial discounts.

All the retailers trade under a nationally known 'label' (such as Wavy Line and Spar), and as this is supported by advertising to make the name well known the retailers benefit. Over 3000 retailers 'sail' under the Spar 'flag'.

To maintain the reputation of the group certain conditions are laid down with which the retailers must comply. Their premises must be maintained at a high standard, a minimum range of goods must be stocked and there is some control on the prices which may be charged.

5.11 MOBILE SHOPS

These are vans which make regular calls on customers. There has been a decline in travelling shops which deliver bread, fruit and vegetables but most milk and heating oil continue to be sold by this method. For obvious reasons, mobile shops are more frequently used in remote country areas.

5.12 MAIL–ORDER HOUSES

Under one form of this system consumers order through the post from wholesalers. A considerable amount of goods is purchased through agents of the sellers. Many of these are housewives working in their spare time who take catalogues to customers, forward the orders and, in some cases, collect the repayments. For many people the attraction of this way of buying is that credit is allowed. If a buyer has partly repaid the instalments on one purchase and shown herself to be reliable, a further order can be made, so that the new debt is added to the balance of the old one.

Because the mail-order house buys such huge quantities of goods it obtains substantial discounts from the manufacturers. The house operates as a large wholesaler who cuts out the retailers' profits. No expensive shops have to be maintained. It is these factors which account for the large profits it can make. Against this must be set the considerable expense of printing impressive-looking catalogues, the high cost of postage and packing, and the commissions paid to the agents. Also, unless the giving of credit is strictly controlled the house will incur a lot of bad debts.

This method of trading expanded considerably in the early 1970s. Buyers like it because they can order goods 'in the comfort of their own homes'. They know they will receive goods of a satisfactory standard because most of the products are well-known makes which are available in shops.

Clothing accounts for over half the sales. There are also large sales of textiles, bedding, furniture, garden tools, toys, etc.

Another form of mail-order trading is carried on by *manufacturers* who sell direct to the public. They obtain their orders by advertising in newspapers. Among the many goods sold in this way are furniture, books, clothes and bedding.

5.13 DISCOUNT STORES

This is another method which has developed considerably in recent years. Discount stores are very large warehouses to which consumers go to buy goods. Like mail-order houses, they are wholesalers who buy in very large quantities at favourable prices and sell direct to the public. No money has to be spent to make the warehouse as attractive as a shop, the customer has to provide his own transport, no credit or after-sales services is provided and only a few people have to be employed. Consequently, the prices charged by these stores are much lower than they are in shops. Some stores sell items such as television sets, deep-freezers and refrigerators, carpets, etc. Others specialise in 'do-it-yourself' goods. There is a separate type of store which sells groceries but only to approved retailers. Such stores are often referred to as *cash-and-carry* stores.

5.14 RETAILING UNDER FRANCHISE

Some retailers have 'concessions' to sell or use the products of a particular maker. Examples are bars selling hamburgers, fried chicken, doughnuts, etc., where the retailer agrees to buy his materials from one supplier only. All the bars selling one product are decorated in the same style and use the same name (such as 'Wimpey'), so that the retailers benefit by having an easily recognised shop. The giver of the franchise trains the retailer and helps him further by advertising.

Launderettes also usually operate under franchise.

5.15 VENDING MACHINES

Slot machines for chocolate have been a familiar sight on railway stations for many years. The method now extends to a wide range of products, including drinks, cigarettes, food items and even packaged meals. These are 'shops' which never close and which require no serving staff. To be profitable they must only offer goods which are in constant demand, the machines must not be allowed to stand empty and they must be kept in good operating order.

5.16 HOW RETAILING HAS CHANGED

We have seen that in the retail trade there are various forms of shops and that some retailing is done without shops. In recent years the proportions taken by each form of retail outlet have altered considerably. Some have declined and others have increased. This may be summarised as follows:

(a) There has been a continuous and marked increase in the size of large retailers. The number of small firms continue to decline.

(b) Amalgamations are increasing, so that trading is in fewer hands.

(c) In Britain, shops set up by immigrants from certain countries flourish because of the long hours the owners are prepared to keep the shops open.

(d) Self-service, which was originally confined to grocery stores, is now a feature of a high proportion of shops in general.

(e) Shops, even small ones, sell a wider variety of goods, so that there is less specialisation.

(f) Packaging has increased, so that articles previously sold loose are widely available in labelled packs. Examples are screws, electrical fittings etc. Even furniture can be bought in sealed packs of components to be assembled by the buyers.

(g) There has been an increase in the sale of 'do-it-yourself' materials and equipment. An example is the range of plumbing fitments available.

(h) 'Shops within shops' are increasing. This occurs when a well-known firm (such as retailer of photographic equipment) has the right to

(i) 'Shopping precincts' are increasing in number. These are shopping areas specially designed to be 'traffic free', so that shoppers may walk in comfort and in attractive surroundings.

5.17 LARGE–SCALE RETAILING

Earlier, we saw that most businesses tend to grow in size. In recent years this has been particularly so in the retail trade. Most of the grocery and provisions trade is in the hands of such large companies as Sainsbury and Tesco. Well-known names in other areas include W. H. Smith & Son, Halfords, F. W. Woolworth & Co. and Austin Reed.

5.18 THE ADVANTAGES OF LARGE–SCALE RETAILING

These include the following:

(a) Buying in bulk
A shop selling huge quantities will obviously buy in large amounts. The result is that the goods can be purchased much more cheaply than would be the case for smaller orders.

(b) The use of 'own branding'
In large stores many well-known products are sold under the name of the store, while others appear under the name of the manufacturer.

Packets of the same product are sold side by side, some with the store's name on them and some bearing the manufacturer's usual label. Those with the store's name will usually be a little cheaper than the others. An example is given in Figure 5.1. This arrangement arises from an agreement between the store and the manufacturer whereby the store agrees to buy a large quantity of goods bearing its own name. Manufacturers welcome such a system because it assures them of large purchases by the retailer. Therefore, 'own branding' is only possible where a retailer is large enough to be able to promise very large orders.

Another version of this system is where a manufacturer undertakes to produce goods to the specification of the retailer. The retailer then sells the goods under his own brand name. Such goods are produced *only* for the particular retailer. The best example is provided by Marks & Spencer Ltd, which has a number of manufacturers producing goods only for the store. All the goods are sold under the name 'St Michael,' a name which is exclusive to the store. The manufacturers benefit because they are certain to be able to sell large quantities of their products. They have no costs of advertising to meet; distribution expenses are reduced because they have only one buyer. Again, such a system can be operated only by a very large retailer.

(c) Specialist buying

A small retailer selling a wide variety of goods can choose only from those offered him by a wholesaler or a manufacturer's salesman. Large retailers have specialist buyers who have a wide market to choose from. Obviously, this must result in more efficient buying. (This is discussed in more detail in Chapter 13.)

(d) Fewer shop staff

Most large retailers use the self-service method. Customers choose their own purchases instead of giving orders to assistants. Most of the staff required will be those filling the shelves and those operating 'check-out points'. Specialisation of labour in other parts of the shop will result in economies. For example, some staff will concentrate on cutting meat and others will weigh and wrap it.

(e) The use of aids to efficiency

A large retailer can afford aids which will reduce costs and increase efficiency. For example, computers can be used to control stock and to analyse trends of sales as between one product and another.

Fig. 5.1 *proprietary brand and 'own brand'*

(f) Quick turnover
Because so much is sold, the large retailer can take a small profit on each sale, thereby attracting customers with low prices. The sheer *volume* of sales will provide the retailer with a good *total* profit.

(g) The popularity of self-service
Because a large retailer can offer self-service, a customer knows what he is buying and the price of it because it is there for him to see. Although he has to queue to pay, he does not have to wait to be served.

5.19 THE DISADVANTAGES OF LARGE-SCALE RETAILING

The disadvantages can include the following:

(a) Only standard goods are stocked
A large retailer will stock only those items which are in regular demand. A shopper who requires any other item must search for a small retailer who has it.

(b) Little personal service
This has relevance to the preceding item. A customer will get only the service which is offered to everyone; no one gets 'special treatment'.

(c) Losses by pilfering
A self-service shop is likely to suffer from the activities of 'shoplifters'. On a national scale the losses due to pilfering are considerable.

5.20 ESTABLISHING A RETAIL BUSINESS

In setting up a business which deals directly with the public the following matters must be taken into account:

(a) The amount and type of competition
If a similar type of business already exists in the area, it must be decided if there is enough custom for two businesses. Unless the newcomer is to be so strong that he will eliminate the established business it must be accepted that the 'battle' will be to get the major share. The newcomer must therefore be able to offer something which the other business does not – such as lower prices, a wider range of goods, some special service, etc.

(b) The site
Some shops must be in the main shopping centre, while others would be in areas where customers would expect to find them. For example, shops selling popular ranges of dresses must be in a prominent position, but an 'exclusive' dress shop would be elsewhere. A person looking for a shop which sells only books or one specialising in lampshades would not expect to find it in the main streets. The rents of 'High Street shops' are certain to be very high, so if one sets up business in that area one must hope to make large trading profits.

The proximity of car-parking facilities is always an advantage.

(c) Suitability of the premises

Accommodation which is specific to the type of business must usually be provided, such as refrigerated rooms for butchers' shops, dispatch departments where a delivery service is provided, changing cubicles for clothing shops, etc. Almost invariably there must be provision for storing stock.

(d) The type of custom

In many businesses there is a choice between standards offered to the public. It must therefore be decided what sort of appeal is to be made to prospective customers. A wine shop can concentrate on the better-quality products: it may offer popular wines at normal prices; or it may sell them at cut prices. The choice will influence the layout of the shop, the services given and the amount of stock held.

EXERCISES

1 'A retailer breaks bulk.' How does this benefit the person he buys from and the person to whom he sells?

2 If you buy a fresh fish from a shop, what service does the shop-keeper give you?

3 Why do small grocers continue to exist in towns where there are supermarkets?

4 How do you account for the declining number of small chemist shops?

5 X Ltd owns a number of chemist shops, selling drugs, cosmetics and toilet requisites. Why should it be decided to now trade as a variety chain?

6 How would a small grocer benefit from joining a voluntary retail chain? What advantages do wholesalers get from belonging to such groups?

7 If you wanted to buy a rare sort of cheese, why would it be unlikely that you could get it from a grocery supermarket?

8 Explain the statement that 'in a supermarket the shopper does most of the work'. If this is true, why do people use them?

9 Why do people buy from mail-order firms goods they have not first examined?

10 In what ways do co-operative retail societies differ from other retailers selling the same sorts of goods? What is the relationship of a retail society to the Co-operative Wholesale Society?

11 What is meant by 'own brands'? How does the system benefit the shopper and the producer?

12 Give examples of businesses: (a) which eliminate the wholesaler and the retailer; and (b) which eliminate the wholesaler.

13 Why can supermarkets offer goods at comparatively low prices and yet make substantial profits?

14 Describe the distinguishing features of: (a) discount stores; (b) franchise trading.

15 What are the chief differences between shops in the main shopping centres and those near an outlying house estate? Why should there be these differences?

16 In recent years in what ways have the following altered as regards the grocery trade: (a) delivery of purchases; (b) packaging of goods; (c) shop opening hours; and (d) the speed of shopping?

17 Assume that different people are aiming to set up the following businesses. In each case state where the business is likely to be suited and why that site would be chosen: (a) antique furniture shop; (b) grocery supermarket; (c) cash-and-carry store selling electrical goods; (d) stamp dealer.

CHAPTER 6

THE WHOLESALE TRADE

Traditionally, the wholesaler buys in large quantities from manufacturers and sells in smaller quantities to retailers. We have seen that the *function* of the wholesaler is often undertaken by manufacturers who sell direct to consumers and by retailers who buy direct from manufacturers. These practices are increasing so that wholesaling *as a separate activity* is declining. Nevertheless, the work of storing large amounts of goods, breaking them into smaller amounts and distributing them still has to be done, even though it may not be a wholesaler as such who does it. In this chapter, however, we are mainly concerned with individual wholesalers and the service they provide.

6.1 HOW THE WHOLESALER SERVES OTHER TRADERS

To see how the wholesaler provides advantages to manufacturers and retailers we can consider what risks and expenses those two groups would be faced with if the wholesaler did not exist. The benefits they receive can be summarised as follows:

(a) Manufacturers do not have to store their products
The wholesaler removes the goods from the manufacturer as they are made. Warehouses cost a lot in rent and wages; all the time goods are in store there is the risk of damage, theft and, for some goods, deterioration. These risks and expenses are taken on by the wholesaler.

(b) Manufacturers and retailers do not have to find each other
A shopkeeper may know a score of firms which make the kinds of goods he sells. Without the services of a wholesaler he would have to make enquiries of all those producers. Instead, he has to consult only the wholesaler because he has the goods of all the manufacturers.

A manufacturer may have, say, 500 retailers who buy his kind of product. If there were no wholesaler, he would have to have salesmen visiting each retailer in the hope of getting orders. If he used a wholesaler, however, that person would be the only buyer he would have to deal with.

Figure 6.1 first shows the number of 'contacts' which would have to be made if there were merely 4 manufacturers and 8 retailers and no wholesaler. It will then be seen that the number of contacts is considerably reduced if a wholesaler exists.

(c) Administration and transport costs are reduced

Every sale by a manufacturer involves a lot of paperwork. Prices must be quoted, orders processed, accounts written up, deliveries made, debts collected, etc. There is no more administrative work required to deal with a large order than there is for a small one, however. Referring again to Figure 6.1 one can see that if there is a wholesaler there are fewer buying and selling transactions. Consequently, both manufacturers and retailers spend less on administration.

Transport costs, too, are reduced because there will be fewer deliveries made by the manufacturer. The wholesaler could make one delivery of goods supplied by several manufacturers to a retailer.

(d) Manufacturers' risks are reduced

It takes time to produce goods, so products are made well ahead of their sale to retailers. There can be the risk that when the goods have been produced there will be little demand for them. This may be because fashions have changed or it may be impossible to sell the goods at a profit because a competitor is selling at a lower price. The wholesaler is in closer contact with the buying public than the manufacturer is. He is therefore able to order goods from the manufacturer before the retailers order from *him*. It is then the *wholesaler* who runs the risk of misjudging the market.

(e) The cash problems of manufacturers and retailers are reduced

The wholesaler pays the manufacturer promptly. The latter therefore receives payment shortly after each batch of production and does not have to wait for payment from a lot of small buyers. He therefore has a regular inflow of cash, reducing the amount he has to borrow.

The wholesaler usually grants credit to the retailers. As a consequence, they have time to sell the goods before they have to pay for them.

(f) The wholesaler smooths out fluctuations in supply and demand

Where sales of a particular good varies according to the time of the year, the trade is said to be 'seasonal'. For example, a high proportion of indoor toys and games are sold only at Christmas. A manufacturer, however, wants to be in production throughout the year. Indeed, because the sales

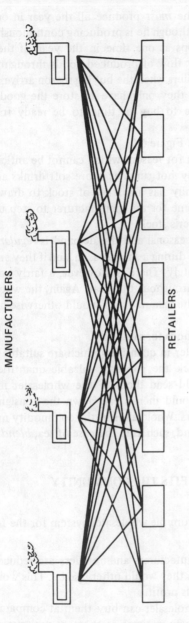

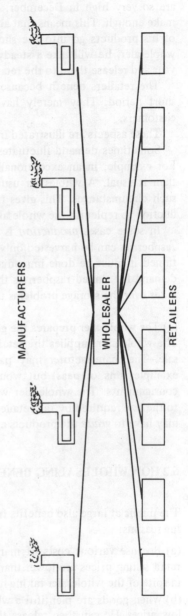

Fig 6.1 *how a wholesaler reduces the costs of administration and transport*

are so very high in December, he *must* produce all the year in order to make enough. This means that although he is producing continuously most of his products go into the shops at one time in the year. If there is a wholesaler, he will take a steady flow of produced goods throughout the year and release them to the retailers when the buying season arrives.

The retailers benefit because they only have to store the goods for a short period. They merely have to buy in time to be ready for their customers.

These aspects are illustrated in Figure 6.2.

Sometimes demand fluctuates for reasons which cannot be anticipated. For example, in an exceptionally hot summer more soft drinks are sold than is usual. A wholesaler usually has a reserve of stock to draw on in such circumstances. This gives time for the manufacturer to step up production to replenish the wholesaler's stock.

In some cases *production* is seasonal and the demand is *regular*. Thus raspberries can be harvested only during a short season, and if they are to be tinned it must be done immediately. There is, however, a fairly constant demand for tinned raspberries throughout the year. Again, the wholesaler takes over the storage problems the manufacturer would otherwise have.

(g) The wholesaler prepares the goods for sale

The wholesaler supplies the retailer in quantities which are suitable for resale. The manufacturer may pack the goods in saleable quantities (for example, tins of peas) but would send them to the wholesaler in large consignments. The wholesaler would then break down the consignments to the size required by the retailers. Wholesalers in the commodity markets may have to *grade* the products and, such as in the case of tea, *blend* them.

6.2 HOW WHOLESALING BENEFITS THE COMMUNITY

The public at large also benefits from the wholesaler system for the following reasons:

(a) Because various costs of manufacturers and retailers are reduced the retail selling prices are lower than they would otherwise be. This would be in spite of the wholesaler taking his profit.

(b) When goods are plentiful a wholesaler can buy them at comparatively low prices. He can then release them in times of shortage without raising prices unduly. (He could, of course, abuse his position by deliberately charging very high prices when supplies are scarce. This would be possible, however, only in the unlikely event of him controlling all the supplies.)

(c) Because less transporting is required the community benefits by a

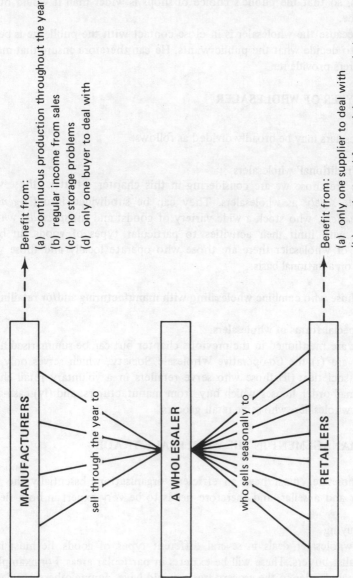

Fig 6.2 *how a wholesaler assists in a seasonal trade*

MANUFACTURERS

sell through the year to

A WHOLESALER

who sells seasonally to

RETAILERS

Benefit from:
(a) continuous production throughout the year
(b) regular income from sales
(c) no storage problems
(d) only one buyer to deal with

Benefit from:
(a) only one supplier to deal with
(b) goods stored for a minimum period
(c) payment made after sales

lesser use being made of the roads. Not so much has to be spent on maintaining the roads and less time is wasted in traffic jams.

(d) Small retailers are better able to withstand competition from the big shops, so that the public's choice of shops is wider than it would otherwise be.

(e) Because the wholesaler is in close contact with the public he is better able to decide what the public wants. He can therefore ensure that manufacturers provide it.

6.3 TYPES OF WHOLESALER

Wholesalers may be broadly divided as follows:

(a) 'Traditional' wholesalers
These are those we are considering in this chapter – that is, those who operate *solely* as wholesalers. They can be subdivided into (i) *general wholesalers*, who stock a wide variety of goods; and (ii) *specialist wholesalers* who limit their activities to pàrticular types of goods. In both types of wholesaler there are those who operate locally and those who trade on a national basis.

(b) Those who combine wholesaling with manufacturing and/or retailing.

(c) Special forms of wholesalers.
These are mentioned in the previous chapter but can be summarised here. They are (i) the Co-operative Wholesale Society, which serves only the retail societies; (ii) those who serve retailers in a voluntary retail chain; (iii) mail-order houses which buy from manufacturers; and (iv) cash-and-carry wholesalers who serve retail grocers.

6.4 MANAGEMENT IN THE WHOLESALE TRADE

A wholesaler must have an efficient organisation. Essentially, he is a buyer and a seller, and therefore needs to be very expert in both fields:

(a) Buying
If a wholesaler deals in several different types of goods, he must have specialist buyers. These will be experts in particular areas. For example, a large wholesaler to the grocery trade would have, among others, specialists buying cheese and wine. The principles of efficient buying by wholesalers are the same as those which apply to retailers. These are discussed more fully in Chapter 13.

(b) Selling

The wholesaler must be in constant touch with retailers, so that salesmen must be employed. He must have his 'finger on the pulse' of the buying public so that he can quickly notice any change in demand. It may be necessary to have showrooms in which to display the goods.

6.5 ARE WHOLESALERS NEEDED?

A wholesaler is one link in the chain of distribution. Every link must have its reward in the form of profit. Why, then, must there be a reward for this particular link? The wholesaler does not produce anything and he has no contact with the consumers. One could say that all he does is bring producers and retailers together – for which he makes a profit.

First, there is the unavoidable fact that no one in business pays for anything which is not necessary. If there *are* wholesalers, we must therefore assume they provide a service which is worth paying for. This we can accept because we have seen that the wholesaler provides benefits for manufacturers and retailers. We have also seen that the wholesaler can reduce the prices paid by the consumer.

Nevertheless, there has in recent years been a considerable reduction in the number of wholesalers – and this trend seems certain to continue. This does not contradict the statement above because, as we have already seen, the wholesaling *function* is essential – although it is not always done as a separate activity. 'Traditional' wholesalers have declined in number because more and more companies add wholesaling to their other activities. The individual wholesaler will always be eliminated where it is more economic for one of the other parties to take over his activities.

Wholesalers are 'middlemen' because they come between manufacturers and consumers. As we shall see in the next chapter, there are *other* middlemen who extend the chain of distribution. We will also see how wholesalers are often grouped into markets.

6.6 WAREHOUSING

We have seen how other traders benefit if the goods are stored by a wholesaler. Because of the decline in the number of wholesalers, however, much warehousing is now provided by the manufacturers. Large retailers also have warehouses but these are only used for storing goods for a short period. Thus a chain of shops will have a central place for receiving and sorting its purchases and from which it will dispatch them to its branches as the goods are required.

Efficient management of a warehouse requires the following:

(a) Firm stock control

Goods must be stored in an orderly manner, so that any item can be found easily. There must be an efficient system for 'checking in' goods as they are received into store and 'checking out' goods as they are dispatched, so that it is always known exactly how much there is of any one item.

(b) Protection

Goods must be stored in such a way that they do not deteriorate or become damaged. In certain instances this will mean providing cold-storage units. All goods must be protected against fire. Many goods have to be kept at a certain temperature and other goods must not be capable of being affected by damp. All goods must be safeguarded against theft and pilferage.

(c) Efficient distribution

There must be efficient methods of dealing with sales (to customers or branches, as the case may be) so that orders are dealt with quickly and accurately. Accounts of sales to customers must be kept in such a manner as to reduce the occurrence of bad debts. There must be an efficient transport system so that few half-filled vehicles are sent out and no journeys are duplicated.

(*Bonded warehouses* are used for some imported goods. They are discussed in Chapter 10.)

EXERCISES

1   How does a wholesaler reduce the storage costs of a firm which makes refrigerators and of those who retail them?

2   What are the problems of firms engaged in seasonal trades? How can wholesalers help solve these problems? Give two examples of seasonal fluctuations in trade.

3   How true is it to say that 'the wholesaler is dying out'?

4   Explain the statement that 'a wholesaler pays his bills promptly and receives payment less promptly'. Who benefits from this?

5   Why may it cost a retailer no more to buy from a wholesaler than from a manufacturer? Who benefits from this?

6   Discuss the statement that 'a wholesaler must be very aware of what is being produced and what consumers want'.

7   What is necessary for a warehouse to be efficient?

8   'Wholesaling is a form of specialisation'. Explain this statement and also discuss the amount of specialisation which may exist *within* a wholesale firm.

9   A company makes electrical fitments for the domestic market. These

are sold in hardware shops. If the goods are marketed through wholesalers, how does this reduce the administration costs of (a) the manufacturer, and (b) the retailers?

10 How does the owner of a delicatessen benefit if he buys cheese and spices from a wholesaler?

CHAPTER 7

MIDDLEMEN AND MARKETS

The word 'middlemen' is a general one, referring to all those people who come between manufacturers and consumers. Middlemen therefore include retailers and wholesalers. We have studied both of these in previous chapters and we now have to consider other middlemen.

Many middlemen operate within organised markets, so these will also be studied in this chapter.

7.1 TYPES OF MIDDLEMEN

There are many different businesses which act as middlemen. These (excluding wholesalers and retailers) can be divided into the following types (see also Figure 7.1):

(a) **Merchants** buy goods for resale at a profit. Many of them buy goods produced abroad and then import them for sale in this country. A merchant therefore *owns* the goods and trades *on his own account.*

(b) **Mercantile agents** are persons who act on behalf of other in making business deals. They may find buyers on behalf of the owners of goods, or they may find sellers on behalf of would-be buyers. Therefore, unlike a merchant, *an agent does not own the goods but acts for a principal.* Whereas a merchant hopes to make a profit, an agent's reward is in the form of commission.

An agent will be one of the following types:

(1) Brokers
These agents *never have possession* of the goods they deal in. Their job is to put buyers and sellers in touch with one another. They operate in most organised markets.

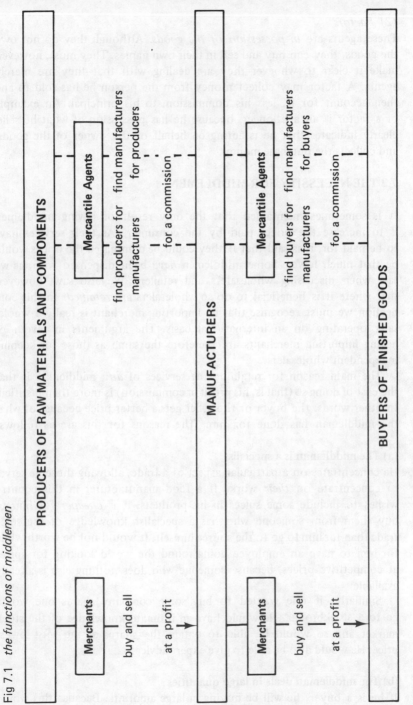

Fig 7.1 the functions of middlemen

(2) Factors

These agents are *in possession of the goods.* Although they do not own the goods, they can buy and sell in their own names. They must, however, make it clear to whoever they are dealing with that they are merely agents. A factor may collect money from the person he has sold to and then account for it, less his commission, to his principal. An example of a factor is an auctioneer, because he has possession of what he sells, clearly indicates that he is acting on behalf of the owner of the goods, and collects the purchase money.

7.2 THE NECESSITY FOR MIDDLEMEN

It is sometimes maintained that the only result of having middlemen is to increase the prices paid by the consumer. As their services have to be paid for, it is said that if they could be eliminated the prices would be that much lower. Some middlemen *have* been dispensed with, as we saw when discussing wholesalers and retailers. We also saw, however, that where it is beneficial to do so wholesalers are *retained.* In this connection we must recognise that an importing merchant is really a wholesaler operating on an international basis. The arguments in favour of having importing merchants are therefore the same as those for keeping independent wholesalers.

The main reason for retaining the services of *any* middleman is that the cost of doing so (that is, his profit or commission) is more than justified. In other words, the buyer or the seller gets a better price because of what the middleman has done for him. The reasons for this are as follows:

(a) The middleman is a specialist

He concentrates on a particular aspect of a trade, allowing those he serves to concentrate on *their* work. If a food manufacturer in this country wishes to include some spices in his products, it is *cheaper* for him to buy them from someone who has a specialist knowledge of the spice trade than for him to go to the source himself. It would not be worth while for him to have an employee going round the world looking for spices at competitive prices, because someone who does nothing else is already available.

Similarly, if one wanted to buy some company shares one would go to a stockbroker. He would have an intimate knowledge of the stock market and so would be able to obtain the shares at the very lowest price. He would also be able to give expert advice.

(b) The middleman deals in large quantities

If he is a buyer, he will be buying in large amounts. Because this would result in a lower unit cost, *his* buyers should get the goods cheaper than if they had bought comparatively small amounts from the producer.

Like any other businessman, a middleman incurs administration costs. The larger his business is, the wider he can spread those costs. The more units he deals in, the lower the amount of costs attributable to each unit. (This is one of the benefits of large-scale trading discussed in Chapter 4.) As a consequence, the amount he will charge a client would be less than the client's overheads would be if he did not use the middleman.

(c) The middleman encourages competition between buyers or sellers

Because the middleman buys from several sellers, he is able to purchase at the lowest possible price. He can go to all the suppliers, and as they all wish to sell to him they will compete against one another to get his custom. Obviously, therefore, he will buy from the one quoting the lowest price. If he is selling, he will meet buyers who are in competition with one another. If you wanted to sell some of your household furniture, you would ask an auctioneer to be your selling agent. All those wishing to buy second-hand furniture would compete against one another so that your furniture would be sold at the highest possible price.

7.3 MARKETS

A market is a place where buyers and sellers of specified goods meet in order to trade. The characteristics of a market are as follows:

(a) As mentioned above, the best price is obtainable if buyers or sellers are in direct competition with one another. In a market *all* the buyers and *all* the sellers meet in the same place. By the basic law of economics, if demand is stronger than supply then prices will rise; in the reverse circumstances prices will fall. In a market the forces of supply and demand are brought together so that, allowing for competition between buyers and between sellers, *a common price will emerge.* It follows that at any one moment there can be only one price for a particular commodity.

(b) A market is a *known source for specific commodities.* A person wishing to buy a product knows there is an established place he can go to get it. A seller knows where he can dispose of such a product. For example, all those wishing to buy shares and those wishing to sell shares will use the Stock Exchange.

(c) Organised markets have all the *administrative facilities* which are necessary. They have offices where the clerical work can be done; where appropriate, there are facilities for transporting the goods (in a fruit market the goods are brought in, sold and taken out); communication systems are available so that in many cases information can be instantly passed to and from all parts of the world.

(d) Markets have *procedures and rules*. For example, the Stock Exchange has elaborate regulations for the conduct of business in stocks and shares. Many markets have a code of conduct for those who deal there, so that there are no dishonest or otherwise unacceptable practices. There are usually procedures for settling disputes.

(e) The workings of most markets result in various forms of measurement being possible. For example, because the market price for each commodity is known, it is possible to *publish prices*. (The prices of some commodities are given in daily newspapers.)

The system also allows for goods to be *graded,* there being standards set for each grade. Thus there are prescribed sizes for potatoes, metals are classified according to the degree of purity, wheat is graded by type and quality, etc. Consequently, everyone knows exactly what the specifications are whenever a product is said to be of a certain grade. There is no need to inspect graded goods, so that deals can be made about goods which are not present in the market. Thus it is possible to buy in England wheat which is still in Canada awaiting shipment.

In this chapter we are concerned only with the major market institutions. Each such market specialises in particular commodities, so we are not considering small *general* markets such as a town's street market. Specialist markets deal only in very large amounts and are not open to the public. The members are all experts; indeed, some markets (such as the Stock Exchange) even restrict the number of experts who may be members. Many of the markets are very old, with traditions going back to when they were established in the days of Britain's pre-eminence as a trading nation.

(Care must be taken in the use of the word 'market'. In this chapter we are referring to highly organised market- *places*. We are not, therefore, discussing the 'retail market', for example. Also, the 'money market' is not an institution; it is a loose term covering finance generally. Similarly, the 'insurance market' relates to Lloyd's and the many insurance companies.)

7.4 TYPES OF MARKET IN THE UNITED KINGDOM

There are a considerable number of markets but we need to concern ourselves only with the larger ones:

(a) The *London Commodity Exchange*. This old-established market at the Corn Exchange, Mark Lane, deals in a wide variety of commodities. These include coffee, cocoa, jute, rubber, copra and vegetable oils.
(b) The *London Metal Exchange.* Here metals such as copper, lead, zinc and tin are traded.

(c) The *London Tea Auctions*. This was once part of the London Commodity Exchange.

(d) The *Baltic Exchange*. This is one of the oldest and most important markets in London. In fact, it consists of four markets:

   (i) The *Freight Market* deals with the chartering of ships (that is, the hiring of them) and of cargo space in them. A merchant requiring to move goods will use the Exchange to find an appropriate vessel to ship them in. The market enables the requirements of shippers to be matched to the available vessels. This can be a very complex operation because there will be many types of vessel operating different routes all over the world.

   (ii) The *Air Freight Market* provides a similar service in respect of goods transported by air.

   (iii) The *Grain Futures Market* is concerned with wheat, barley, etc. ('futures' are explained below).

   (iv) The *Oil and Linseeds Market* deals with linseed, soya beans, cotton seed, etc.

(e) Wool is marketed on the *London Wool Exchange* and the *Bradford Wool Exchange*.

(f) Raw cotton is bought and sold on the *Liverpool Cotton Exchange*. The *Manchester Royal Exchange* deals with yarn and cloth.

(g) The institutions in the financial market will be considered in Chapters 18 and 19.

(h) *Fresh produce markets*. Producers of fresh food bring their products to such markets and then they are sold. The produce is brought to the market early in the day, sold and quickly taken away by the buyers. These markets must therefore have extensive facilities for accommodating transport vehicles.

In London, certain markets remained on the same sites for centuries (e.g. Covent Garden for fruit and vegetables, Smithfield for meat and Billingsgate for fish). For obvious reasons, fish wholesalers have markets at fishing ports so that they can deal directly with the fishermen.

7.5 'SPOT' MARKETS

These are concerned with goods which are available for immediate delivery ('on the spot') upon payment. The goods are sometimes inspected before the purchase is made because not all goods can be graded. The quality of raw wool, for example, can vary considerably, so that standards cannot be set. Fresh produce is bought and sold on spot markets.

7.6 REDUCING THE RISKS OF PRICE FLUCTUATIONS

A manufacturer runs two possible risks from price fluctuations. First, the price of his *raw materials* may rise during production. Second, the price *at which he can sell his product* may fall. In either case market prices have moved against him. The measures which can be used to reduce these risks are explained below.

7.7 DEALING IN FUTURES

Before a manufacturer can go into production he needs to know what his costs will be. When he has established that figure he can then decide if his proposed selling price will give him a reasonable profit. Included in the costs will be the amount he will have to pay for his raw materials. These he may not require immediately, however, possibly because he is only *planning* production at this stage. Alternatively, he may require this knowledge because he is quoting a price for his product in the hope of getting a contract to make it for someone.

His risk is that the price of the raw materials may have risen by the time he requires them. If he has to buy at a price higher than the one in his estimate, his anticipated profit may well turn into a loss. He could, of course, buy the materials *now*, but this would mean that much of his capital would be 'tied up' in stock which is merely being stored for some time.

A solution to his problem may be to *buy futures*. This means that he enters into an agreement to take and pay for his materials in, say, three months' time at an agreed price. No matter what the market price of the materials is when they are delivered he will pay the price which was agreed upon when the contract was made. From the outset, therefore, he knows exactly what the materials will cost him, so that his original calculations cannot be upset.

Assume that in January the agreed price was £1000 for materials to be delivered in March. If in March the market price of those materials were £1100, the manufacturer would still pay only £1000. The seller would suffer, of course, because had he been free to do so he would have sold the materials on the market in March for £1100. If, instead, the market price fell to £900, the seller would gain because if he had not had the contract with the manufacturer he would have had to accept a lower price in the market in March.

In either instance the manufacturer would not be affected because his costs remain unaltered. The attitude of the seller would have been that in January he had made a definite sale. This is important in industries which produce goods which have an unpredictable demand. He runs the risk of having to sell below the market price but at least he is protected against a severe fall in market prices.

Dealing in futures, therefore:

(a) insures the buyer against a rise in prices;
(b) makes supply of the goods certain;
(c) insures the seller against a fall in prices; and
(d) provides the seller with a positive sale.

7.8 HEDGING

A manufacturer selling on the open market also runs the risk that when he has completed production the price at which he can sell will be below his anticipated price. Production is often a lengthy process, and the longer it is the more difficult it is to estimate what the product can be sold for. He is therefore trying to relate a *known* figure (his costs) to an *unknown* figure (what he can sell at).

If the market price of his product falls by the time he is ready to sell it, it may be at least partly due to the price of the raw materials having fallen. For example, if the price of cocoa beans falls, then one would expect the price of chocolate to fall as well. In such a situation the manufacturer will have paid for his raw materials at a price higher than the current one and will have to sell his product below his anticipated price.

Some safeguard against this is possible by hedging. (A hedge is a protection against wind and, similarly, a hedging operation aims to provide a shield against the harsh winds which can blow through the world of commerce.)

This can be illustrated by taking the example of a manufacturer of cloth. In January he plans to produce cloth for sale in March. The market price of that amount of cloth in January is £10 000 and he hopes the same price will prevail in March. He buys the yarn he will require for £5000, and as he estimates his other production costs will be £3000 he anticipates a profit of £2000.

He decides to protect himself against a fall in selling prices in March. Having purchased the yarn 'spot' (for immediate delivery) he makes an agreement to *sell* the same amount of yarn to a third party *in the future*. This is known as a *forward sale*. He therefore undertakes to deliver the yarn in March at today's price (£5000). If the market price of yarn in March is the same as it was in January, he will buy it in the market for £5000 and sell it for the same price. He will therefore make neither a profit nor a loss on the hedging transaction.

The anticipated results of the two transactions are set out in the first part of Figure 7.2, showing a profit of £2000.

Fig 7.2 *a demonstration of hedging*

Anticipated results				
Manufacturing			*Hedging*	
Sale of cloth in March		10 000	Sell yarn forward in January	5000
less			Buy yarn in March	5000
cost of yarn in January	5000		Profit/loss	. . . . .
other costs	3000	8 000		
Profit		£2 000		

Total profit £2000

Actual results on a falling market			
Manufacturing		*Hedging*	
Sale of cloth in March	9 000	Sell yarn forward in January	5000
less costs	8 000	Buy yarn in March	4000
Profit	£1 000	Profit	£1000

Total profit £2000

Actual results on a rising market			
Manufacturing		*Hedging*	
Sale of cloth in March	11 000	Sell yarn forward in January	5000
less costs	8 000	Buy yarn in March	6000
Profit	£3 000	Loss	£1000

Total profit £2000

Now consider what the position would be if in March he finds he can sell the cloth for only £9000. His manufacturing profit would then be only £1000. If the price of cloth has fallen, it is very probable that the price of yarn has also dropped. The illustration shows that the manufacturer can buy the yarn on the market in March for £4000. As he is paid the agreed price for it (£5000), he makes a profit of £1000 on the hedging transaction. His total profit is therefore £2000 - which was his anticipated figure.

The illustration also shows what would be the position if both sets of prices *rose* in March. If the market price of the cloth rose to £11 000, the manufacturer would make a profit of £3000. However, he would have to buy yarn at the inflated price of £6000, leaving him with a loss of

£1000 on the hedging transaction. Again, his total profit would equal the anticipated figure of £2000.

7.9 FUTURES MARKETS

Deals in which goods are to be delivered and paid for at a future date take place in what are known as *futures markets*. They are sometimes called *terminal markets*.

The procedures outlined above indicate only the principles of the system. In many dealings in futures actual delivery does not take place. Instead, the party who has lost on a deal pays the difference between the two prices to the other party. The purpose of futures is to insure against losses due to price movements, and any payments which have to be made are regarded as being the cost of that insurance.

There are speculators, however, who do aim to make profits from futures transactions. They enter into contracts with no intention of ever holding the goods. How well they fare depends upon how accurately they forecast prices. The speculators 'trade' contracts between themselves, and with buyers and sellers of goods who finds themselves in difficulties because of adverse price movements. As a contract may pass through many hands before it matures, speculating in futures can become very complex. Settlement between speculators usually consists of setting off the liabilities of one trader to another against contrary liabilities.

7.10 SPECULATION

The word 'speculator' is often used in an uncomplimentary manner. To talk of 'property speculators', for example, often implies grasping landlords or those indulging in dishonest property deals. Strictly speaking, however, to speculate means to conjecture, so that one may 'speculate about the prospects of peace', for example. Speculation therefore means attempting to look into the future. Almost all business activity is concerned with this. A manufacturer produces goods in *anticipation* of selling them at a profit; a company *hopes* its advertising will be successful.

In its most usual form, however, speculation means buying or selling *now* with the intention of selling or buying at a profit *in the future*.

What may be called 'acceptable speculation' includes a form of insurance. We have seen that hedging and dealing in futures reduce the risk of future price movements. If prices move the wrong way, the insurance provides at least partial compensation. If the compensation is not required, then the 'premium' paid for the insurance has still been worth while. (If your house has *not* yet burned down, you do not necessarily regret having taken out an insurance policy on it!)

Speculators can also benefit the market generally:

(a) They buy when prices are low and sell when prices are high. The effect of the buying is to put up a price which is particularly low; selling when the price is very high reduces the price. Therefore, *speculation smooths out price fluctuations*.

(b) If there is an excess of goods on the market, their price will be low. If a speculator buys at that price, it has the effect of absorbing some of the excess so that eventually more will be produced. Prices will be high when there is a shortage of goods. If a speculator then sells, the goods are released on to the market. Therefore, *speculation can smooth out fluctuations in supply*.

(c) *Speculators specialise in risk-bearing*. Other traders receive the benefits mentioned above, while the speculator accepts the dangers of his forecasts being wrong.

Speculation can, however, be unacceptable. Sometimes a market is upset by people 'dabbling' in something about which they are not knowledgeable. Occasionally, people will buy a share or a commodity on a 'hunch': that is, without making a careful assessment. This is a form of gambling. Alternatively, there can be 'panic selling' when there is no justification for apprehension.

The real evil of speculation, however, is when it is done by experienced operators manipulating the market. A market may be 'rigged' by spreading rumours so that the price of a share, for example, moves in a way which does not reflect the true situation. For instance, a story may be 'leaked' to the effect that a mining company has struck a rich lode when in fact it has not. In the past it was occasionally possible to 'corner a market': that is, to get control of all the supplies of a commodity and so force up prices. Today this is almost impossible, though it can sometimes be done for a very short period. 'Cornering' is more likely to take place in a society which is not highly organised or where conditions are exceptional, such as in a famine area where transport is disrupted.

7.11 MARKETING BOARDS

These are institutions set up by a government to handle all the sales of a particular type of product. A large proportion of the producers must agree to the scheme before it is established. After that, all producers (except those producing less than a very small amount) must register with the Board and comply with its regulations. The Board controls all aspects of marketing, including the fixing of prices. It can control the amount of production so that, for example, the Milk Marketing Board can increase or reduce the amount of cattle a farmer may have. It will establish systems of grading and set standards of quality. It may carry out research into more efficient methods of production.

Most of the management members of a Board are elected by the producers. The administration costs are paid by the members.

Marketing Boards operate in co-operation with the government and there are direct links between the Board and a Minister. For example, the government will be concerned about the effect on the cost of living of prices set by the Board; it may be necessary to give subsidies to some producers; and the Board may wish the government to place restrictions on some imported foods.

EXERCISES

1 'Some middlemen make money dealing in goods they never see. All they do is increase the price paid by the consumer.' Comment on this statement.

2 How does a *factor* differ from a *broker?* In what ways does a *merchant* differ from both? Give an example of each.

3 In what ways does the existence of a fish market benefit: (a) producers; (b) retailers; and (c) consumers?

4 The price paid for meat in a butcher's shop is far higher than that paid to a farmer for his dead animals. Why?

5 If you had a valuable picture to sell, would you sell it privately or would you pay for it to be auctioned? Give reasons for your answer.

6 Why does an organised market produce a common price for a product?

7 Give examples of goods sold by grade and those which are not. Are goods always inspected before they are purchased?

8 Where would a businessman go to: (a) charter a ship; (b) buy cotton; (c) sell meat; (d) buy copper?

9 What is meant by buying 'spot'?

10 Discuss the importance of *futures* to a company contracting to build a major road.

11 How can a manufacturer reduce the risk of a fall in demand for his goods by hedging?

12 Do you consider hedging to be a form of gambling?

13 Give examples of 'acceptable' speculation and speculation which is 'unacceptable'.

14 Name a Marketing Board in your country. How do the activities of that Board benefit (a) the members of the board, and (b) the community generally?

INSURANCE

No matter how accurately a businessman plans for the future there is always the possibility that some unexpected event will upset those plans. By means of insurance it is possible to obtain protection against the consequences of some of those events. No one would venture into business unless he knew that he would receive some help if an accident occurred which caused him financial loss. Industry would be brought to a standstill unless it had this confidence.

In many respects insurance differs from other commercial activities and we will consider these unique features in this chapter.

8.1 THE 'POOLING' OF RISKS

The way in which insurance works is based on long-established truths. To illustrate these we will assume there are a number of companies which wish to be protected against financial loss caused by damage to or destruction of their factories.

First, the possibility of damage or complete loss to any one company is small. During a year only a few of the factories will be harmed.

Second, if, however, a factory *is* damaged, the cost to its owners may be considerable.

The companies *could* arrange that if any company suffered a loss the others would join together to provide the unlucky one with compensation. The danger in this plan is that there may be several losses during the year, and in any event no one would know at the beginning of the year how much he would have to contribute.

The solution is provided by the insurance companies. They arrange for each company to pay a fixed amount into a fund held by an insurance company. If a company suffers a loss, the insurer will provide compensation, even if there is not enough money in the fund. Each company therefore pays a certain amount, known as a *premium*, to the insurance company.

This is a *known* expense as compared with the *unknown* expense of having to repair or replace a damaged factory. The 'lucky' companies will get nothing in return for what they have paid except the comfort of knowing that the insurance company had *guaranteed* to compensate them if they had been 'unlucky'.

This pooling of risks therefore means that each company *must* pay a comparatively small sum, but that *if* it suffers loss it will receive a much larger sum. They therefore share the risks but with the additional advantage of the insurance company's guarantee to compensate where necessary.

8.2 HOW PREMIUMS ARE FIXED

We have seen that the insurance company must compensate any company which suffers a loss and that the money to do so comes out of the premiums contributed by the companies. Obviously, the insurance company will not want to pay out more than it receives. It must therefore know *how likely* it is that a factory will be damaged. This is sometimes known as the 'probability of loss'. An insurance company can estimate this and the probability of other sorts of losses by using records which it has accumulated over the years and from official statistics. For example, it is known how many people are killed in car accidents every year. As the number of people driving cars is also known, it is possible to calculate what proportion of them are likely to be killed.

To give a simple example of how an insurance company calculates what premiums it must receive, let us assume that for a particular risk the probability of loss is 5 per cent:

(a) If 100 people each takes out insurance for £1000, the *maximun possible* loss is £100 000. This would be the amount to be paid by the insurance company if every person suffered a total loss.

(b) The insurer knows that, in fact, losses will most likely amount t only 5 per cent of that figure. Therefore, the *probable* loss is £5000.

(c) Accordingly, the insurance company must have £5000 in the pool. It will therefore ask each person to contribute by paying £50 as his premium. The premium rate will be 5 per cent of the amount insured.

This example is illustrated in Figure 8.1.

8.3 INSURABLE AND NON-INSURABLE RISKS

As an insurance company has to use statistics to assess the probability of a loss, it will not undertake a risk it cannot calculate. A businessman cannot insure against trading losses because there are no statistics which will take account of the many possible causes. For example, a trading loss may be

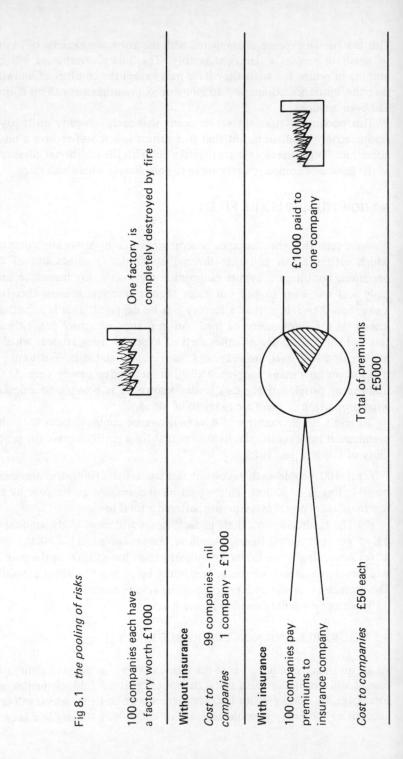

Fig 8.1 *the pooling of risks*

100 companies each have a factory worth £1000

One factory is completely destroyed by fire

Without insurance

Cost to companies 99 companies – nil
                     1 company – £1000

With insurance

100 companies pay premiums to insurance company

£1000 paid to one company

Total of premiums £5000

Cost to companies £50 each

due to the businessman's stupidity or rashness, or because he has been swindled.

If *some* statistics are available, however, insurance can be taken out against even the most uncommon risks. If one wanted to cross the Sahara by car, an insurance company could provide the necessary cover. One can also insure against being struck by lightning while playing golf or against being kicked by a horse.

8.4 HOW INSURANCE COMPANIES MAKE PROFITS

On studying the example in Section 8.2 one might say: 'But suppose claims on the insurance company *exceed* 5 per cent?' In that case, of course, the insurance company must nevertheless pay. It must be explained, however, that the high losses sustained this year will be added to the insurance company's statistics, so that next year (if losses are expected to go on rising), the probability of loss will be higher – and so will the premiums. If there are two major oil-tanker disasters in one year, the claims on the insurers may be greater than they had anticipated, so they will attempt to recoup by charging higher premiums in the next year.

In many cases, however, above-average losses of one year are compensated by below-average losses the following year. In an exceptionally bad winter more sheep will be lost than usual so that more will have to be paid to farmers who were insured. It is unlikely, however, that such bad weather will be repeated next year.

Insurers will charge higher premiums than normal where the risks are higher than average. On a national basis it will be known what proportion of factories are likely to be damaged by fire, but a factory making inflammable material is likely to suffer a greater loss if it has a fire than would another factory. Premiums are therefore 'loaded' where extra risk is involved.

Finally, insurance companies do not only rely on the premiums to provide money for claims. They are very large investors, and the millions of pounds they receive are invested (see Section 19.3).

8.5 INSURANCE AND ASSURANCE

As there is sometimes confusion about these two terms, it is necessary to explain the difference:

(a) **Insurance** provides cover for events which *may* happen. A factory may or may not be damaged, for instance.
(b) **Assurance** relates to events which *will* happen. The only certainty in life is death, because we must all die. An assurance policy is one on

which a claim will definitely be made because that will occur when the assured person dies. To be 'assured of something' is to be 'certain of something'.

8.6 THE PRINCIPLES OF INSURANCE

Because of the nature of insurance there are certain principles which do not apply elsewhere. They are necessary because without them the system of pooling risks would collapse. Before considering them in detail they may first be listed as follows:

(a) *Indemnity*, which includes the doctrines of *subrogation* and *contribution.*
(b) *Utmost good faith.*
(c) *Insurable interest.*
(d) *Proximate cause.*

8.7 INDEMNITY

The basic purpose of insurance is to restore a person who has suffered a loss to the position he was in immediately before the loss. To *indemnify* means to compensate or make good. If an insured article is destroyed, the compensation will be that sum of money which represents the value of the article *at the time of the accident.* If you bought a car for £2000 three years ago it will not be worth that figure today. Therefore, if it is destroyed today, what you will lose is *today's* value - say, £850. This will be the amount the insurance company will pay. The principle of indemnity cannot be strictly applied to personal accident insurance and life assurance, however. No money can compensate for the loss of a limb or for death. Such policies provide a 'benefit': that is, some financial relief.

Subrogation. It is a fundamental of insurance that a person making a claim must not profit thereby, which is why, as shown above, the insurance company will only pay for the *true* loss. It is for the same reason that the insured may receive nothing beyond the cash paid to indemnify him. If the wrecked car could be sold for £50 as scrap, you could not take the £850 *and* get another £50 by selling the wreckage. The doctrine of subrogation gives all the rights to the car to the insurance company. Subrogation means that the insurer 'takes the place of' the insured.

Contribution. Another way the assured could make a profit would be to insure the same article with two insurers. In the unlikely event of this happening (because double insurance would appear to be an attempt to defraud), the two insurers would share the compensation.

The *average clause.* Almost invariably, insurance policies contain an average clause. Suppose you bought a house five years ago at its then market value of £10 000 and you insured it for that sum. If you did not increase the amount of cover the maximum claim you could make on the insurance company today would be £10 000. If, therefore, the house is worth £15 000 today, you could not get full compensation. In fact, because the house is insured for only two-thirds of its current value you would get only two-thirds of *any* loss. Thus, if damage were suffered to the extent of £9000, you would only receive £6000.

8.8 UTMOST GOOD FAITH

The legal term for this is *uberrima fides.*

As the amount of the premium partly depends upon any circumstances which are specific to the risk, the insurance company must know of those risks. Some of that information must come from the person who is applying for the insurance. (Figure 21.3 later in the book shows the sort of form which must be completed when asking for life cover.) If the applicant were engaged in motor-racing, the insurance company would be taking a greater risk than normal if it insures him. If, however, the applicant said he did *not* race, the insurance company would be unaware of its extra risk. If it knew the truth, it would either refuse to insure or charge a higher premium.

Consequently, an applicant must show the 'utmost good faith' in disclosing any information he is asked to which may influence the attitude of the insurer. If this is not done, the insurer can refuse to pay on a claim.

8.9 INSURABLE INTEREST

You can insure against a risk only if *you* would suffer if the event insured against happened. Obviously, you are entitled to insure your own house against fire but you cannot insure a neighbour's house. Again, the intention is to prevent profit being made from insurance. If you could collect money because your neighbour's house was destroyed, it would not be because *you* had lost anything.

8.10 PROXIMATE CAUSE

The doctrine of proximate cause states that a claim will be met only if the loss suffered was a *direct consequence* of the insured risk happening. Suppose you insure against structural damage to your house. On most policies you would be able to claim if subsidence of the earth caused the walls to crack. If, however, your house was near some old mine workings, the policy would probably exclude this particular risk. You would, however, normally be able to claim if a runaway lorry crashed into the side of your house. It is therefore important to study carefully the exact wording of a policy.

8.11 TAKING OUT AND CLAIMING ON INSURANCE

Before applying for insurance the benefits offered by the insurance company and any exceptions or conditions it makes must be carefully considered. For a standard risk the insurance company will set this out in its literature. For example, one section of a 'home-risks' policy may provide an indemnity against damage to food kept in a deep freezer. The conditions relevant to that section and the conditions applicable to all sections of the policy will be similar to those shown in Figure 8.2.

Cover can then be applied for by completing and submitting a *proposal form*. The importance of answering each question honestly has already been mentioned.

If a claim has to be made, the insured must notify the insurer without delay. A written claim must then be submitted. Usually the insurer will inspect the damage, investigate the circumstances of its occurrence and estimate the amount of the loss. The insured may have to give evidence that he has not broken any of the conditions (such as wilfully damaging the freezer). The insurer will then offer an amount as compensation, and when the figure has been agreed (or settled by arbitration if agreement is not possible) the insured will receive payment.

8.12 TYPES OF INSURANCE

The main types of *commercial* insurance are explained below. There are also, as we have seen, *household policies* which provide cover for risks to homes and their contents. In addition, there are forms of insurance too numerous to list here. These range from those which will provide compensation if wet weather results in an outdoor event being ruined to one giving indemnity to those who would have suffered financial loss if the 1980 Olympic Games were cancelled.

8.13 MARINE INSURANCE

Hull insurance relates to the vessel and its fixtures, providing cover for loss or damage at sea. A *time policy* gives cover for a specified period, usually one year. A *voyage policy* relates to a particular voyage.

Cargo insurance provides cover for loss or damage of the cargo while it is in transit. As explained in Chapter 10, it promises indemnity to the *purchaser* of the goods being shipped.

Freight insurance. In this context 'freight' means the *charge* for carrying

Fig 8.2 *terms in a 'home-risks' policy*

SECTION 7—DEEP FREEZER CONTENTS

Cover

The Society will indemnify the Policyholder against loss of or damage to

1. Goods in the Deep Freezer in the Policyholder's Private Dwelling
2. Goods elsewhere in the Policyholder's Private Dwelling which would have been in the Deep Freezer but for the happening of an event giving rise to deterioration or putrefaction

due to

(a) A rise or fall in temperature as a result of
    (i) breakdown of or accidental damage to the Deep Freezer
    (ii) failure of any thermostatic or automatic controlling device of the Deep Freezer due to inherent defect
    (iii) failure of the public electricity supply not due to the deliberate act of the Supply Authority
(b) Contamination by refrigerant or refrigerant fumes

up to an amount not exceeding in any one Period of Insurance the Sum Insured under this Section stated in the Schedule of the Policy

Provided that:-

    (i) the age of the Deep Freezer does not exceed 10 years
    (ii) the Deep Freezer shall be maintained in efficient condition and good repair.

GENERAL EXCEPTIONS
APPLYING TO ALL SECTIONS

The Society shall not be liable in respect of

1. (a) loss or destruction of or damage to any property whatsoever or any loss or expense whatsoever resulting or arising therefrom or any consequential loss
    (b) any legal liability of whatsoever nature

    directly or indirectly caused by or contributed to by or arising from
        (i) ionising radiations or contamination by radioactivity from any nuclear fuel or from any nuclear waste from the combustion of nuclear fuel
        (ii) the radioactive toxic explosive or other hazardous properties of any nuclear explosive assembly or nuclear component thereof

Radio-activity

2. (a) any consequence of war invasion act of foreign enemy hostilities (whether war be declared or not) civil war rebellion revolution insurrection military or usurped power

Enemy Action

    (b) loss or damage to any property due to its confiscation requisition or destruction by order of any government public or local authority

Confiscation

3. loss damage or liability occasioned by or happening through riot or civil commotion arising in Republic of Ireland or Northern Ireland or elsewhere other than in Great Britain the Isle of Man or the Channel Islands.

Riot Civil
Commotion

4. loss or damage directly occasioned by pressure waves caused by aircraft or other aerial devices travelling at sonic or supersonic speeds

Sonic Bangs

5. loss or damage caused by the wilful act of the Policyholder or any member of his family

Wilful Acts

the cargo. The shipowner is paid this charge at the commencement of the journey, though strictly he is not entitled to it until he delivers the goods. This insurance provides him with indemnity in case he has to repay the charge because of his failure to deliver.

Shipowners' liability insurance gives the shipowner cover for a variety of possible liabilities. These would include those for damaging another vessel in a collision, injuring the crew or passengers, polluting beaches, etc.

8.14 FIRE INSURANCE

Most fire insurance policies provide cover not only for losses due to fire but also those caused by explosions, floods, burst pipes, burglary, etc.

If premises are badly damaged, they will not be usable for some time, so that profits will suffer. A *consequential loss* policy will indemnify the owner for the profits he would otherwise have earned during the period of disruption.

8.15 ACCIDENT INSURANCE

Liability insurance provides cover for claims which may be made against the insured person: employers may have to compensate workmen who are injured; a shopkeeper may have to pay damages to someone who is hurt in his shop; a motorist may be liable to a 'third party' he injures, such as a pedestrian. (Third-party insurance is compulsory for all motorists.)

Property insurance relates to a wide range of risks to any form of property. It includes accidental damage to vehicles and machinery, deliberate damage caused by burglary or vandalism, loss of animal stock for a variety of causes, etc.

Personal accident insurance relates to physical damage to a person or group of persons. It provides for losses due to physical disability. For a sportsman this could, of course, be particularly costly.

8.16 LIFE ASSURANCE

A *whole life policy* provides a 'benefit' upon death. The premiums are usually payable to at least the age of 60.

An *endowment policy* provides a 'benefit' at the end of a specified period or at death if that occurs first. (The features of such policies are discussed in Chapter 21.)

If an assured person ceases to pay the premiums on an endowment policy, he *may* be entitled to a partial refund. This figure would be its 'surrender value'. No refunds are paid on whole life policies which are allowed to lapse.

8.17 THE INSURANCE MARKET

This market consists of the following:

(a) *The insurance companies.* Between them these companies offer a wide variety of insurances. *They aid the community* in the following ways:

(i) they insure individuals against personal risks which they would not otherwise be able to bear. In the main these are those relevant to householders and motorists;

(ii) they provide a means of saving in the form of endowment policies;

(iii) they encourage industry by taking on many of the risks of business; and

(iv) as institutional investors they provide a source of capital for industry.

(b) *The members of Lloyd's of London.*

8.18 LLOYD'S OF LONDON

Lloyd's is a market-place and it is its *members* who undertake insurance. Its original area was solely marine insurance, but to this has been added other types. It does not deal in life assurance, however. Its two types of members are as follows:

(a) Underwriters

These members are the only persons allowed to accept insurance at Lloyd's. Each has to have extensive financial resources because every underwriter is personally responsible for the amount of risks he accepts. The risks are shared, however, because each underwriter willing to do so agrees to accept a stated proportion of a particular risk. In addition, underwriters are grouped into 'syndicates', so that an individual acceptance is in fact an acceptance by a number of underwriters.

(b) Brokers

A person requiring insurance through Lloyd's must first approach a broker, who then has the responsibility of getting cover for his client on the best possible terms. The broker makes out a 'slip' which gives details of the cover required. He obtains quotations from several underwriters and accepts the most advantageous. The first underwriter writes on the slip the amount of cover he is prepared to provide and the rate of his premium. Other underwriters add to the slip (each charging the same premium as the first one did) until the risk is fully covered. The policy is then prepared and signed by the parties involved.

EXERCISES

1 For ten years a company has paid an annual premium of £1000 on a fire insurance policy and has never made a claim. Has that expense been justified?

2 Two small firms pay different premiums for fire insurance on their factories. Both factories are insured for the same amounts. What could be the reasons for the difference in the premiums?

3 How can an insurance company pay in full every claim it admits, even when the claims for one year are exceptionally heavy?

4 A friend has bought a second-hand car for £800 and intends to insure it against accidental damage. Advise him how he may be affected by the term 'utmost good faith'.

5 Two years ago you bought a silver ornament for £200 and insured it for that sum. A fire has badly damaged it. What factors will influence the amount you will receive if you make a claim on your policy?

6 Mr Smith owns a small grocery store. What insurance would you advise him to take out?

7 You own a shop which is next door to a store holding inflammable material. Because of the danger to your shop, can you take out insurance on the store?

8 What sort of risks are uninsurable? Give three examples.

9 Mr Brown owns a village shop, valued at £30 000. If he insures it against fire, how is he affected by the principle of *indemnity* and the doctrine of *proximate cause*?

10 What must you prove if you make a claim under an insurance policy?

11 How does insurance assist industry?

12 What is the difference between (a) a time policy and a voyage policy; (b) cargo insurance and freight insurance?

13 Give four examples of *liability* insurance.

14 Explain the difference between *insurance* and *assurance*.

15 How is an insurance contract completed at Lloyd's?

16 Why are statistics vital to an insurance company and what are their sources?

CHAPTER 9

TRANSPORT

Transport is an essential part of commerce, and as economic activity becomes more complex so the importance of transport increases. Increasing specialisation in industry means that production becomes more centralised. The result is that goods have to be sent longer distances from a few areas to consumers who are scattered. Specialisation also means that components are made in a few areas and therefore have to be moved to central areas for assembling. Transport plays an even larger part today because of the increase in trading between countries.

The costs of transport have to be added to the costs of production. To make goods competitive in the market it is therefore necessary to keep transport costs as low as possible.

In this chapter we will consider how the different forms of transport each play their part.

9.1 THE PLACE OF TRANSPORT IN COMMERCE

As part of commerce, transport is concerned with the following:

(a) The distribution of goods

Produced goods must be distributed from centres of production to sales outlets and then to widely spread consumers. Raw materials must be brought into the country and distributed to producers. Makers of components receive raw materials from sundry sources and distribute finished products to manufacturers.

The vehicles of transport range from giant oil tankers to vans delivering bread to householders. There is specialisation between the transport systems, so that, for example, some traffic is always by road and others by rail. There is specialisation *within* transport systems, such as between the different types of sea transport.

(b) The movement of people

Commerce requires that people can be moved quickly. Businessmen travel to all parts of the world; salesmen move within their territories, everyone has to travel to his work.

9.2 TRANSPORT EFFICIENCY

If a transport system is to be efficient, it must satisfy certain conditions. There is no one system which can be said to be the most efficient in every respect. The most efficient system is the one which best meets the needs of the person who requires it. For some operations one system will be better than the others, but for other operations it may be the least efficient. The general requirements of an efficient system are as follows:

(a) Economy

Transport costs must be as low as possible. The cheapest method is not necessarily the one which will best benefit the user, however. If an oil pump was urgently required in the Middle East, the cheapest method may be to send it by road or by sea. Because of the urgency it would be sent by air as speed would be more important than cost-saving.

How a system is used can sometimes affect the cost. For example, it is cheaper by any method to make up 'loads' instead of sending individual consignments.

(b) Speed

Again, the importance of speed must be balanced against the cost. To send goods by air is obviously the swiftest method, but a less expensive method would be used if there were no urgency. On the other hand, it is not unduly expensive to send small packages (such as diamonds) by air.

(c) Convenience

An important factor is how conveniently placed are the terminals: that is, where the transport system begins and ends. If goods are sent by rail, they must first be transported to the departure terminal and then from the arrival terminal. This entails extra time and cost, so that it has some relevance to the two requirements mentioned above.

(d) Regularity

Except where he uses his own service or one specially provided, the consignor is bound by the travel schedules of the transporter. Trains, planes and regular road services operate to time-tables. It is therefore essential for the service to be frequent and punctual.

9.3 RAIL TRANSPORT

The railways have long lost their position as the leaders in inland transport. This is due to (i) the disadvantages which are specific to the system and which cannot be removed; (ii) the high cost of staffing and maintenance, so that insufficient funds are available to improve the service; and (iii) the improvements in road transport, helped by an extensive road-building programme.

9.4 THE ADVANTAGES AND DISADVANTAGES OF RAIL TRANSPORT

(a) **Travelling speed** is greater than it is in road transport *while the train is moving*. Trains not only travel faster but they are not held up by traffic congestion. Trains even have a speed advantage over inland airlines because they collect and deliver their passengers at city centres and not at distant airports. The advantage is particularly so on 'Inter-City' trains, which run between major towns at high speeds.

(b) **Transport time** is often slow, however. This is because goods have to be taken to and collected from terminal points. Besides adding to the transport time, this increases the risks of breakages and pilfering. Because of the nature of railways an interruption on a line will cause delays; unlike road traffic, a train can rarely take an alternative route in an emergency.

(c) **Time-tabling** imposes some rigidity because goods and people can be moved only in accordance with railway schedules.

(d) **Operating costs** are low when only the actual transporting is considered. A two-man train can convey a load many times greater than could be carried by a whole fleet of lorries. However, because so many other staff have to be employed, and because the expense of maintaining the track is so enormous, the true cost is high. In fact, almost every railway in the world operates at a loss.

9.5 DEVELOPMENTS IN RAIL TRANSPORT

Over the years the railway has fought its competitors by improving its services. It is undoubtedly superior in passenger transport because of its speed and comfort, but it is in goods transport it has had to try hardest. The following are some of the ways it has sought to compete against road transport:

(a) Containerisation
The problem of having to load and unload at terminals has been reduced by containerisation. A factory will load its consignment into a large con-

tainer. The container is then taken by lorry to the departure terminal and there lifted straight on to a specially built waggon. At the destination terminal it is off-loaded on to another vehicle. The railway has further improved this method by providing its own lorries, so that it collects, conveys and delivers container loads. The British Rail system is called *Freightliner*. The system is made more successful by the use of huge freightliner *terminals* where sophisticated equipment swiftly sorts the consignments and makes them into train-loads.

Containers can also be loaded on to *liner trains*, which run regularly between major centres.

(b) Special transporters

The railway provides fleets of specially designed waggons where there is a large amount of specialised traffic. Train-loads of vehicles are carried from car-makers' factories; special tankers move grain and chemicals; holiday-makers' cars are taken to resorts. Some materials (such as coal and oil) are moved in waggons provided by the producers. These are known as *company trains*.

(c) Parcel deliveries

British Rail has improved its parcel delivery service by introducing new methods. It is possible to take parcels to certain railway stations with the assurance they will be transported by passenger train without delay to another station. The disadvantage is that parcels can be sent only from specified stations and have to be collected from stations which provide the service.

9.6 ROAD TRANSPORT

The increase in the amount of road transport in recent years has been considerable. Whereas the mileage of railway track has been reduced since the early 1960s, there has been a considerable expansion and improvement of the roads network. A prominent feature has been the development of motorways linking the major centres. This has meant that motor traffic can travel faster because of the open roads and the by-passing of congested traffic areas.

It has also resulted in larger vehicles being used, thereby reducing unit costs.

A feature has been the increase in the number of *trans-continental* vehicles. Goods can be onloaded at a factory in the north of England, quickly taken by motorway to a port, driven on to a ferry and driven off in northern Europe. From there it can go to any part of Europe and the

Middle East. All this can be done with no loading and unloading on the way. Figure 9.1 gives an outline of how the major roads link with the ports.

Containerisation is used extensively, particularly for goods going to and from abroad.

9.7 THE ADVANTAGES OF ROAD TRANSPORT

(a) Door-to-door service
The goods are loaded on to a vehicle and off-loaded at the destination point. All the disadvantages of having railway terminals are eliminated.

(b) Flexibility
A lorry load can be moved whenever it is necessary to do so. The timing does not depend upon the scheduling of services.

Exceptional loads can be moved by using special transporters. A train cannot take a load if it is wider, longer or higher than a certain amount.

A lorry will take the shortest route, whereas trains are restricted to where the tracks go.

(c) Economy
Strong competition between the hauliers keeps the costs down. An efficient haulier will plan his deliveries so that he has few empty return journeys. If he is making several deliveries by one vehicle, he will plan the most economical way of doing so.

A very large load only requires a one-man crew, though many lorries would be required to carry the amount which could be transported by a train with a two-man crew. However, road hauliers have very much lower costs for other labour.

They have to pay for vehicle maintenance but 'track' maintenance is paid for by the government (partly by taxing the hauliers).

(d) Regular services
Besides making special journeys, road hauliers provide regular services, including container terminals.

There is also a national network for parcels delivery with a sophisticated sorting system. In many cases the costs are less than for postal services.

9.8 THE DISADVANTAGES OF ROAD TRANSPORT

(a) Diseconomies
It would, in some instances, be uneconomic to transport very heavy loads over long distances by road. For example, a train can carry a huge load of coal in a long line of waggons. To move it by road would require a con-

98

Fig 9.1 *road and sea links*

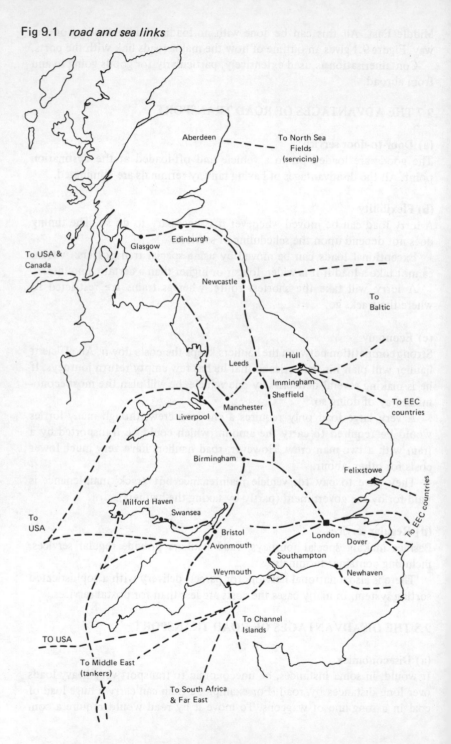

siderable number of lorries. The saving would not only be in cost, because the train could travel across the country at night very much faster than lorries could.

(b) Travelling time

A train journey will take less time than a road journey. Lorries may travel at high speeds on motorways but there are always areas of congestion, particularly at the departure and arrival points.

(c) Social costs

Although of no direct concern to the user and the haulier, there are considerable costs to the community. Roads have to be maintained and improved; police have to be employed; accidents burden hospital services. There are environmental losses due to pollution, noise and road-building. Much time is wasted because of traffic congestion.

9.9 OWN-VEHICLE TRANSPORTING

Many firms use their own vehicles for moving their goods. Whether or not it is wise to do so depends upon the circumstances of the trader. Certainly, a firm which transports a lot of goods at very frequent intervals would normally use its own fleet. A company owning a chain of supermarkets must deliver every day to each branch, so it would have to use its own transport.

A firm using its own vehicles does not have to rely on anyone else. It therefore does not run the risk of a haulier being inefficient or being unable to make himself immediately available.

Against this must be counted the capital which must be spent in buying vehicles. To this must be added the cost of maintenance and repair facilities. If a firm is to use its own vehicles it is therefore essential they be kept fully employed. The firm which makes irregular deliveries will, in general, do better to use the services of the road or railway hauliers.

9.10 OTHER FORMS OF INLAND TRANSPORT

(a) **Canals** have been in decline for many years. Where they are used the traffic is confined to bulky goods where speed is not important; for example, moving cement.

(b) **Pipe-lines** are used for carrying gas and oil over long distances.

(c) **Air travel** in Great Britain is mainly confined to passenger traffic. Within some other countries, however (such as Australia), there is an established cargo service.

9.11 SEA TRANSPORT

An efficient sea transport system is essential, particularly for a country (such as Great Britain) which has no land boundaries. Such a country must provide facilities for visiting ships as well as for its own vessels if it is to have an efficient service:

(a) There must be *terminals* with the necessary equipment for loading and unloading vessels. Speed is an essential factor because ships must have a quick 'turn round'. When a ship is at a terminal it incurs costs and earns nothing.

(b) There must be *premises* for warehousing goods, for keeping goods in bond, for forwarding goods, etc.

(c) *Offices* are required for dock officials and for customs, immigration and police officers.

(d) *Docks* must be available for repairing and refitting ships.

9.12 INLAND AND SEA LINKS

There must be adequate road and rail networks running directly to the ports. Figure 9.1 has shown how the main roads provide connections between industrial centres and ports. In recent years there has been a considerable increase in *direct* traffic between the United Kingdom and the rest of Europe. This reduces the amount of loading and unloading, for the following reasons:

(a) Road vehicles can be transported across water on *'roll-on-roll-off'* ferries.

(b) *Containerisation* enables consignments to be lifted from vehicle to ship without 'breaking' the load (see Figure 9.2).

Both systems reduce the costs of handling because stevedores are not required for unloading individual items. Also, there is no danger of loss due to pilfering.

Specialisation by UK ports takes the following forms:

(a) *Passenger traffic* has declined considerably because of the increased use of air travel. Most of those travelling by sea do so for pleasure. The main port for cruises is Southampton.

(b) *Short sea traffic* is mainly to the continental mainland, so the ports are on the south and east coasts. Some ports, such as Felixstowe and Immingham, have expanded rapidly because they have installed sophisticated equipment for handling containers.

(c) *Local trade traffic*. Specialist facilities are available for quickly moving perishables, such as flowers and tomatoes from the Channel Islands. There is a fast rail service from Weymouth to inland centres.

Fig 9.2 *containerisation for overseas transport*

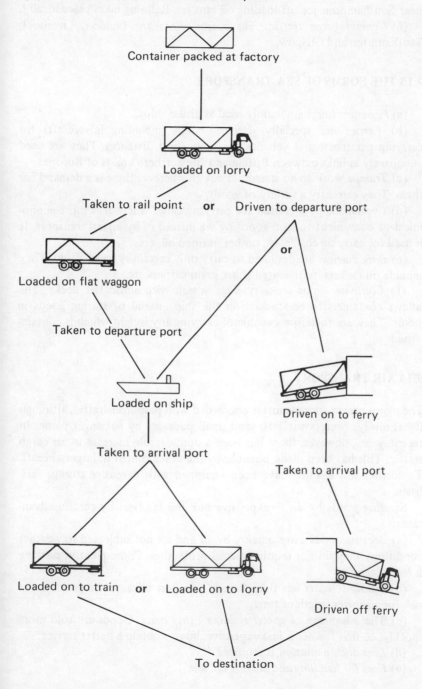

(d) *Oil traffic*. There are special deep-water berths at Milford Haven and near Southampton for off-loading oil tankers. Refining takes place locally.

(e) *General cargo traffic*. The major ports are London, Liverpool, Southampton and Glasgow.

9.13 THE FORMS OF SEA TRANSPORT

(a) *Passenger liners* are mainly used as cruise ships.

(b) *Ferries* are specially designed ships (including hovercraft) for carrying passengers and vehicles for fairly short distances. They are used extensively as links between Britain and the northern coasts of Europe.

(c) *Tramps* work to no schedules but go wherever there is a demand for them. They can carry a variety of goods.

(d) *Coastal shipping* is used for carrying cargo where it is more economical or convenient to send goods by sea instead of by inland transport. It is used for carrying coal, clay, timber, refined oil, etc.

(e) *Bulk carriers* are designed to carry only certain types of cargo. They include oil tankers, refrigerated ships, grain carriers etc.

(f) *Container ships* are very large vessels with single flat decks. This allows containers to be stacked *on* the ship instead of storing goods in holds. They are therefore capable of carrying any freight which is containerised.

9.14 AIR TRANSPORT

The major part of air transport is concerned with passenger traffic, although it has always been possible to send small packages by passenger plane. In recent years, however, there has been a considerable increase in air cargo traffic. This has been made possible by the development of larger aircraft. To further this airports have been equipped with extensive storage facilities.

Sending goods by air is expensive but this is offset by certain advantages:

(a) Because goods move quickly by air and are not subjected to weather conditions they do not require special protection. Consequently, *packing is less expensive*.

(b) *Insurance costs less* than for sea transport because the goods are at risk for a shorter length of time.

(c) The advantage of *speed reduces other costs*. Goods are sold more quickly, so that finance is less expensive; buyers obtain a better service.

(d) *Less documentation* is required.

(e) *Fees for handling and storing are less*.

9.15 THE CHOICE OF TRANSPORT METHODS

Where there is a choice between the methods of transport the decision will depend on (i) the nature of the goods, and (ii) the priorities, i.e. for speed, cost, etc.

In many instances there is *no* choice. There is only one method of transporting oil abroad; some goods cannot go by rail; and so on. In other cases account must be taken of the following:

(a) True cost

What is the *total* cost of moving the goods? As we have seen, air transport is less expensive than may at first appear to be the case. If goods have to be unloaded and reloaded at terminal points, the costs will increase.

(b) Speed

How essential is quick delivery? If there is no urgency, it will usually be best to send by the slowest method. Regular services are cheaper than special deliveries, so that if goods are transported frequently the former method should be used.

(c) Security

What are the risks of loss due to damage, deterioration and pilfering? In general, the risks will be smaller the less the goods are handled.

(d) Reliability

How certain is it that the goods will be delivered on time? Ships and aircraft may be delayed by bad weather. Generally, rail transport is less affected by weather conditions than road transport and it is not disrupted by traffic congestion.

9.16 PASSENGER TRANSPORT

(a) Almost all overseas travel is by air.
(b) Because of improved service to passengers (in comfort, speed, frequency, terminal facilities etc.), long-distance coaches are used more extensively in many countries.
(c) In some countries (such as Britain) the railway service is declining. In others (such as France) the system has been improved to provide high-speed trains, greater comfort, etc.

9.17 TRANSPORT DOCUMENTS

(a) Delivery Note
(see Section 13.7).

(b) Charter Party
This is a document containing an undertaking by a shipowner to provide a vessel to carry a shipper's load from one port to another. Alternatively, it may be an agreement to provide a ship for a specified period. The former is known as a 'voyage charter'; the latter is referred to as a 'time charter'.

The sum to be paid by the shipper is known as 'freight'. On a voyage charter this is calculated on the weight of the cargo. On a time charter it is based on the tonnage of the ship.

The shipowner will of course wish his ship to complete the voyage as quickly as possible so that he may use it again to earn more freight. The Charter Party will therefore limit the number of days allowed for loading and unloading. These are known as 'lay days'. If the number of days is exceeded, the shipper may have to pay a further amount, known as 'demurrage'.

(c) Consignment Note
This is a document, provided by a road or rail carrier, which a person sending goods must first complete. Particulars must be given of the description and weight of the goods, the name and address of the consignee and whether it is to travel at owner's risk rate or carrier's risk rate. A higher charge is made for carrier's risk because it makes the carrier responsible for any loss or damage in transit. When the goods are delivered the consignee signs the Note to acknowledge their receipt.

(Document specific to overseas trade are discussed in Section 10.10.)

EXERCISES

1   If an exporter wished to hire a ship to move his goods from London to Hong Kong, what form would the agreement take? How would his *certain* hiring charges be calculated and what *further* costs may he incur?

2   In sending goods by rail, what document must the consignor sign and what would it contain? What factors would determine the cost of carriage?

3   Explain why the relative efficiency of transport affects costs to the consumers.

4   Discuss the effects of rail and air traffic having to use terminals.

5   What factors must be considered when comparing the time it takes to deliver goods by rail with delivery by road?

6 How do you account for the considerable increase in the use of containers?

7 Explain the following: (a) liner trains; (b) freightliner terminals; (c) company trains.

8 What methods are available for delivering parcels?

9 Explain the advantages of using transcontinental vehicles and roll-on–roll-off ferries.

10 A wholesaler makes deliveries twice a week to each retailer in an area within a 100-mile radius. Three vehicles are required each time. Should he use his own vans or the services of a contractor?

11 What services must a country provide for shipping lines which move goods into and out of the country? Give reasons.

12 What special features are relevant to the transport of crude oil by sea?

13 Compare the transport services provided by coasters, tramps and container ships.

14 To what extent is it expensive to transport goods by air?

15 State, with reasons, the form of transport you would use for each of the following:

(a) Coal from Newcastle to an electricity power station near London.
(b) A canister of film from Los Angeles to London.
(c) Rare birds from Cape Town to London Zoo.
(d) China clay from Falmouth to Stoke-on-Trent.
(e) Milk from Dorset to the Midlands.
(f) Daffodils from the Channel Islands to Birmingham.
(g) Steel girders from Wales to a building site in Liverpool.

CHAPTER 10

FOREIGN TRADE

During our studies we have encountered various forms of specialisation. We have seen that even in a primitive society there is specialisation of labour; that firms specialise in sections of an industry; that different parts of the country specialise in what they produce. This principle of specialisation extends to international trade, in that each country does those things it is best suited to do. Like the small community on its island, this results in a country producing more than it requires of those things it specialises in. This surplus is sold to other countries in exchange for the surplus production of those countries. Consequently, each country gets the goods it wants from the most economical source: that is, from its own production or from another country, as the case may be.

10.1 THE BASIS OF FOREIGN TRADE

No country can produce all the goods it requires. Britain has no gold or copper; it cannot grow rice or tea commercially. It must therefore buy such goods from those countries which are able to supply them. On the other hand, it is better able to produce some goods (such as whisky, for example) than other countries can. Therefore, it has surplus goods it can sell in exchange for the surpluses of other countries.

Where a country produces something which another cannot it has an *absolute* advantage over that country. Britain has oil, France has no oil. Therefore, Britain has an absolute advantage over France in respect of oil. An advantage can also be *relative*. Britain is able to produce wine, but because it is not easy to grow grapes in Britain it produces only a small amount. The climate and soil of France is particularly suited for growing grapes so that it produces vast quantities of wine. French wine is therefore less expensive and is of a better quality than British wine. Consequently, large quantities of French wine are exported to Britain in spite of the availability of British wines.

Expertise and experience can also be exchanged between countries. For instance, Britain has technical 'know-how' in electronics, so it can sell direction-finding equipment to airlines all over the world.

The basis of foreign trade, therefore, is as follows:

(a) Each country exploits its natural advantages.
(b) Each country concentrates on those things it does best.
(c) Each country sells its surplus production.
(d) Each country uses its surpluses to buy things it does not produce itself.

10.2 VISIBLE TRADE

This relates to the export and import of *goods*. These are tangible things, such as motor-vehicles, oil, butter, etc. The major proportion of Britain's visible exports are manufactured goods: that is, goods which have been made and assembled. Many of the raw materials used in production are visible exports of other countries (such as timber and chrome, for example), so that, of course, they form part of Britain's visible imports.

The balance of trade is the difference between the value of *visible* imports and the value of *visible* exports of a country. Britain consistently has an 'unfavourable' balance of trade: that is, she imports more goods than she exports.

10.3 INVISIBLE TRADE

This relates to the import and export of *services*.

Invisible imports of Britain include air fares paid by British people to foreign airlines, spending abroad by British holiday-makers, and dividends to foreign companies which own British companies.

Invisible exports of Britain are, fortunately, very high. They always exceed invisible imports. Britain is the insurance centre of the world and a leader in banking, and these industries bring in large sums. Others come from shipping and air transport, foreign investments, visiting tourists, etc.

10.4 THE BALANCE OF PAYMENTS

Goods and services which are exported provide the country with an income – and, of course, the reverse applies to imports. The important thing about the difference between the two totals is the effect it has on the *balance of payments*. This is the record of all the financial transactions between a country and the rest of the world. It is a sort of national cash book.

If an Englishman buys a British car, he will pay for it in pound notes and this will have no effect on the balance of payments. If he buys a Japanese car, he will still pay pound notes but the importer he pays them to will have to pay the Japanese producer in *Japanese* money. Therefore, if the car costs the importer £2000, he will have to pay the equivalent of that sum in yen which his bank will obtain for him. The importance of this is that it will reduce the Bank of England's reserve of foreign currency.

Because Britain's balance of trade is always in deficit it causes a strain on the currency reserves. Fortunately, invisible earnings are much higher than invisible imports and the difference is often enough to cancel the adverse balance of trade. Figure 10.1 shows that in 1978 Britain had an unfavourable balance in visible trade, but a favourable balance in invisibles. The two balances are brought together to produce what is known as the *balance of payments on current account.* As the table indicates, this balance was favourable.

Fig 10.1   *the balance of payments on current account, 1978*

Visible trade	(£m.)
Exports	35 432
Imports	36 607
Visible balance	− 1 175

Invisibles	
Credits	18 335
Debits	16 128
Invisible balance	2 207

Current balance	1 032

Another part of the national accounts records the movements of capital in and out of the country. When the balance on this 'capital account' is taken with the current account balance the result is known as the *over-all balance of payments.* That figure therefore includes *all* money coming into and going out of the country.

Figure 10.2 illustrates the make-up of the balance of trade and the two balance-of-payments figures.

Fig 10.2 *balance of trade and balance of payments*

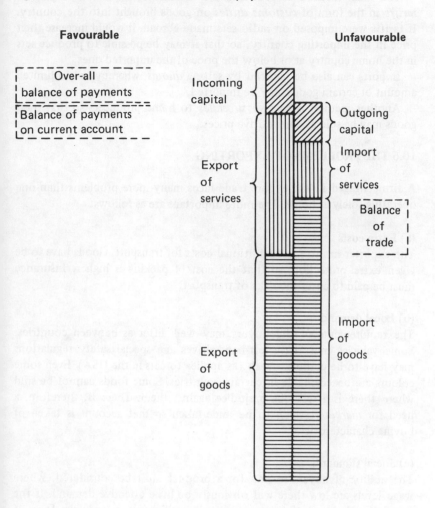

10.5 PROTECTION AND FREE TRADE

We have seen that an unfavourable balance of trade causes a drain on the country's currency reserves. Importing too many goods also results in unemployment in those home industries which could have produced goods which were imported. Those in favour of *free trade* say that economic forces should be allowed to operate without hindrance. *Protectionists*, on the other hand, say that imports should be controlled.

The main method of reducing the amount of imports is to impose *tariffs* in the form of *customs duties* on goods brought into the country. If tariffs were imposed on radio sets made abroad, it would increase their price in the importing country, so that it may be possible to produce sets in the home country at or below the price of the imported ones.

Imports can also be reduced by setting *quotas*, whereby only a limited amount of certain goods may be imported.

Another method is to give *subsidies* to home producers so that their goods may be sold at competitive prices.

10.6 THE PROBLEMS OF EXPORTING

A firm engaged in the export trade faces many more problems than one operating solely at home. The more important are as follows:

(a) Extra costs
The exporter has to meet additional costs for transport. Goods have to be given extra protection, so that the cost of packing is higher. Insurance must be paid to cover the risks of transport.

(b) Local demand
The requirements of the buyers may well differ as between countries. Some vehicles must have left-hand drives and special safety regulations may have to be complied with (as applies to cars in the USA). Even some colours are unacceptable in certain countries. Some foods cannot be sold where there is a religious prejudice against them. There is, therefore, a need for *market research* to be undertaken so that account is taken of buying characteristics.

(c) Social standards
The ability of buyers to pay for a product must be considered. Where wage levels are low there will obviously be little effective demand. If the population is largely illiterate advertising will have to be in the form of pictures and symbols. In other cases advertising must be expertly translated into the local language.

(d) Measurement
All forms of measurements as to size, weight, capacity, etc., must be in local units. Prices must be quoted in the relevant currencies.

(e) Documentation
In addition to the amount of paperwork involved in transporting goods abroad, there are the documents required by the importing country.

Customs duties may be imposed and frequently licences are required before goods will be admitted.

(f) Receiving payment

The risk of non-payment is higher for exports than it is for home trading. The protective measures which are available are discussed later in the chapter, but whatever steps are taken they will mean incurring costs.

The Department of Trade provides 'export intelligence' to help British traders meet these problems. Because of information received from government offices abroad it can provide exporters with data about the following:

  (i) the market potential for particular goods;
 (ii) regulations of overseas countries concerning their imports;
(iii) the financial standing of an overseas trader;
(iv) the economic, financial and political stability of a country;
 (v) statistical information about a particular country; and
(vi) details of any contract put out for tender by a foreign country.

10.7 METHODS OF SELLING ABROAD

(a) Selling to buying agents

An exporter can remain in his own country to do all his selling by dealing with overseas buyers. These are agents, resident in this country, of foreign companies or members of a visiting buying mission.

(b) Selling to export houses

Export houses are usually merchants who buy from the home manufacturers and then sell the goods to overseas buyers. Thus all the *exporting* is done by the house because it finds the market and deals with exporting procedures.

(c) Employing overseas agents

An exporter may have agents permanently resident in overseas countries who obtain orders. Frequently they are nationals of the countries concerned, so this method has the advantage of using people with local knowledge. An agent may act for more than one exporter, but obviously it is preferable to have an agent who deals with a single exporter. When an agent has more than one principal there could be a conflict of interest.

(d) Licensing overseas manufacturers

By this method goods are not *physically* exported. The manufacturer licenses a foreign manufacturer to produce goods of the home manufacturer's design. In return the foreign manufacturer pays a proportion of the sales income in the form of *royalties*.

(e) Running an export department
A large exporter may have a specialist staff which does all the work of exporting. It will find its own markets and will probably have a team of overseas salesmen. It will, of course, deal with all the documentation.

10.8 BILLS OF EXCHANGE

These are used extensively for securing payment for goods which have been exported. The reasons for this are because of circumstances which are specific to exporting. They can be demonstrated if we assume that a British exporter, Maker Ltd, has received an order for machine components valued at £15 000 from Dinkum Ltd in Australia:

(a) Having made and despatched the machinery, Maker Ltd will require early payment. However, the goods will not reach Australia for some time and Dinkum cannot be expected to pay for them before then.
(b) Dinkum Ltd intends to assemble the components in a machine which it will then sell. Because of the length of time elapsing before the machine can be sold and payment received for it, Dinkum would like to pay for the components as late as possible.

The solution could be for Maker Ltd to give credit to Dinkum Ltd, but this would be expensive and risky. Instead, Dinkum Ltd signs a promise to pay at a specified future date. This promise is known as a *Bill of Exchange*, which is legally defined as

an unconditional order in writing, addressed by one person to another, requiring the person to whom it is addressed to pay on demand or at some fixed or determinable future time, a sum certain in money, to, or to the order of, a specified person, or to bearer.

The stages in the transaction will be as follows:

(1) The exporter will draw a Bill similar to the one shown in Figure 10.3. It will be noted that: (a) it is *signed* by the drawer, Maker Ltd, and *addressed* to the drawee, Dinkum Ltd, (b) the drawee is *ordered* to pay; (c) the date of payment is determinable; and (d) it is *unconditional*.
(2) Dinkum Ltd would indicate its agreement to pay by 'accepting' the bill: that is, by signing it. However, the company could not be expected to do this until it knows it will be able to obtain the goods when they are available. Therefore, the bill will be accompanied by a *Bill of Lading*. This

Fig 10.3. *a Bill of Exchange*

£15 000

Bulldog Works
Blackton Road
Birmingham
1 November 19 . .

Ninety days after sight pay British Bank Limited account of Maker Limited the sum of Fifteen Thousand Pounds.

(Signed) J. Williams
Director

Dinkum Ltd
Sydney

Maker Ltd

---

document gives legal title to the goods (see section 10.10 below). There will also be attached an insurance policy covering the goods during transit. Because the bill has these documents attached it is known as a *documentary bill.*

Maker Ltd would not let Dinkum Ltd have these documents until it is certain it will be paid. Accordingly, Maker Ltd will ask its bank to send the documents to a bank in Sydney.

(3) The Sydney bank will inform Dinkum Ltd of the arrival of the documents. Dinkum Ltd will not be able to obtain the goods when they arrive unless it has the Bill of Lading. To get this document it must accept the Bill of Exchange held by the bank.

(4) The accepted bill will then be sent to the exporter's bank. Maker Ltd can then *discount* the bill with its bank, receiving an amount somewhat below £15 000.

(5) When the bill falls due, Dinkum Ltd will pay the exporter's bank £15 000.

These movements are illustrated in Figure 10.4.

It is not always necessary to send the documents to the importer. Instead, there may be an arrangement whereby the importer's agent in the exporting country will accept the bill and then send the other documents to his principal. Alternatively, an *acceptance house* (see Chapter 18) may agree to accept the bill. Such a bill is regarded as being safer than one accepted by importers (and which are known as *trade* bills) and can be discounted at better rates.

114

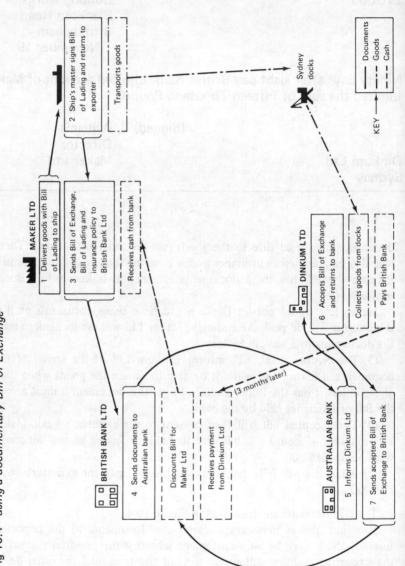

Fig 10.4 *using a documentary Bill of Exchange*

10.9 **THE EXPORT CREDITS GUARANTEE DEPARTMENT (ECGD)**

There are risks in exporting which do not apply to the home trade. It is not always as easy to obtain information about the creditworthiness of overseas buyers as it is for those in the home country. A foreign buyer may fail to pay through no fault of his own because he may be affected by a sudden political upset in his own country. The overseas country may, without warning, impose currency regulations so that money cannot be sent out of the country. A war may interfere with normal commercial activities.

These are the sort of unpredictable risks which insurance companies cannot accept. The Department of Trade has a more informed knowledge of conditions abroad and is therefore better able to assess the risks. The ECGD of the Department of Trade undertakes most of the insurance of exports. It operates on the same principles as insurance companies do: that is, premiums are kept as low as is possible without endangering the 'fund'.

This insurance also makes financing of exports easier because banks are willing to lend on the security of ECGD policies. In approved cases the Department will guarantee the repayment of bank loans to exporters.

10.10 **EXPORT DOCUMENTS**

(a) Bill of Lading
As already stated, this is the 'document of title' to the goods, so that the holder may claim possession of the goods when they reach the destination port. It contains details of the goods to be shipped, the names of the sender and the recipient, the destination port and the name of the ship. Three copies are made out; one is kept by the ship's master, one is attached to the Bill of Exchange, and the other is signed by the ship's master and returned to the consignor as confirmation that the goods are on board. The Bill sets out the terms under which the goods are to be carried and serves as the contract of carriage.

If there are any signs of damage when the goods are delivered to the ship the bill is noted with the details so as to protect the shipowner against any claim for damage. Such a bill is known as a 'dirty' bill; others are 'clean' bills.

A Bill of Lading can be endorsed and passed to another person so that that person acquires the right to the goods.

(b) Air Waybill
This document is used instead of a Bill of Lading for all goods sent by air. It is in·three parts. The first part is signed by the consignor and retained

by the carrier; the second part is signed by the consignor and the carrier, and accompanies the goods; the third part is signed by the carrier and handed to the consignor as his receipt.

(c) Certificate of Insurance

This provides proof that the goods have been insured against loss or damage during transit. The exporter usually takes out the insurance and sends the certificate to the importer for him to use in the event of a claim having to be made.

(d) Shipping Note

This document is addressed to the port authorities and accompanies the goods when they are delivered to the docks. It details the goods, the port of destination and the ship in which they are to be carried. A copy is signed and returned to the consignor. This copy is known as a *dock receipt.*

(e) Certificate of Origin

If a country imposes tariffs on imported goods, it may do so at different rates, so that the duty on goods from one country is lower than that on goods from another country. Also, the country may have a free-trade agreement with some countries and scales of tariffs for others. For example, no duty is payable on goods passing *between* members of the European Economic Community, but a member may levy tariffs on goods imported from non-members. A non-member could send his exports to a member country with a low tariff rate against him and then arrange for the goods to be exported duty-free from there to a member country. To avoid this it is usual for imported goods claiming to be duty-free to be accompanied by a Certificate of Origin, signed by an official body, certifying that the goods were made in the country stated.

10.11 METHODS OF IMPORTING

(a) Import department

A business regularly engaged in importing will have a specialist staff to deal with it. This would particularly apply when the same raw materials are continuously used (such as cocoa beans by a chocolate manufacturer) and when there is a positive link with a producer (such as a motor agent specialising in one make of foreign car).

(b) Import merchants

These buy on their own account, usually specialising in certain types of goods or commodities or in the products of a particular country.

(c) Import agents
These act in the importing country for foreign sellers. They sell the goods at the best possible price, taking advantage of their knowledge of the local market. They are paid commission on their sales.

(d) Import brokers
These middlemen act as the link between home buyers and foreign sellers. They specialise in particular goods or commodities, and because of their experience they are used in order to find goods for buyers and to find buyers for available goods.

10.12 DEALING WITH THE CUSTOMS

Goods will not be released to the holder of a Bill of Lading until the Customs have been paid any duty which may be due. It must first be decided *if* any tariff is payable and, if it is, how much it amounts to. To do this the importer will file an 'entry', giving details of the goods:

(a) *An entry for free goods form* is used if the goods are duty-free. The Customs officers will compare the details on the form with the list of all the goods carried in the ship (known as the *Ship's Report*) submitted by the master before the cargo was unloaded. An endorsement on the form by a Customs officer is proof that the goods can be released.

(b) *An entry for home use ex ship form* is used if duty is payable. The amount of duty is determined, and when it has been paid the goods can be released.

Bonded warehouses are used when the importer prefers not to pay the duty immediately. The duty payable on a consignment of tobacco or whisky may be considerable. If the importer does not expect to sell the consignment in the immediate future, it would 'tie up' a lot of his capital if he paid the duty at once. The goods are released from the bonded warehouse when the duty has been paid.

10.13 THE CUSTOMS AND EXCISE DEPARTMENT

The duties of this department are as follows:

(a) To examine incoming goods and check them with the covering documents, and to assess and collect any duty payable.
(b) To ensure that the amount of certain imported goods does not exceed the limit of any relevant quota.
(c) To produce statistics concerning imports and exports. These are com-

piled from import and export licences issued by the Department of Trade. Open general import licences are given for goods which are allowed unrestricted entry. For other imports individual licences are required.

(d) To control bonded warehouses.

(e) To prevent the import of prohibited goods (such as drugs).

10.14 QUOTING PRICES IN FOREIGN TRADE

When an import duty is payable the cost to the importer is increased by the amount of the charge, of course. There are also a number of other costs to be met. Some of them may be paid by the exporter and would therefore be included in the price paid by the importer; others will be met separately by the importer. What charges are included in a quoted price will be indicated by the terms of the contract:

(a) Free on board (f.o.b.)

The exporter pays the costs only up to and including the point of loading the goods on to the ship. All subsequent costs are the responsibility of the importer.

(b) Free alongside ship (f.a.s.)

This means the exporter will pay the charges only *up to* loading on the ship.

(c) Cost, insurance and freight (c.i.f.)

A price quoted c.i.f. includes the insurance premium and the cost of transporting by sea.

EXERCISES

1 Why does Britain always have an unfavourable balance of trade?

2 Give six examples of Britain's invisible exports and explain their importance to the economy.

3 Define (a) balance of trade; (b) balance of payments on current account; (c) over-all balance of payments.

4 Explain the effect on Britain's balance of payments of each of the following: (a) British people holidaying in Spain; (b) using copper in the manufacture of electronic equipment in Britian which is then sold abroad; (c) Lloyd's underwriters insuring against earthquakes in California; (d) American tourists to Britain; and (e) the British owner of a patent allowing a foreign manufacturer to use it.

5 Almost all television sets used in Britain are made elsewhere. In this respect, what are the arguments for and against protectionism?

6 What special problems face an exporter of baby foods to Nigeria ?

7 Why is market research particularly important in exporting?

8 Explain how the Department of Trade provides export intelligence.

9 In what ways can a manufacturer's products be purchased abroad without him having overseas contacts?

10 Explain the difference in exporting between using overseas agents and granting licences to foreign producers.

11 Explain the significance of the following words in the legal definition of a Bill of Exchange: (a) 'unconditional'; (b) 'addressed by one person to another'; (c) 'requiring the person. . . to pay'; (d) 'at some fixed or determinable future time'.

12 A British furniture manufacturer buys timber from Canada. What advantages do the importer and the exporter get if the transaction is covered by a Bill of Exchange?

13 Concerning Bills of Exchange, explain the following: (a) acceptance, (b) documentary bill; (c) discounting; (d) acceptance house; (e) trade bills.

14 How can an exporter ensure that his buyer does not get possession of the goods before the importer binds himself to pay for them?

15 Explain the part played by banks in respect of transactions in which Bills of Exchange are used.

16 What sorts of risks are covered by policies issued by the Export Credits Guarantee Department? Why do insurance companies not provide such cover?

17 What are the similarities and the differences between a *Bill of Lading* and an *Air Waybill*?

18 What is a *Certificate of Origin* used for?

19 What are the differences between (a) import merchants, (b) import agents, and (c) import brokers?

20 Explain the purpose of (a) entry forms, (b) Ships' Reports, and (c) bonded warehouses.

CHAPTER 11

PUBLIC ENTERPRISES

Throughout the book our concern has been with *private* enterprise: that is, commercial activities carried on by firms ranging from one-man businesses to multinational companies. In addition, central and local government play a major part in providing goods and services, i.e. via *public* enterprises.

11.1 THE FORMS OF PUBLIC ENTERPRISE

(a) Public corporations

These are bodies, each established and controlled by an Act of Parliament, which run particular commercial activities. Some were *set up* to provide services which were not previously available. These include the British Broadcasting Corporation, the United Kingdom Atomic Energy Authority, the Forestry Commission and the Arts Council. Others were established to *take over* industries which were previously privately owned. These are known as *nationalised* industries and are discussed below.

(b) Government shareholdings

The government has a financial 'stake' in some companies as a shareholder.

(c) Trading by government departments

A small amount of trading is done by the Civil Service. For example, the Stationery Office sells official literature.

(d) Local authorities

These provide services to a local community which could otherwise be offered by private enterprise. For some of these there is no *direct* charge, though the community at large pays for them in the form of local rates and national taxation. For example, education is the responsibility of the state and much of the cost is met from taxes. Education is administered *locally*, however, and the remainder of the costs are met from local rates. Other 'free' services include street-cleaning and refuse collection, street-lighting, etc. Other services are partly paid for by those who use them and include recreation facilities, car parks, airports, etc.

11.2 THE REASONS FOR PUBLIC OWNERSHIP

The justification for taking an industry out of private ownership is not the same in all cases. Some of the reasons are given below, though it may be said that the first one *is* a common factor. As public ownership includes activities other than those which have been nationalised, the following reasons apply to public enterprises *generally*:

(a) Political attitudes
Some people maintain that many forms of private ownership should be abolished. They hold the view that the means of production should belong to and be developed for the people as a whole. This particularly applies to the 'gifts of nature', such as land itself and natural resources such as coal, oil and gas. Some would extend this further to include banks, insurance companies and large manufacturing concerns.

(b) Basic importance
Certain industries and services are basic, in that everything else depends upon them. All forms of power come in this category, as does steel, sewerage, ambulance services, etc. They must be operated for the good of the community and industry generally because everyone would suffer if private owners were allowed to act in their own selfish interests.

(c) National security
Certain services *must* be provided by the state for the safety of the public because it would be dangerous to leave them in private hands. Obviously, the police and the armed forces must be controlled by the government. Strange as it may now seen, there were once a number of privately owned fire brigades! Nuclear energy is an obvious example of where security demands it be in the hands of the government.

(d) Where services cannot be profitable
There are many essentials which cannot be provided by private enterprise because they cannot operate at a profit. Therefore, such facilities as health services, drainage, state schools, subsidised housing, etc., must be the responsibility of public enterprise.

(e) For financial reasons

Some privately owned industries were not profitable because they were not large enough to provide the benefits of large-scale trading. This was often because a number of businesses in an industry were competing against one another. The only way to prevent their collapse was to integrate them into one national service. British railways, for example, were uneconomic partly because so many companies were operating, some of them in direct competition with one another. Nationalising the railways brought them all under one control, thereby making them more economical to run.

Other private industries were in danger because they could not afford the heavy costs required to make them efficient. This was one reason for nationalising the coal industry. Other industries could not be *established* because of the enormous capital costs, so that the state became responsible for setting up airlines, airports, atomic energy stations, etc.

11.3 PRIVATE AND PUBLIC CORPORATIONS COMPARED

(a) The profit motive

Unless a private undertaking makes a profit it will eventually cease to exist. A public corporation aims primarily to provide essential goods or services, so that profit-making is not its objective. Any excess of income over expenditure is called a 'surplus' and is used to pay interest on the capital it has borrowed from the government. Where possible, surpluses are used to finance expansion of the industry and to reduce the charges it makes.

If a private corporation makes no profit in a year, it will be the shareholders who will suffer. If a public corporation makes no profit, the amount of the interest it is unable to pay is added to its debt to the Treasury. In some circumstances the corporation will be lent further capital.

(b) Pricing

A private corporation can charge only what its customers are prepared to pay. It cannot increase its prices if a competitor is charging lower prices. A public corporation, however, is usually a monopoly. Its customers have no option but to pay the prices demanded, though the government can apply pressure on the corporation to avoid large increases. The problem is made more difficult by the fact that a public corporation must provide certain services even if to do so involves it in making a loss. For example, if the postal service was in the hands of a private corporation it might refuse to make daily deliveries to remote places. The Post Office, as a public body, cannot, however, fail to provide the service for which it was formed.

(c) Management and accountability

A private corporation is managed by directors appointed by the shareholders. The directors are accountable to the shareholders as owners of the company. The owners of a public corporation are the members of the public at large. Obviously, they personally cannot appoint the managers of the corporation, so this is done by the government acting on behalf of the public. Similarly, the managers are answerable to Parliament as representatives of the public. Annual accounts must be submitted to Parliament and they are scrutinised by specially appointed committees. Day-to-day control of a public corporation is exercised by a Minister of State.

The government has a firmer control over a public corporation than shareholders have over a private corporation. Often, the attitude to a Public corporation will alter when the government is changed. Decisions are sometimes made for political considerations rather than financial ones.

(d) Capital

The capital of a private corporation is provided by investors, some of it at fixed rates and some in the form of shares. The capital of public corporations is borrowed from the Treasury at fixed rates of interest.

11.4 SOME PUBLIC CORPORATIONS

The more important public bodies may be summarised as follows:

Power

The National Coal Board was formed in 1946 to nationalise the coal mines.

The British Gas Corporation was established in 1973 to provide a national network to distribute North Sea natural gas. The gas industry was nationalised in 1948.

The Electricity Council has general responsibility for the supply of electricity. The generating and transmitting of electricity is the responsibility of the Central Electricity Generating Board. Nationalisation took place in 1947.

The British National Oil Corporation, formed in 1976, controls the development by private enterprise of North Sea oil.

The National Water Council is responsible for water supplies, sewerage and the protection of rivers and estuaries. The water industry was nationalised in 1948.

The United Kingdom Energy Authority was established in 1954 to undertake research and set up atomic power stations.

Transport

British Rail is responsible for the railway network, which was nationalised in 1947.

Many urban bus services and all underground train services are operated by local authorities or by public bodies established for that purpose.

The British Waterways Board is responsible for inland water navigation.

The Civil Aviation Authority is generally responsible for controlling air services in and out of the country. British Ariways is state-owned. The British Airports Authority manages the national air terminals.

The British Transport Docks Board deals with those docks which have been nationalised.

Communications

The Post Office was a government department until 1969, and is now a public corporation.

The British Broadcasting Corporation provides radio and television services. Its income derives from the sale of licences to the public. It was established in 1926.

The Independent Broadcasting Authority licences and controls private concerns which operate television services in return for income from advertisers.

EXERCISES

1 How does a public limited company and a public corporation differ as regards (a) the provision of capital, (b) ownership, (c) control, (d) accountability, and (e) allocation of profits and surpluses?

2 Name some of the services provided by a local authority which could otherwise be supplied by private enterprise.

3 Why are railways in Britain allowed to continue to operate although they do so at a loss?

4 What is the difference between a corporation being owned by the government and one in which it has shares?

5 Give reasons for the nationalisation of the coal mines.

6 Give examples of nationalisation for the sake of national security.

7 Why were some industries put under state control largely because of their size?

8 Many public corporations operate as monopolies. What effect does this have on consumers?

9 Why were the following established: (a) the British National Oil Corporation; (b) the British Gas Corporation; (c) the Independent Broadcasting Authority?

8 Many public corporations operate as monopolies. What effect does this have on consumers?

9 Why were the following established: (a) the British National Oil Corporation; (b) the British Gas Corporation; (c) the Independent Broadcasting Authority?

10 Who pays for the following: (a) state schools; (b) municipal car parks; (c) passenger train services; (d) domestic gas; (e) television programmes?

CHAPTER 12

COMMERCE AND THE GOVERNMENT

In the previous chapter we looked at the ways in which the government takes part in commercial activities. We now need to consider the actions of the government which have an effect on those engaged in commerce. As we shall see, the government has responsibilities to the commercial world and the business community has obligations to the government.

12.1 GOVERNMENT INVOLVEMENT

The government is involved in commerce in the following respects:

(a) Maintaining the social structure
As we saw at the very beginning of our studies, commerce can flourish only in a stable society. The government is responsible for ensuring that the conditions for this exist. It has to strive for peaceful relations with other countries. It must also provide security *within* the country, so that a fair legal system and the means to operate it has to exist. It must play its part in encouraging co-operation between workers and management. It must attempt to reduce conflict between social classes.

(b) Economic planning
The government must have economic policies which aim to benefit the whole community. It will therefore intervene in the commercial world to impose conditions which are necessary to achieve those objectives. These would include measures to improve the balance of payments, to reduce unemployment, to control the supply of money and credit, etc.

(c) Financing services
The government has to provide enormous sums of money to pay for the services it provides. It therefore follows that it must impose taxes and take other steps to obtain the required revenue.

(d) Departmental services

Various government departments provide services to the commercial world and to the community generally. These operate within the policies of whatever government is then in power.

(e) Legislation

Commerce must be controlled so that there are no abuses by those with financial power. Legislation is also required in order to impose the government's policies on the commercial community.

12.2 GOVERNMENT EXPENDITURE AND INCOME

Like any commercial undertaking, the government has to forecast what its expenses will be in the forthcoming year. Unlike a business, however, the government can *demand* that it be provided with the funds to meet those expenses.

The government's estimate of its expenses and the methods it intends to use to raise money to pay them are presented to Parliament as the *Budget*. This is usually done annually in early April, though where necessary 'mini-budgets' are presented between the annual ones. Invariably, a budget proposes tax changes. This is necessary because the amount required differs from year to year, but changes are often made for other reasons. For example, it may be decided to make companies pay more tax and for individuals to pay less tax; it may be necessary to remove unfairness to some taxpayers; wealthy people may be required to pay a higher rate of tax than in the past; measures may be taken to favour certain parts of industry.

The main items of income are shown in Figure 12.1. (These are taken from government statistics for 1978.)

Fig 12.1 *central government receipts on current account for 1978*

	(£m.)
Gross trading surplus	47
Rent, dividends and interest	3 805
Taxes on income	22 321
Taxes on expenditure	17 545
National insurance contributions	10 023
	53 741

12.3 TAXATION

It will be seen that a large proportion of the government's income is in the form of taxes. Taxation can be used for purposes besides meeting expenses, however. For example, if the government wishes to reduce spending by the public it can increase taxes, so that people have less money to spare. If not all that income is used by the government, it is known as 'budgeting for a surplus'. On the other hand, to 'budget for a deficit' means to tax lightly, so that business will be encouraged because people will be able to buy more goods.

As explained below, taxes are either 'direct' taxes (shown in the table as 'taxes on income') or 'indirect taxes' ('taxes on expenditure').

12.4 DIRECT TAXES

These are taxes which are paid *directly* to the government by the persons on whom they are levied.

Direct taxes are based on *gains* in the form of income and capital.

(a) Income tax

This is assessed on what a person receives during the year in the form of wages or salary, fees, interest on investments, rents, profits from a non-corporate business, etc.

It is known as a *progressive* tax because the tax rate increases in stages as income increases. A person is allowed to receive a certain amount before he pays any tax at all. Further allowances are given so that, for instance, a married man pays less than a single man. Other allowances are given for a variety of reasons. The remaining income is known as *taxable* income.

A person who is employed pays through the Pay As You Earn system (PAYE). He is given a code number which represents the allowances to which he is entitled. By means of tax tables his employer deducts the amount of tax payable each time he pays the employee. The total of the amounts deducted from all the employees is paid by the employer to the Inland Revenue.

(b) Corporation tax

Companies pay this tax on their profits after various adjustments have been made. There is a fixed rate, except that small companies pay a lower rate than large companies.

(c) Capital gains tax

If a profit is made on selling an asset, a tax is payable on it. Therefore, a speculator who buys and sells shares would pay no income tax in respect of those activities because they do not provide what the authorities call 'income'. Instead, he pays a fixed rate of tax on the gains he makes. Any losses in buying and selling can be set off against the gains.

(d) Capital transfer tax

This is imposed when property is transferred upon the death of the owner and replaces what was known as 'death duties'. The tax is also levied on gifts of property.

12.5 INDIRECT TAXES

These are those taxes which a person does not pay directly to the government but which he pays *in effect*. Indirect taxes are taxes on *spending*. They are paid when a person buys something at a price which includes a tax. The person receiving the payment has to pass on to the government that part of the price which consists of tax.

12.6 VALUE-ADDED TAX (VAT)

This is a 'sales tax' and it is imposed on most goods and services. It is based on the value which is added to anything at the various stages on its way to the final consumer.

This can be shown by a simple illustration. Assume you bought a domestic appliance before VAT was brought in. For the purpose of the example we will say that the raw materials cost £20. Having made the appliance the manufacturer sells it to a wholesaler for £25 and he sells it to a retailer for £30. You buy it from the retailer for £40. If, however, VAT were imposed at 15 per cent, the position would be as follows:

(a) The providers of the raw materials will charge the manufacturer £20 + 15% (£23). £3 would be passed to the government by the raw materials producers.

(b) The manufacturer will charge the wholesaler £25 + 15% (£28.75). The manufacturer will account to the government the £3.75 he has received (the 'output' tax) *less* the 'input' tax he has paid of £3: that is, 75p.

(c) The wholesaler will charge the retailer £30 + 15% (£34.50). He will pay the government £4.50 less £3.75: that is, 75p.

(d) The retailer will sell to you for £40 + 15% (£46). He will pay the government the £6 tax he has received less the £4.50 he has paid: that is, £1.50.

The government therefore receives the tax in four sums – £3 + 75p +

75p + £1.50 – a total of £6. The whole of the tax is, however, paid by you because you pay £46 for something which, were it not for VAT, would have cost £40. (See Figure 12.2.)

Fig 12.2 *levying value-added tax*

Seller	Buyer	Price free of tax (£)	Added value (£)	Price including VAT (£)	Tax payable by seller (15% of added value) (£)	(£)	(£)
Producer	Manufacturer	20	20	23			3.00
Manufacturer	Wholesaler	25	5	28.75	3.75	– 3.00	0.75
Wholesaler	Retailer	30	5	34.50	4.50	– 3.75	0.75
Retailer	Consumer	40	10	46	6	– 4.50	1.50
							6.00

12.7 EXCISE DUTIES

These are imposed on such goods as petroleum products, tobacco and alcoholic drinks. Taxes are also levied on all forms of gambling.

12.8 OTHER SOURCES OF GOVERNMENT INCOME

(a) Local rates
Local authority services are partly financed by grant from the government and by securities issued to the public. A large proportion is met from the 'rates'. This is a 'local tax', based on the rateable values of private dwellings and business premises.

(b) National insurance contributions
Social security benefits are largely met from contributions by employers and their employees and by those who are self-employed.

(c) Import duties
These provide some income but, as already explained, their main purpose is to improve the balance of payments.

12.9 GOVERNMENT SERVICES TO COMMERCE

The titles and the functions of government departments change from time to time but, in total, certain services are always provided. We have already seen how the Department of Trade (and the Export Credits Guarantee Department in particular) helps exporters. Some of the other areas of service are as follows:

(a) Economic development
Sundry committees of representatives of the government, employers and trade unions exist to study the problems of individual industries. From time to time there are consultations between the government, the Trades Union Congress (TUC) and the Confederation of British Industry (CBI) about industry generally. Where necessary, schemes are established to encourage the development of industry in areas which are economically depressed.

(b) Financial aid
The government will, in certain instances, provide the capital to establish new companies or support existing companies where it is not possible to obtain finance from private sources. Tax concessions may be made where new machinery is purchased. Grants and subsidies are made to encourage new industries in depressed areas. Various training schemes are financed.

(c) Labour relations
There is machinery available whereby the two sides in an industrial dispute can be brought together in an attempt to settle their differences.

(d) Information
A monthly digest of statistics about most aspects of the economy is published. Information about new legislation and regulations, and sundry guides, are provided continuously. The Central Office of Information deals with all sorts of enquiries.

12.10 LEGISLATION

(a) Companies
Some of the longest and most complicated legislation is contained in Companies Acts. This is necessary in order to protect investors and those who do business with companies.

(b) Employment
In recent years there has been a considerable increase in legal measures to protect employees. They cover such matters as disputes, working conditions, dismissals, etc.

(c) Social attitudes

There is legislation to reduce the unfairness of sex discrimination, racial discrimination, etc.

(d) Monopolies

A business which controls 25 per cent of a market is regarded in Britain as being a monopoly. Legislation permits the government to break up a monopoly or prevent one being formed if it is considered to be in the public interest to do so.

(e) The environment

Acts of Parliament and local regulations exist to prevent dispoiling of the environment. Controls relate to a variety of matters, ranging from alterations to privately owned houses to the routing of motorways.

EXERCISES

1   Name five possible reasons for altering taxes in a Budget.
2   Explain why the amount of income tax a person pays depends upon his personal circumstances and not on what he spends.
3   Why may one person earning £5000 a year pay more income tax than someone else earning the same amount?
4   Explain why direct taxes and indirect taxes are so described.
5   Explain in outline the PAYE system of taxation.
6   Mr A is a company director who holds an executive position in his company. Occasionally he buys and sells shares as a private venture. What forms of taxation does he pay?
7   Why is indirect taxation known as a tax on spending?
8   X Ltd buys rubber from Planations Ltd and makes motor tyres from it. Some of the tyres are sold to retailers. If the price you have to pay for a tyre includes VAT at 15 per cent, how does the government receive the tax?
9   How does a local authority receive the money to pay for the services it provides?
10   Give examples of how the government will intervene in the conduct of a business.
11   Give three examples of how government departments will help a particular business.
12   Why are the Companies Acts among the longest there are?

CHAPTER 13

BUYING AND SELLING

All businesses are engaged in buying and selling. Although they include those which 'sell' services, in this chapter we will be concerned only with trading in *goods*.

13.1 BUYING AS A SPECIALIST ACTIVITY

Buying is a job for experts because unwise buying can badly damage a business. In a small business probably all the buying will be done by one person. Because the range of purchases is not wide and the buyer is knowledgeable about the business he will be able to buy expertly. For example, a man running a small shop selling materials for artists will obviously have a lot of experience in that field. The work is very specialised and the fact that his customers often ask for his advice indicates he is an expert. He will therefore be an efficient buyer.

In large businesses, however, the amount and variety of purchases is so extensive that no one person can be expert in every area. The solution is to divide the work between separate buyers, each being responsible for his own types of purchases. Thus a large provision store would have separate buyers of meat, bread, fruit, frozen products, etc. Again, if one considers the enormous variety of purchases to be made by a motor-car manufacturer, it is obvious that the services of many buying experts are required. Such a system provides the advantages of specialisation, so that each buyer concentrates on his own area. *Having specialist buyers gives the following advantages*:

(a) Each buyer will have a lot of technical experience. Consequently, he can assess accurately the quality of the available goods. He will be as knowledgeable as the sellers are, so there will be no possibility of them deceiving him.

(b) A buyer will have a sound knowledge of conditions in his market. A good buyer can anticipate price changes, shortages and surpluses, and he will know where there are 'bargains' to be had.

(c) An experienced buyer will know the sellers personally. He will know who he can trust, who delivers promptly, who can be relied on for quality, etc.

The work of specialist buyers would be centralised in a *Purchasing* or *Buying Department.* This section would be responsible for the clerical work of ordering, keeping records and authorising payment to the sellers. It would 'chase' suppliers who were late in making deliveries and would check incoming goods.

13.2 THE PRINCIPLES OF EFFICIENT BUYING

Some businesses will buy *goods for resale,* these being *wholesalers and retailers.*

Manufacturers will buy *raw materials, machinery* and, in some cases, *components.*

All businesses will buy *equipment* and *office supplies.*

The *principles of efficient buying* may be summarised as follows:

(a) A business buying goods for resale must be guided by the preferences of its customers. There is no point in buying goods which are unpopular. Therefore, a business *must* react to a demand by its customers. If the public insists of buying something which the shopkeeper knows is not the best product, he must remember that 'the customer is always king'. For example, a retailer knows that coloured stripes in toothpaste do not improve it, but if customers, pursuaded by advertising, insist on coloured toothpaste, he would be foolish not to stock it.

(b) Obviously, the selling price must exceed the buying price by an amount sufficient to cover expenses and provide a profit, but it is not always best to sell those goods on which the difference is greatest. For instance, if there is a 'profit margin' of only 5 per cent on article A and it is 15 per cent on article B, it is better to stock article A if it sells four times as well as article B.

(c) Goods should be bought in large amounts because suppliers give discounts for large purchases. There are limits to this, however. Unless goods can be sold quickly a large purchase will result in the buyer having to meet heavy storage costs. The expense of storing goods is high (particularly in rent) and some goods will deteriorate unless sold within a short time. A supermarket sells vast quantities of goods every day, so it will buy in large amounts in the knowledge that they will be quickly taken out the shop.

It must also be remembered that ordering a large amount means that a large sum has to be paid. If it takes some time to sell all the consignment, the seller will be receiving his return slowly. So long as stock is unsold it represents 'tied-up' capital.

(d) Machinery and equipment bought for use *within* a business must be 'cost-effective'. The savings they provide by improving efficiency and reducing other costs must be more than the purchases cost (including their maintenance). A firm may buy a computer because it would result in fewer clerks being employed, and so less would be paid in wages. However, total costs may *rise* because computer experts will have to be employed, and other unanticipated costs may show themselves. Many a manager has been persuaded by a salesman to buy a piece of office eqipment and then found his costs had *increased*!

13.3 THE DOCUMENTS USED IN BUYING AND SELLING

Firms regularly engaged in buying and selling all use the same *types* of documents. *Each document serves two purposes*:

(a) To give information to the other party – for example, to tell a supplier what goods are required.
(b) To enable it to keep its own records – for example, to know what goods have been ordered.

The documents are therefore linked to records kept by the buyer and the seller. Thus, after goods have been sold, the seller, using his document, will have a record of what he has supplied and how much he is owed for it. The buyer's record, taken from the same document, will tell him what goods he has received and how much he owes for them. As each document travels between the two parties, each will keep its own records.

Figure 13.1 shows the movement of documents and the records kept by buyer and seller. You should refer to this diagram when studying the following explanations of the documents used in buying and selling. Before that stage is reached, however, it may be necessary for buyer and seller to agree on a price. We will therefore first look at the documents which may be used before the goods are actually ordered.

13.4 THE INQUIRY

If a buyer regularly buys the same goods from the same seller, he will know what the prices are. In other cases, however, it will be necessary to *ask* what the price would be. To get the best price he would probably approach more than one supplier.

By way of illustration we will assume that in the past a manufacturer

Fig 13.1 *documents used in buying and selling*

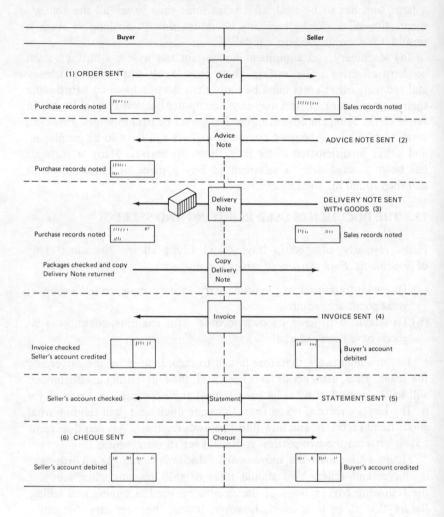

has purchased small amounts of certain goods from a supplier and now requires to know what savings he would make if he were to buy in larger quantities. Figure 13.2 shows the letter of inquiry he may send. Points to note about the letter are as follows:

(a) It is addressed to the person who can give the required answer.
(b) It contains a reference to the inquirer's records.

Fig 13.2   *the inquiry*

A.B. Producers Limited

Western Road   Eastville   Sussex

Mr D. McLean   Our ref.: P/852/JS/OT
Sales Manager
Lawson Chemicals Ltd   Your ref.:
Overton Road   5 March 19..
Blackton Lancs

Dear Sir,

As you will be aware, we have in the past ordered from you small
amounts of Emulsifier and Axton Refiners. Because of a change
in our production methods we will in future require larger amounts
of these fluids. We anticipate that each month we will use 20
litres of Emulsifier and 10 litres of Axton Refiners.

We would be pleased to receive your quotation for these larger
quantities.

Yours faithfully

A.B. Producers Ltd

J. Smithers

J. Smithers

Purchasing Manager

13.5 THE QUOTATION

In response to the inquiry the supplier would send a quotation and a
covering letter similar to the ones illustrated in Figures 13.3 and 13.4.
The following should be noted in respect of those documents:

(a) The supplier repeats the inquirer's reference and gives his own
reference in his letter.

(b) The quotation is set out on a standard form. It is numbered so that
the supplier can file a copy for future reference. If later there was a
dispute about the price charged, the buyer would refer to this number
in his letter of complaint.

Fig 13.3 *the reply to the inquiry*

LAWSON CHEMICALS LIMITED
OVERTON ROAD BLACKTON LANCS

Mr J. Smithers
Purchasing Manager
A.B. Producers Ltd
Western Road
Eastville Sussex

Our ref.: D25/770/DM/AS

Your ref.: P/852/JS/0T

10 March 19..

Dear Sir,

I thank you for your inquiry and attach our quotation for the products you require. You will note that the 5-litre cans are relatively less expensive than the 2½-litre cans you had previously and that there is a further reduction for orders of 20 litres or more of any one fluid.

I have quoted on the assumption that you will require the same grades as before but if you require any advice as to their suitability for your new process I would be pleased to ask John Masters, our local Technical Officer, to discuss the matter with you.

Yours faithfully

D. McLean

D. McLean

Sales Manager

(c) For each item the supplier's description of it and the code he uses are given.

(d) The terms of sale are set out. These show that a discount of 2½ per cent will be granted if the account is paid within 30 days; that delivery can be promised within 14 days after an order is received; and that the price includes the cost of carriage.

13.6 THE ORDER

If the prospective buyer is satisfied with the terms given in the quotation, he will send an order. This is made out on his own form, such as that shown in Figure 13.5. The following points should be noted about the document illustrated:

Fig 13.4 *the quotation*

```
                          QUOTATION              No. 72561/9

                   LAWSON CHEMICALS LIMITED
                   OVERTON ROAD BLACKTON LANCS

   To A.B. Producers Ltd
      Western Road
      Eastville  Sussex                          10 March 19..
```

Code	Description	Units	Price per unit	Quantity discount
			£	
XL55/B	Emulsifier Grade B	5-litre cans	17.45	10% on 4 cans or over
AB6/A	Axton Refiners Grade A	5-litre cans	18.25	10% on 4 cans or over

Prices exclusive of VAT
Terms: 2½% 30 days   Per pro Lawson Chemicals Ltd
Delivery: 14 days
Carriage paid   *D. McLean*
                                            Sales Manager

(a) It contains the reference number of the order form. The buyer would enter this number on his purchase records as indicated at (1) in Figure 13.1.

(b) In specifying the items he quoted the *supplier's* descriptions and codes.

(c) It is on a standard form, a copy of which the buyer will file.

(d) The address to which the goods are to be delivered is given. This is necessary because, for example, the goods may be ordered by a head office for delivery to a branch or outlying factory.

The buyer's records will now show that the goods have been ordered. They will also show when they are to be delivered so that the buyer can 'chase' the supplier if delivery is not on time. When the seller receives the order he will record that he has the order to fulfil by a stated date. He can thus identify outstanding orders at any time.

The seller may send an *Advice Note* to say that the order has been received and perhaps to give a delivery date. As in the example delivery should be made within 14 days, however, it may be unnecessary to send this document. If it *is* sent, then the buyer will note his records as shown at (2) in Figure 13.1. An Advice Note may sometimes be sent to say that the goods have been dispatched.

Fig 13.5 *the order*

A.B. Producers Limited

Western Road   Eastville   Sussex

Lawson Chemicals Ltd
Overton Road
Blackton Lancs

Order No.: F/3572/25

3 April 19..

Please supply the following

Item	Code	Quantity
Emulsifier Grade B	XL55/B	8 x 5 litres
Axton Refiners Grade A	AB6/A	4 x 5 litres

J. Smithers

Deliver to: above address

Purchasing Manager

13.7 THE DELIVERY NOTE

This document is sent with the goods. It is usually a copy of the invoice, except that the prices are omitted. A common practice is to type both documents together but the Delivery Note would contain only the first two columns of the invoice shown in Figure 13.6. It therefore allows the purchaser to check the items received against those listed in the Note. The purchaser will sign a copy of the Note to say that the goods *appear* to be in good order and then hand it to whoever delivered the goods. Later, he will open the packages and examine the contents.

As shown at (3) in Figure 13.1, the buyer will then note in his records that the purchase is completed. The seller would already have recorded that he had dispatched the goods, and when he receives back the copy of his Delivery Note he will know that delivery has been acknowledged.

Fig 13.6 *the invoice*

INVOICE

LAWSON CHEMICALS LIMITED
OVERTON ROAD BLACKTON LANCS

A.B. Producers Ltd
Western Road
Eastville Sussex

No.: 2778/264

Your Order No.: F/3572/25

18 April 19..

Delivered 17.4.19.   to above address   by our vehicle

Quantity	Description	Price per unit (£)	Total price (£)	Quantity discount (£)	Cost (£)	VAT at 15% (£)	Amount payable (£)
8 x 5 litres	Emulsifier Grade B XL55/B	17.45	139.60	13.96	125.64	18.84	144.48
4 x 5 litres	Axton Refiners Grade A AB6/A	18.25	73.00	7.30	65.70	9.85	75.55
			212.60	21.26	191.34	28.69	220.03

Terms: 2½%   30 days

13.8 THE INVOICE

This is the bill for the goods supplied. It is usually sent after the goods
have been delivered, but some firms send invoices with the consignments.
In our example the invoice would be similar to that shown in Figure 13.6.
In studying the illustration the following should be noted:

(a) The invoice has a number. The seller will keep a copy of his invoice
and use it to debit the account of A.B. Producers Ltd with the total
of £220.03. The ledger entry will be referenced to the invoice number to
identify the source of the entry.

(b) The buyer's order number is also given. This enables A.B. Producers
Ltd to 'tie up' the invoice with the order so that it can see it is being
charged for exactly what was ordered. The buyer will use the invoice
to credit the account of Lawson Chemicals, showing that £220.03 is owed
to that company. The entries made by both companies are shown at

(4) in Figure 13.1.

(c) Added to the cost of the goods has been value-added tax at 15 per cent. At this point it is sufficient to say that after payment A.B. Producers can produce the invoice to show it has paid £28.69 in VAT and the copy invoice indicates that Lawson Chemicals has collected that sum.

(d) The invoice repeats the terms given in the quotation.

13.9 THE STATEMENT

We have seen that the seller debited the amount of the invoice to the buyer's account, adding it to any amount which was previously owed. At the end of each month Lawson Chemicals will send a copy of that account to its customer, showing the amount owed (if any) at the beginning of the month, the transactions which took place during the month and the resulting amount owing at the end of the month. Reference to Figure 13.7 will show that A.B. Producers owed £170 at the beginning of the month. It settled that amount on the 4th, having been given a credit of 2½ per cent for paying within 30 days of the invoice being received.

It then received a further consignment and was charged £72.60 for it. (Note that the invoice number is quoted.) The buyer disputed this figure and the seller agreed there had been an overcharge of £6. Lawson Chemicals

Fig 13.7 *the statement*

STATEMENT
LAWSON CHEMICALS LIMITED
OVERTON ROAD BLACKTON LANCS

A.B. Producers Ltd
Western Road
Eastville Sussex

Account No.: 4/17720
Terms: 2½% 30 days

			Debit	Credit	Balance
1	April				170.00
4	April	Discount		4.25	165.75
4	April	Cheque		165.75	—
8	April	Invoice 2778/250	72.60		72.60
12	April	Credit Note 653		6.00	66.60
18	April	Invoice 2778/264	220.03		286.63

Fig 13.8 *a credit note*

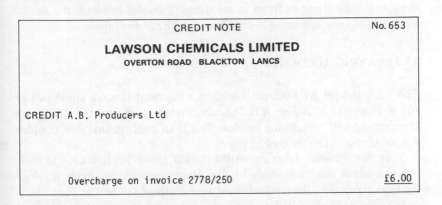

thereupon issued a *credit note* for that sum. This document would be used by A.B. Producers to debit the seller's account and, as can be seen in the illustration, Lawson Chemicals credited the buyer's account.

The credit note is shown in Figure 13.8. Such documents are also used when damaged goods are returned or where a buyer, having been charged for packing crates, returns them to the seller. A *debit note* is issued when the buyer has been undercharged or he has to pay some extra sum.

It will be seen that the final item in Figure 13.7 refers to the invoice we have been studying. A.B. Producers has been debited with the full amount of £220.03 and it now owes £286.63. This sum will be reduced by 2½ per cent if the outstanding invoices are paid within 30 days of their dates.

As will be seen at (5) in Figure 13.1, the buyer will check that the statement agrees with the account in his books.

13.10 KEEPING ACCOUNTS

We have seen that each party to a transaction keeps an account in the name of the other party and that a statement is a copy of the account as it appears in the creditor's books. The ledger accounts as set out in Figure 13.1 are in the 'traditional' form. Such accounts list the debit items on the left-hand side and the credit items on the right-hand side. To find out what is owing at any time it is therefore necessary to subtract the total of one side from the total of the other side. Today, most ledgers are kept in the style shown in the statement in Figure 13.7. It will be seen that as each item (debit or credit) is written, the resulting balance is entered at the same time.

The account of the debtor in the creditor's book must, obviously, show the same items as those in the debtor's books, but with the debits and credits in one appearing as credits and debits in the other.

13.11 PAYING ACCOUNTS

The records kept by both parties when a payment is made are shown at (6) in Figure 13.1. Before A.B. Producers sends its cheque the Purchasing Department will 'vouch' the invoice. This is to confirm that it is in order for its Accounts Department to pay.

Very few business debts are settled in cash, this being restricted to such items as minor purchases made locally. Most payments are made through the banking system; the methods used are explained in Chapter 16.

It is not normal practice to give receipts for payments made by cheque. Indeed, it is not necessary, because the Cheques Act 1957 states that a cheque paid by the banker on which it is drawn is evidence of its receipt by the creditor.

13.12 DISCOUNTS

In the specimen transactions we saw that the buyer would have his debt reduced by 2½ per cent if he settled his account within 30 days. This is known as a *cash discount.*

It is expensive for a seller to have money owed him. This is partly because of the extra clerical costs involved in making further demands for payment. The main reason, however, is that a creditor needs his money in order to pay his own bills. If he has to wait for it, he may be forced to borrow so that he can carry on in business. As he would have to pay interest on any money borrowed, it is more economical for him to allow a lower rate of interest to his debtors as an inducement to pay promptly. In fact, while money is owing to him, *his debtor* is using the creditor's money.

Some suppliers invoice goods at the price the retailer will sell them at. For example, a manufacturer may advertise that certain of his goods can be purchased in shops for £20 each. If he charges a retailer £20, then obviously the shopkeeper will make no profit. Instead, the invoice quotes the figure of £20 *less* a *trade discount* of, say, 25 per cent. The retailer therefore pays £15.

Tradesmen (such as decorators) often obtain their supplies from shops below the price paid by the general public. This, also, is a form of trade discount.

13.13 CREDIT CONTROL

If a buyer does not pay for goods he has purchased, the seller will have to write off the amount as a loss. This is known as a *bad debt*. Even if the purchaser *does* eventually pay (probably after being sued for the debt) the seller will have been put a lot of expense. A supplier must therefore do all he can to avoid dealing with people who will not pay or who pay very late. Before he will agree to sell goods to someone he has not dealt with before he will try to establish that person's 'creditworthiness'. To do so he may ask for a reference from the would-be buyer's bank. A more useful method would be to ask a trade enquiry agent to investigate and report on the firm's financial standing. These agents can find out the financial status of a firm and give a report within a few days.

If the supplier agrees to allow credit to his new customer, he will usually place a limit on the amount. If the buyer subsequently builds up a good reputation for paying promptly, the seller may increase the amount of credit if the customer requests it. On the other hand, a 'good payer' may later run into difficulties. His supplier must therefore keep a close watch on the accounts of his customers because it is there that any clue about slow payers will be found.

13.14 METHODS OF FINDING OUT PRICES

We have already seen the form in which a quotation may be given in response to an inquiry. Another method of finding out the price of goods is to refer to *price lists* issued by suppliers. These are merely *offers* to sell at specified prices. There is no *promise* to sell, because the goods may be out of stock when an order is received.

In some circumstances a supplier will submit a *tender*. This is sometimes in response to an advertisement inviting suppliers to offer to provide goods or services. For example, a local authority may wish to buy large quantities of stationery and will ask suppliers who wish to do so to quote prices. Such a method ensures there will be competition between interested suppliers, so that the buyer purchases at the lowest prices.

An *estimate* is a quotation for making something or providing a service. For example, a manufacturer may offer to build a machine for a certain price or a contractor may agree to clean office windows for a stated annual charge.

Prices current is a term referring to the prevailing market prices of commodities. They are often published in newspapers. They show the prices as they were when they were printed; for many commodities these may change within a very short time.

A *pro forma invoice* means it is an invoice sent 'as a matter of form'. It indicates what the invoice would look like if the buyer ordered the goods. (The term is also used as a copy invoice – for example, to show Customs officers details of goods imported.)

13.15 PRICING TERMS

In the specimen quotation (Figure 13.4) there was the term 'carriage paid'. This means the price includes all transport costs. Other terms which may be used include the following:

Loco. This is the factory price and does not include transport costs. Motor-cars are usually priced this way.

Free on rail (F.O.R.) means that the seller bears all costs up to a named railway station.

Carriage forward. This indicates that the seller pays all costs up to a stated point.

Cash on delivery (C.O.D.) indicates that the price must be paid to whoever delivers the goods.

Cash with order (C.W.O.) means that payment must accompany the order.

(Terms used in overseas trade are listed in Chapter 10.)

EXERCISES

1 Why is buying a job for experts?

2 The owner of a local photographic shop is contemplating purchase of a supply of a new type of camera. What must be bear in mind before making a decision?

3 If *A* Ltd sells goods to *B* Ltd, how does each company know: (a) when the goods are due to be delivered; (b) when the goods have been delivered; and (c) how much is owed at any one time?

4 Mr Jones owns a small grocery store. He has the opportunity of buying, at a particularly low price, a consignment of sugar sufficient to serve his customers for three months. Would you advise him to take this 'bargain'?

5 A business is shortly to be opened under the name of County Shops Ltd. The owners wish to order a large stock of headed letter paper. Draft the inquiry they would make of a printer.

6 Give the printer's reply to the above inquiry, using a formal quotation.

7 Diddums Ltd, a babywear shop chain, orders the following goods from Cozy Ltd: 500 bonnets; 1000 pairs of booties. The supplier has

quoted £50 for 100 bonnets and £30 for 100 pairs of booties. The goods are ordered from the head office in London and are to be delivered to the firm's warehouse in Birmingham. Draw up the order.

8 Draft the invoice sent by Cozy Ltd to Diddums Ltd following the above order. A discount of 5 per cent is offered for payment within 30 days.

9 Explain the purpose of each of the following documents: (a) Delivery Note; (b) statement; (c) credit note; (d) tender; (e) estimate.

10 Some goods are invoiced at '£1000 less trade discount 20 per cent. Cash discount 5 per cent 30 days'. First, distinguish between the two types of discount. Second, how much will the buyer pay?

11 Goods were invoiced to *XYX* Ltd as follows:

Iron shackles	240	
Packing crates	50	(refundable)
Total	£290	
Discount 5% 30 days		

XYZ Ltd returns the crates immediately after the goods are unpacked and pays the account after 20 days. What items relevant to the transaction will appear in the statement subsequently received by *XYZ* Ltd from the suppliers?

12 Newcomer Ltd wishes to place regular orders for frozen foods from Iceberg Ltd. (1) To avoid bad debts, what should Iceberg Ltd do (i) before accepting orders; and (ii) after accepting orders from Newcomer Ltd? (2) If Newcomer Ltd persistently pays it bills late, how does this affect the supplier?

CHAPTER 14

ADVERTISING

Both consumers and sellers are affected by advertising. Sellers must first make their products known and they may then have to persuade consumers to buy their products in preference to those of other sellers. Consumers, at whom advertising is aimed, require information, but there is the possibility of deception in the ways they are persuaded. There are therefore moral as well as practical considerations in the practice of advertising.

14.1 THE PURPOSES OF ADVERTISING

These are as follows:

(a) To inform
Advertising can be used to place facts before the public. An advertisement for a car may include some technical details, so that part of the advertisement is informative. Another advertisement may be *entirely* informative, such as the announcement of the opening of a new shop.

(b) To persuade
Although the advertisement for the car may give some facts, its over-all objective is to persuade people to buy the car. To do this various subtle methods may be used. The illustration, for instance, may give an exaggerated impression of the car's power. The wording and the lay-out may be designed to appeal to the emotions rather than the mind. If you study some advertisements for practical products, you will find that they contain little or no technical information. One would not expect to find a scientific analysis in an advertisement for a lipstick, of course, but an examination of advertisements for medicinal goods will show that the appeal is mainly to the emotions.

(c) To remind

Some advertisements aim merely to keep the name of the product before the public. A newspaper advertisement may consist only of a picture of a packet of cigarettes; a bus may carry the name of an insurance company; a hoarding may display a well-known advertising phrase. They *say* nothing but serve a useful purpose in constantly reminding the public of the name of the product.

14.2 ADVERTISING MEDIA

The term 'media' means the forms used to carry advertisements.

The choice of media depends upon the product and the audience the advertisement is aimed at. For example, very few people are interested in stamps. A stamp dealer would want to appeal to that small number of people and to no one else. He would therefore advertise in a magazine which most stamp enthusiasts read.

(a) Newspapers

The cost of advertising in newspapers largely depends upon the circulation of each newspaper. If a newspaper sells a million copies, it is possible (although not probable) that a million people will read an advertisement in it. Some pages in a newspaper are more expensive to advertise in than are others, because most people will read the general news pages but only some will read the pages devoted to sport, fashion, the arts, etc.

Different types of people read different newspapers, so an advertiser will use those papers whose readers are likely to be possible buyers of his product. For example, an art gallery would not advertise in a 'popular' newspaper because few of its readers would be likely to be visitors to art galleries. Figure 14.1 is a subtle indication of what sort of people read a 'quality' newspaper.

(b) Magazines

The same principles about which media to use also apply to magazines. There are magazines which men read, those which women read and those which both read. Within each group there is specialisation, so that one magazine will be read by one 'social group' and not by another.

(c) Radio and television

These are the most expensive of advertising media. A broadcast at a 'peak time' will be heard or seen by millions of people. If only a tiny fraction of them respond, the huge cost will have been justified. One reason for the success of such advertising is that it is difficult to ignore. A broadcast will be heard or seen by everyone using a radio or television set; even if only

Fig 14.1 *'social groupings' and the media*

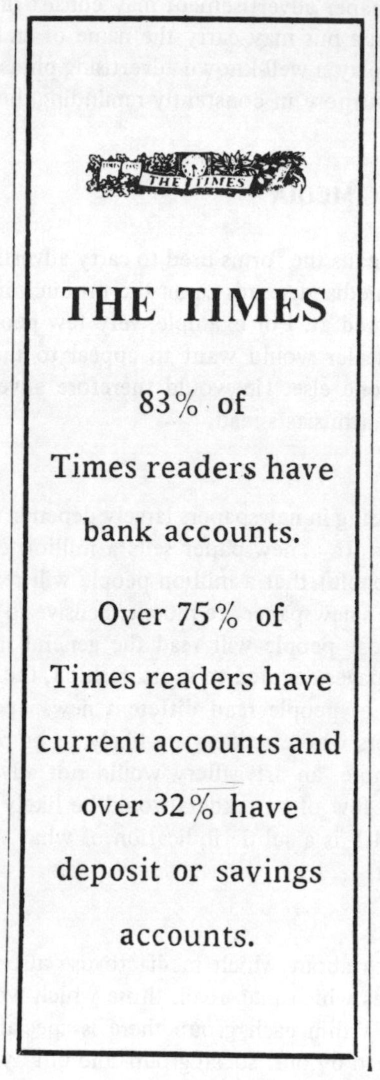

THE TIMES

83% of

Times readers have

bank accounts.

Over 75% of

Times readers have

current accounts and

over 32% have

deposit or savings

accounts.

subconsciously, it will make an impression. On the other hand, when you read a newspaper or magazine you will not even notice most of the advertisements.

A radio or television advertisement must make an *instant* appeal. There may be only 30 seconds to get the message across, so its impact must be immediate.

(d) Outdoor advertising

This includes posters, advertisements on vans and buses and in trains. The message must be simple and short, perhaps with an immediately recognisable illustration.

14.3 MARKET RESEARCH

How *do* advertisers know what sort of people read certain newspapers and magazines? The information comes from market researchers. They also find out what people's personal preferences are. You may have been stopped in the street and asked some questions by a market researcher. These questions are carefully drawn up and the answers to thousands of questionnaires are totalled and analysed. From this it is possible to get the views of a cross-section of the public. (see the example in Figure 14.2.)

Fig 14.2 *questionnaire for market research on smoking*

1	Do you smoke cigarettes?	YES/NO
	(If 'no', terminate.)	
2	How many do you smoke a day?	
3	What size of cigarette do you smoke?	MINOR/STANDARD/LARGE
4	Do you smoke filter tips?	YES/NO
5	Do you smoke menthol cigarettes?	YES/NO

Market research is often done in advance of an advertising campaign – and sometimes it is done even before a product is made. The aim is to find out the preferences, likes and dislikes of the public, so that the product is presented in such a way as to appeal to the most people. It also makes it possible to stress in advertisements those features which will get the best response.

Market research will also establish why the sales of a product are falling. By asking questions and summarising the answers an indication of the cause can be obtained.

14.4 DOES ADVERTISING INCREASE PRICES?

The two conflicting answers to this question may be summarised as follows:

(a) Advertising is very expensive. Whoever pays the cost must pass it on to the consumers. Therefore, advertising *increases* prices.

(b) Advertising increases sales. The more a manufacturer produces, the lower his costs per unit. This allows him to *reduce* prices.

14.5 IS THE COST OF ADVERTISING JUSTIFIED?

The arguments *against* the second statement above are as follows:

(a) Advertising will increase sales only if it is *successful*. An unsuccessful campaign will merely increase costs. Also, a manufacturer may spend thousands of pounds simply to defend himself against another manufacturer's advertising. He incurs huge costs merely to stand still.

(b) There must be a limit to the amount of sales. The population can eat only a certain amount of breakfast cereal, for example. If the sales of one brand increases, the sales of another must decrease.

(c) Advertising is not honest when there is no genuine competition. For example, there are many brands of soap powder, all apparently fiercely competing against one another. In fact, almost all the soap powders are made by *three* manufacturers.

The defenders of advertising say that (in addition to reducing prices) advertising is necessary for the following reasons:

(a) *To inform the public.*

(b) *To encourage competition.* To increase sales, advertising must offer lower prices and improved products. Successful advertising will therefore ensure that the public gets the most efficiently produced goods.

(c) *To increase the standard of living.* Advertising encourages people to buy things which will make their lives easier and more enjoyable. Thus, if advertising increases the sale of washing-machines, the amount of household drudgery is reduced.

14.6 THE MORAL ASPECTS OF ADVERTISING

The aim of advertising is to *persuade* consumers, and in that respect it can be very successful. It has been shown that, in spite of the huge cost, a two-minute television 'commercial' can produce an amazing response; the number of applications for a job advertised in a newspaper is often remarkable. One may therefore put the following questions about advertising:

(a) Are people persuaded to buy things they cannot afford and which they do not really need?

(b) If advertising increases the amount of smoking and drinking, is it a harmful practice?

(c) Does sex appeal have to play a large part in advertising some products?

(d) By publicising only the favourable aspects of a product, is advertising honest?

14.7 PROTECTING CONSUMERS AGAINST ADVERTISING

Because of complaints that some advertisments are misleading, offensive or morally wrong, the industry has set up its own body to deal with them. The Advertising Standards Authority will investigate complaints that an advertisement is misleading or offends against the British Code of Advertising Practice. A newspaper announcement about the Authority is shown in Figure 14.3.

There have been instances where people have sent money in response to mail-order advertisements and then did not receive the goods or a refund of their money because the advertiser had become bankrupt. Members of the Newspaper Publishers' Association insure their readers against this risk, as is shown in the newspaper statement shown in Figure 14.4.

EXERCISES

1   Give an example of each of the following advertisements: (a) one which gives information only; (b) one which contains no factual information; (c) one which informs and persuades.

2   Give two examples of products or services which would use each of the following advertising media in preference to others: (a) women's monthly magazines; (b) posters on buses; (c) 'quality' newspapers; (d) radio.

3   Which media would you concentrate on if you were advertising the following: (a) an expensive camera; (b) a new make of packet soup; (c) a forthcoming 'sale' in a local shop; (d) a 'special offer' of Indian shawls to be sold by post?

4   How can market research make it possible to decide (a) what size to make a new cigarette, (b) why sales of a particular washing-powder are falling, (c) what to concentrate on when advertising toilet soap?

5   Discuss the contention that 'advertising increases the cost of toothpaste'.

6   'Advertising ensures that people will have the things they would not otherwise possess.' Comment on this statement.

7   What are the aims of the Advertising Standards Authority?

8   Give reasons for saying whether or not cigarettes and alcohol should be advertised. Also what is meant by an advertisement being 'morally offensive'? Give examples.

Fig 14.3   *an attempt to control the moral standards of advertising*

Are you legal, decent, honest and truthful?

Advertising has to be. ✓

The Advertising Standards Authority.

Write to: The Advertising Standards Authority Ltd.
Brook House, Torrington Place, London WC1E 7HN.

Fig 14.4 *protection in respect of mail-order advertisements*

Readers' Protection Scheme Mail Order Advertising

With effect from April 1, 1975, national newspapers have set up a Central Fund to refund monies sent by readers in response to mail order advertisements placed by mail order traders who fail to supply goods or refund the money and who have become the subject of liquidation or bankruptcy proceedings. This arrangement does not apply to any failure to supply goods advertised in a catalogue or direct mail solicitation. These refunds are made on a voluntary basis on behalf of the contributors of the Fund and the readers' claims are limited to the Newspaper Publishers' Association on behalf of the contributors.

(a) Mail Order Advertising is defined as direct response advertisements, display or postal bargains, where cash has to be sent in advance of goods being received. Classified advertising and gardening features are excluded.

(b) Classified advertising is defined as advertising that appears under a "Classification" heading (excluding "Postal and Weekend Shopping") or within the classified columns or sections.

For the purpose of the Scheme.

In the unhappy event of the failure of a mail order trader, readers are advised to lodge a claim with the newspapers concerned within three months from the date of appearance of the advertisement. Any claim received after this period may be considered at the discretion of the NPA.

The establishment of this Fund enables you to respond to these advertisements with confidence.

COMMUNICATIONS

In the commercial sense communications are the methods used to obtain information from outside a business, to negotiate with other businesses and to pass information outward. Numerous forms of communication methods are available and a businessman should choose that method which is most effective in a particular situation. To be effective a communication method must be one which is *economical* and *accurate*, and as *rapid* as is necessary.

The basic methods are those provided by the Post Office; for many of these it has a monopoly. The more important of these as well as those provided by private concerns are explained in this chapter.

15.1 THE NECESSITY FOR EFFICIENT COMMUNICATION

A business requires efficient methods of communication for the following reasons:

(a) Information is required about what is taking place outside the business. A firm needs to know the conditions prevailing in markets in order to estimate costs of materials and to fix its own prices. It has to be aware of the plans of the government, what competitors are doing, what is happening in the financial world, what marketing prospects are, and so on. Accordingly, any business must have access to an 'intelligence service'.

(b) It must be able to communicate with those it does business with, such as suppliers, customers, banks, etc. This will include business negotiations and all the procedures for giving and receiving orders for goods, for receiving and dispatching goods, paying and receiving money, etc.

(c) Information must flow out to employees and shareholders and, often, to the Press and the public at large.

15.2 POSTAL SERVICES

These are the services provided by the Post Office for the delivering of letters and parcels:

(a) Ordinary letter post
Britain has a 'two-tier' postal system. 'First-class' mail (for which there is an extra charge) receives priority over other letters, the intention being that first-class letters will be delivered the day after posting.

Automation has been introduced to make sorting faster. Every address is given a 'post code' and this allows letters to be sorted electronically.

(b) The Recorded Delivery service
This provides proof that a letter has been delivered because the addressee has to sign the postman's book when the letter is delivered. This is useful when it is necessary to prevent someone denying they had received a letter. It also provides a limited amount of compensation if the letter is lost or damaged. An extra fee has to be paid and the letter must be handed in at a Post Office. In exchange, the consignor receives a certificate. If at a later date he wishes to have proof of delivery, this will be provided by the Post Office on payment of a further fee.

(c) A Certificate of Posting
This provides evidence that a letter has been posted, but it does not give proof of delivery. Again, the letter must be handed in at the Post Office in exchange for a certificate.

(d) The Registered Post service
This promises indemnity in the event of a letter or packet being lost in the post. The amount of compensation paid depends upon the value of the contents and the amount of the fee paid. Packets must be firmly sealed and cash can be sent only if envelopes provided by the Post Office are used. The packet must be handed in to the Post Office and a receipt obtained.

(e) Business Reply and Freepost
A trader can encourage people to reply by providing 'Business Reply' envelopes or postcards. The person replying pays no postage and the trader pays a charge on top of the normal postage. Where a trader offers Freepost the respondent simply includes the word 'Freepost' in the address. The trader has to have the prior agreement of the Post Office and pays a deposit from which the postage charges are deducted.

(f) Special delivery services

The Express Delivery Service ensures that when a letter reaches the office of destination it is immediately delivered by messenger instead of waiting for a postman's routine call. Datapost is a system of transporting packages by road with the intention they be delivered early the next morning.

(g) Parcel delivery service

The Post Office will accept parcels up to a certain size and weight. It does not have a monopoly of parcel delivery because many other services are available.

(h) Cash on delivery service

This enables goods to be sent on the understanding that the postman will not deliver them until he has been paid the amount due on the goods. This ensures that the consignor receives prompt payment.

(i) Air mail

The cost of packets sent by air mail depends upon their weight and the destination country. All mail within Europe travels by air, as it does within certain other countries. *Air letters* can be purchased from Post Offices, the cost of which includes the postage. They must contain no enclosures.

15.3 TELECOMMUNCATIONS

(a) The telephone

Everyone is familiar with the telephone services provided by the Post Office. The most important recent development has been *Subscriber Trunk Dialing (STD)*, whereby a call can be dialled direct instead of going through an operator. It is possible to dial direct to many parts of the world.

Internal telephones for use within a firm can be hired from the Post Office or purchased from manufacturers.

Telephoning has the advantage of providing immediate contact. It allows for matters to be discussed and decisions made personally. To that extent it is superior to other systems. It has the disadvantage that it provides no written record of the communication.

(b) Teleprinters

These can be privately owned, or alternatively the *Telex* system of the

Post Office can be used. A subscriber types his message on a special machine and this is simultaneously typed on to a similar machine in the office of the addressee. Unlike the telephone, it is not affected by any time difference between the two parties. A message typed in London in the afternoon will be recorded in Sydney during its night hours and will await the arrival in his office of the Australian addressee. The cost of sending a message depends on how long it takes to send it. If a code is used, this will shorten the message and the address, thereby reducing the cost of transmission.

15.4 USING THE MOST APPROPRIATE METHOD

No one method is the most suitable for any type of communication. What is the best in one circumstance would be inappropriate in another. Where more than one method could be used with equal efficiency, the choice must be of the most economical one:

(a) Speed of transmission
Generally, the faster a communication the more costly it is. For example, first-class delivery is more expensive than second-class delivery. Consequently, the cheaper method should be used if a postal communication is not urgent (e.g. price lists and circulars). Where, however, speed is essential, the extra cost of using a quicker method is justifiable.

(b) Accuracy of information
Some forms of communication cannot be relied upon to be completely accurate. For example, a remark made on the telephone may be misunderstood; because telegrams must be abbreviated they can be misinterpreted. These disadvantages do not apply to letters and teleprinter messages.

(c) Having a record
If a message is sent by telephone, there is no record of it. Some messages (such as agreements) must be in a permanent form, so that letters or teleprinters would be used.

(d) Safety
In some cases it is essential to ensure that a communication is received. It may be necessary to send it by hand or registered post.

15.5 PUBLIC RELATIONS

This is concerned with 'projecting the image' of a business. It is therefore a form of communication. The aim is to improve or maintain the reputation of a firm and to make its name better known. The methods include the following:

(a) Getting news items published and broadcast which reflect favourably on the firm.
(b) Exhibiting at trade fairs.
(c) Inviting the Press to demonstrations of its products.
(d) Co-operating with other bodies 'in the public interest', such as by providing technical information for newspaper and broadcast articles, advising consumer associations, being represented on official committees, and so on.
(e) Providing a good after-sales service.
(f) Dealing quickly and fairly with any complaints by customers, the public or the Press.

EXERCISES

1 Which communication methods would you use for the following: (a) to send an urgent message from London to San Francisco; (b) to fix an appointment for the next day with someone 200 miles away; (c) to make an offer to buy goods from someone a mile away? Give reasons for your answers.

2 Explain the difference between (a) Recorded Delivery and Registered Post; (b) Business Reply and Freepost; (c) Express Delivery and Datapost.

3 Assume you have to send a message from London to New York. What should you bear in mind in choosing between sending it by telephone or by teleprinter?

4 Give examples of information which goes from a firm to the outside world.

5 Under what circumstances would you decide to (a) obtain a Certificate of Posting, (b) send a parcel cash on delivery (c.o.d.), (c) use the Datapost system, (d) send a letter by second-class post?

6 Give two examples of losses which may be suffered by a firm because of poor communication.

7 How can a company present a 'good image' of itself? Why should it want to do so?

CHAPTER 16

BANKING SERVICES

In the English system banks can be broadly divided into three groups:

(a) *The Bank of England* is owned by the state. As it is the centre of the financial world it is discussed in Chapter 18. Some reference will also be made to it in this chapter.

(b) *Joint-stock* or *commercial banks* are the 'High Street banks' we all know. They are also known as *clearing banks*. In this chapter we will look at the services provided by these banks for business people and private individuals. (The ways in which banks provide credit are discussed in the next chapter.)

(c) *Merchant banks* are financial institutions offering specialist services and these are dealt with in Chapter 18.

16.1 THE BROAD FUNCTIONS OF A BANK

A bank deals with other people's money. It *stores* some of it but most is *circulated*. The funds of a bank are constantly changing, as is illustrated in Figure 16.1. These movements constitute the basic functions of a bank. We can identify these by looking at what a bank does for a particular customer. We will assume him to be a small grocer, named Alan Hardy:

(a) *It provides a safe and convenient place for Hardy's spare cash*. Every day Hardy will receive fairly large amounts of cash from his customers. He will pay out little cash, however, because he will pay most of his bills by cheque. Having set aside enough 'change' to keep in the till, Hardy will have a surplus of cash at the end of each day. Obviously, it would not be safe for him to keep it in his shop, so he pays it into his bank.

(b) *It collects payments on behalf of Hardy from his customers*. Some of Hardy's customers will pay him by cheque. A customer who gives Hardy a cheque is ordering his own bank to transfer money to Hardy's bank account. Instead of Hardy taking the order to the customer's bank

Fig 16.1 *the movements of a bank's funds*

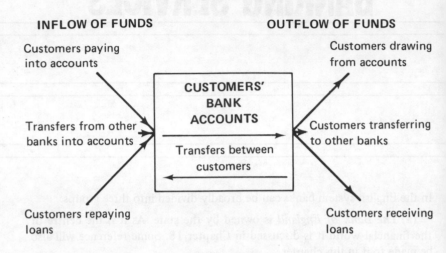

INFLOW OF FUNDS

OUTFLOW OF FUNDS

Customers paying
into accounts

Customers drawing
from accounts

Transfers from other
banks into accounts

**CUSTOMERS'
BANK
ACCOUNTS**

Transfers between
customers

Customers transferring
to other banks

Customers repaying
loans

Customers receiving
loans

he gives it to his own bank. That bank will collect the money from the customer's bank and pay it into Hardy's account.

(c) *It provides Hardy with cash when he needs it.* We have seen that Hardy's bank account has been receiving money in the form of cash and cheques. There is therefore a fund which can be drawn on because it is *his* money and not the bank's. Hardy can obtain cash as he needs it from the bank as quickly as he can take it from his till.

(d) *It will pay Hardy's creditors for him.* When Hardy pays a bill he will give his creditor a cheque. Thus he orders his bank to transfer money to the creditor's bank account. Again, it is his own money he is asking the bank to use.

(If the creditor is a customer of *another* bank, Hardy's money will go out of his bank, reducing the funds of Hardy's bank. The same principle applies in reverse when Hardy *receives* a cheque from someone who banks elsewhere. If, however, Hardy and the other person both use the same bank, the transfer is *within* that bank, so that the amount of its funds is not altered. These points are shown in the illustration.)

(e) *It may provide Hardy with a loan.* If Hardy receives a loan from the bank, he is then, of course, using money which is *not* his. Against this outflow of funds there will be an inflow as Hardy pays back the loan.

16.2 THE TYPES OF BANKING ACCOUNTS

The two main types of banking accounts are *current accounts* and *deposit accounts*. As is explained below, a current account is for daily use because it provides cash immediately. A deposit account is a sort of reserve for holding money which is surplus to daily requirements (see Section 16.4). A third type is the *budget account*, used for paying domestic bills (see Section 16.5).

16.3 CURRENT ACCOUNTS

These are the 'active' accounts. A businessman will pay into and draw out of his current account every day.

No interest is payable on such an account. The bank may impose *charges* for operating the account but no charge is payable so long as a certain minimum balance is in the account.

To open a current account an application form, similar to the one shown in Figure 16.2, must be completed. The applicant must provide the name of a referee and some money (as little as £1) to start the account. The bank will also require a copy of the applicant's signature because, as he will draw cheques, a bank must be able to recognise his signature. If a bank pays out on a cheque which has a forged signature on it, it must refund the money to the customer.

When the bank has approved the application it will open an account for its new customer. At the same time it will provide him with a paying-in book and a cheque book.

The *paying-in book* contains pages similar to that shown in Figure 16.3. Every time sums are paid into a current account the totals of the denominations are entered on a page of the book and its counterfoil. The cheques are listed on the back. The bank cashier checks that the money agrees with the figures and tears off the slip. This is used to enter up the customer's account. The counterfoil is stamped by the cashier and handed back to the customer as his receipt. From this he can write up his own books.

The *cheque book* contains the forms for drawing out money, either for the customer's personal use or for transferring to someone else. The cheque is used to debit the customer's account and for processing through the cheque-clearing system (see Section 16.14). The customer enters details of the cheque on the counterfoil and uses it to enter up his own records. (Current accounts are sometimes referred to as 'cheque accounts'.)

(Money may also be paid into and drawn out of current accounts without using paying-in slips and cheques. This is explained in Sections 16.10–16.12 below.)

At regular intervals the bank will send a customer a *statement of account*. This a copy of his account at the bank and is in a form similar to the one shown in Figure 17.1 in the next chapter.

Shopkeepers are sometimes reluctant to accept a cheque from someone

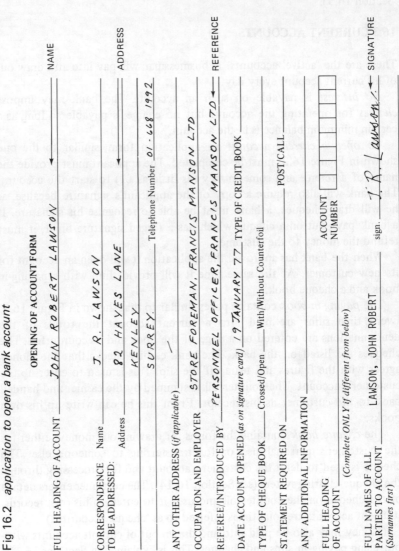

Fig 16.2 application to open a bank account

OPENING OF ACCOUNT FORM

FULL HEADING OF ACCOUNT ___ JOHN ROBERT LAWSON ___ NAME

CORRESPONDENCE Name ___ J. R. LAWSON ___
TO BE ADDRESSED: Address ___ 82 HAYES LANE ___ ADDRESS
___ KENLEY. ___
___ SURREY. ___ Telephone Number 01 - 668 1992

ANY OTHER ADDRESS (if applicable) ___

OCCUPATION AND EMPLOYER ___ STORE FOREMAN, FRANCIS MANSON LTD ___

REFEREE/INTRODUCED BY ___ PERSONNEL OFFICER, FRANCIS MANSON LTD ___ REFERENCE

DATE ACCOUNT OPENED (as on signature card) 19 JANUARY 77 TYPE OF CREDIT BOOK ___

TYPE OF CHEQUE BOOK ___ Crossed/Open ___ With/Without Counterfoil ___

STATEMENT REQUIRED ON ___ POST/CALL ___

ANY ADDITIONAL INFORMATION ___

ACCOUNT NUMBER ☐☐☐☐☐☐☐

FULL HEADING OF ACCOUNT ___ sign. ___ J. R. Lawson ___ SIGNATURE
(Complete ONLY if different from below)

FULL NAMES OF ALL PARTIES TO ACCOUNT ___ LAWSON, JOHN ROBERT ___
(Surnames first)

Fig 16.3 *bank paying-in book*.

they do not know. A person who maintains a satisfactory account can be provided with a *cheque card* by his bank. This is a guarantee to the shopkeeper that a cheque drawn for an amount of up to £50 will be met by the bank. When handing his cheque to the shopkeeper the customer shows his card and enters its number on the back of the cheque. This is not a form of credit because the customer must agree not to draw cheques for more than he has in his account (unless the bank has already agreed he may do so). Cheque cards must not be confused with credit cards (see the next chapter), though some credit cards can be used as cheque cards.

16.4 DEPOSIT ACCOUNTS

These are savings accounts: that is, they are used to hold money which is not needed on a day-to-day basis. Unlike for a current account, the bank pays interest on a deposit account. No cheque book is provided because seven days notice has to be given to withdraw money. However, a bank will usually pay out on demand and will charge interest for the seven days.

16.5 BUDGET ACCOUNTS

An individual has to pay domestic bills at irregular intervals, but his income is usually received at *regular* intervals (as in the case of a monthly salary). For example, in one month he may have to pay bills for gas, electricity and the telephone; there may be large annual items, such as car tax and insurance. To overcome this problem banks offer budget accounts. If you use this system, it works as follows.

You make a list of all the household bills you expect to receive during the coming year. You then divide the total by twelve. (If you are paid weekly, you can divide it into thirteen four-week periods.) You then arrange for the bank to transfer one of these instalments from your current account to a budget account each month. As the bills come in, you pay them by using special budget account cheques.

The method not only evens out your spending but it can also save you money. For example, buying an annual rail season ticket is cheaper than using monthly or quarterly ones.

16.6 THE PARTIES TO A CHEQUE

When a person writes out a cheque he is *ordering his bank* to pay some of his money with the bank *to someone else*. He sends the cheque to the other person, who can then get payment from the payer's bank 'on demand': that is, the money must be paid immediately.

The parties to a cheque are as illustrated in Figure 16.4:

Fig 16.4 *an order cheque*

(a) The party who makes out the cheque (Hardy) is the *drawer*.
(b) The party who is ordered to pay the money (Midland Bank) is the *drawee*.
(c) The party to whom the money is to be paid (Wholesaler Ltd) is the *payee*.

It is possible to write a cheque without naming the payee by making it out to 'bearer'. This is a dangerous practice because anyone who obtains such a cheque can get payment on it. These are known as *bearer cheques*. Where the payee is named the cheque is called an *order cheque*.

Sometimes there are more than three parties to a cheque. Instead of paying a cheque into his bank account a payee may use it to pay someone else. If Wholesaler Ltd wished to use the cheque to pay, say, *OK* Ltd, it may 'endorse' the cheque by writing on the back 'Pay *OK* Ltd' and signing. When it pays the cheque into its bank *OK* Ltd will add its signature to the endorsement. Wholesaler Ltd. would be the *endorser* and *OK* Ltd would be the *endorsee*. (This is why a cheque is made payable to' . . . or order'.)

16.7 THE FEATURES OF A CHEQUE

If we look again at Figure 16.4, there are the following points to note:

(a) In the top right-hand corner there is the branch code number.
(b) The amount to be paid is stated in words in one place (although pence is always given as a figure) and in figures in another. The bank will not accept a cheque if the two versions differ.
(c) Banks usually issue 'personalised' cheques: that is, the customer's name is printed on them. He signs below the printed name.
(d) The figures at the bottom are printed in magnetic ink, so that they can be 'read' by a computer. This allows cheques to be sorted automatically. The first set of figures is the number of the cheque. Next is the branch code number (the same as the one at the top.) Finally, there is the customer's account number.

16.8 DISHONOURED CHEQUES

If a bank refuses to pay on a cheque, the cheque is said to be 'dishonoured'. When that happens the cheque is returned with an indication of the reason:

(a) 'Refer to drawer' means there is not enough money in the account to meet the cheque.
(b) 'Instructions not to pay' means that the drawer has 'stopped' the cheque by telling the bank not to honour it.
(c) A cheque may be returned if the bank learns that the drawer has died or become bankrupt.
(d) 'Words and figures differ' is self-explanatory.
(e) If a cheque is more than six months' old, it is said to be 'stale'. The drawer will then be asked if he still wants it to be honoured.

16.9 CHEQUE CROSSINGS

A crossing consists of two parallel lines (with or without words) drawn across the face of a cheque. *Any* form of crossing is an instruction to a bank *not to pay cash* over the counter. If someone steals a crossed cheque it is possible to find out which account it was paid into. Crossing cheques is therefore a sensible precaution. The various forms of crossings are shown in Figure 16.5 and are explained as follows:

(1) This is a *general crossing*. It *may* contain the words '& Co' but this adds nothing effective to the cheque. A cheque crossed generally can be paid into any bank account.

(2) A *special crossing* on a cheque means it can be paid only into the bank named in the crossing.

(3) '*Account payee only*' indicates that the payee may not endorse the cheque to someone else. (In practice, however, a bank will accept the cheque from the endorsee if it is satisfied he has a right to it.)

(4) A cheque crossed '*Not negotiable*' does not mean it cannot be *transferred*. If, however, the person transferring the cheque has no right to it (that is, he stole it), the endorsee would also have no claim on the drawer. All other cheques are 'freely negotiable'.

(5) Banks usually issue cheques which have crossings already printed on them, so that people will be encouraged to use this safer method. If a drawer requires the payee to have cash, he can 'open the crossing' by writing 'Pay cash' in it and adding his signature. If he himself wishes to draw cash, he must also endorse the cheque.

Fig 16.5   *types of cheque crossings*

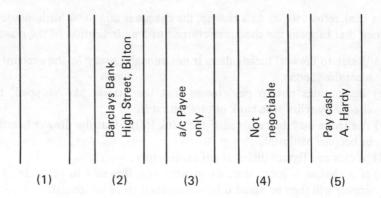

(1)   (2)   (3)   (4)   (5)

16.10 THE CREDIT TRANSFER SYSTEM

This system of paying accounts is also known as *Bank Giro* (not to be confused with National Girobank; see Chapter 21). It can be used to pay single amounts or to pay a number of accounts at the same time.

When you receive a bill there may be enclosed with it a Bank Giro credit slip, similar to the one shown in Figure 16.6. To pay the account you may complete the form and hand it in at a bank with a cheque or cash. If you do not have a bank account, a small charge will be made. This saves you the expense of sending money through the post and is, of course, more convenient. The bank will transfer the amount in the same way it deals with cheques.

Fig 16.6 *a bank Giro slip*

Date	**BARCLAYS BANK LIMITED**		Notes £50
Cashier's Stamp	**bank giro credit**		Notes £20
	CODE NO.	BANK COPY	Notes £10
	20-84-17		Notes £5
			Notes £1
	BARCLAYS BANK LIMITED		50p
	SUTTON, SURREY 43 HIGH STREET		Silver
			Bronze
	ACCOUNT		TOTAL CASH
			Postal Orders
Number of Cheques	Paid in by		Cheques, etc. (Listed overleaf)
			REM £

The method is very frequently used for paying staff. A firm employing 500 people *could* send each one a cheque, spending money on postage and a lot of time. Instead, it can make out a list of the employees, and against each name it will give the bank reference number of the employee and the amount of his pay. With the list will be a transfer slip for each employee. The bank will then transfer the individual items to the appropriate bank accounts and debit the employer's account with the total.

A firm can settle a batch of bills in the same way.

16.11 STANDING ORDER

This is an instruction to a bank to make regular payments to a certain payee. If you have to pay an insurance premium once a year, it is quite easy to forget it. If you have to pay hire-purchase instalments every month, you have the bother of writing cheques and posting letters. A standing order (otherwise known as a *banker's order*) will ensure that the bank pays these items as they become due. Although a charge will be made, you avoid the cost of sending money by post.

16.12 DIRECT DEBITING

Again, this is a method of instructing a bank to make regular payments. One of the problems in using a standing order is that it instructs a bank to pay a *set amount* each time, whereas in practice the amounts may vary. For example, if the annual subscription to an organisation is increased, every member then has to make out a new standing order. In direct debiting you let *your creditor* tell the bank how much is due. To do this you must give clear authority to the creditor and he must inform you that the amount is being changed before he demands the new sum.

16.13 THE ADVANTAGES OF SETTLING DEBTS THROUGH A BANK

(a) Money does not have to be used. The inconvenience and risk of moving cash is eliminated. No time is spent in counting money.
(b) Counterfoils of cheques and paying-in slips are used to write up accounts. These can be checked against statements from the bank.
(c) Once a cheque has been paid it provides proof of its receipt by the payee.
(d) Cheques can be made safer by crossing them.
(e) No matter how far away the other party is, payment can be made locally. There is a saving of the cost of postage and stationery.

16.14 HOW CHEQUES ARE 'CLEARED'

Every day many hundreds of thousands of cheques and other transfer documents go through the banking system. Each document results in increasing someone's bank balance and reducing someone else's by the same amount. Also, as many of these transfers involve two banks (the drawer's and the payee's), the *banks'* own balances change. At the end of each day each bank will have received amounts from each of the other banks and have paid out amounts to each of them. The problem of altering each customer's bank balance and of working out the indebtedness between any two banks is therefore a complex one. The method of doing so is known as *clearing cheques*. It is made easier by the use of computers which can 'read' the magnetic figures on cheques.

Let us first look at what happens to the two people immediately concerned – the drawer and the payee. When Mr. Hardy drew the cheque shown in Figure 16.4 he immediately recorded in his accounts that he had paid his bill. When Wholesaler Ltd received the cheque it paid it into its bank account and recorded that Hardy had paid. Wholesaler's bank then increased its customer's bank balance by the amount of the cheque.

Wholesaler's bank now has to collect the money from Hardy's bank. In other words, it will 'clear' Hardy's cheque. When Hardy's bank has transferred the sum it will reduce Hardy's bank balance; so the bank account will be altered *after* Hardy has altered his own record.

How the two banks will adjust *their* balances will depend on where the two parties bank. To show this we will trace the movements of three cheques drawn by Hardy – who, we will remember, banks with the Midland at Banktown:

(1) *Hardy sends a cheque to Suppliers Ltd, who also banks with the Midland in Banktown.* In this case the cheque will not leave the Banktown branch. All that has to be done is to debit Hardy's account and credit the account of Suppliers Ltd. This is known as a *branch clearing.*

(2) *Hardy sends a cheque to Wholesaler Ltd, who banks with the Midland in Newtown.* When the Newtown branch receives the cheque from its customer it will send it to its head office, together with all the other cheques it has received which were not drawn on Midland Newtown accounts. The Midland head office will put together all the cheques drawn on its Banktown branch and send them there. (Other Midland cheques will go to the relevant branches.)

This will of course reduce the amount held at the Banktown branch, but it is quite likely there will be transfers in the opposite direction: that is, from Newtown to Banktown. The net result will be to change the balances of each branch, but the total held by the *bank* will be unchanged because all the transfers had been between Midland customers.

This is known as a *head-office clearing.*

(3) *Hardy sends a cheque to Services Ltd, who banks with Lloyds in Devenish.* Lloyds Bank Devenish will send all the cheques it receives to its head office. Having disposed of cheques drawn on other branches (as Midland did in (2) above), Lloyds now has to deal with cheques drawn on *other banks.* It divides all the cheques according to the banks they are drawn on – mainly National Westminster, Barclays and Midland. The bundles of cheques are then taken to the *Bankers' Clearing House.* There, Hardy's cheque and all the others drawn on Midland accounts will be handed to a representative of Midland Bank. Midland will then owe Lloyds the total of the cheques in the bundle. Lloyds will, of course, owe Midland for *its* cheques. Therefore, the amount which has to be transferred between the two banks is the difference. This is done through the operations of the Clearing House.

16.15 THE CLEARING HOUSE SYSTEM

All banks have accounts with the Bank of England, so that indebtednesses between banks can be settled by transfers in Bank of England accounts.

If, after all the cheques had been listed, it was found that Lloyds owed Midland £1m. and Midland owed Lloyds £5m, the difference could be settled by Midland paying Lloyds £4m. However, differences between each bank and *all the others* have to be settled, so that although Lloyds is due to receive £4m. from Midland it may have to pay out more than that to the others. The Clearing House system makes individual settlements unnecessary. Instead, the 'net indebtedness' between *all* the banks is settled.

This can be explained if it is assumed that at the end of a day's clearing the position is as shown in Figure 16.7. Instead of calculating the difference between the debts of each pair of banks, it is easier to work out the net position of each bank in relation to all the others. The summary shows that Lloyds and National Westminster each owe £1m. and that Midland owes nothing. Barclays is owed £2m. Therefore, the only transfers which are necessary are for Lloyds and National Westminster to each pay £1m to Barclays.

Fig 16.7 *settling net indebtedness through the Clearing House*

Figures in £m.

Bank owing money	owed to				Total debt
	Barclays	Lloyds	Midland	Natwest	
Barclays		1	4	3	8
Lloyds	3		1	5	9
Midland	2	5		1	8
Natwest	5	2	3		10
Total due to receive	10	8	8	9	35

Summary

Bank	owes	is owed	Net indebtedness
Barclays	8	10	− 2
Lloyds	9	8	1
Midland	8	8	nil
Natwest	10	9	1

16.16 BANKERS' DRAFTS

A banker's draft is, in effect, a cheque which a bank draws on itself on behalf of a customer. There can be instances when a creditor is not prepared to accept a cheque from his debtor. It may be because the amount is particularly large, because the creditor knows nothing about the debtor, or because payment is to be made in a foreign currency. If the bank agrees, it will send the creditor its draft for the amount and debit its customer's account. The creditor would, of course, have no hesitation in accepting such a reliable document.

16.17 OTHER BANKING SERVICES

These (excluding the provision of credit, which is discussed in the next chapter) include the following:

(a) Investment advice; management of investments; buying and selling of investments.
(b) Insurance and life assurance.
(c) Executor and trustee services.
(d) Safe custody of valuables; night safes.
(e) Travellers' cheques and foreign currency.
(f) Cash dispensers.
(g) Exporting advice and services.

EXERCISES

1 Why may a businessman have a current account *and* a deposit account?

2 How is a current account opened?

3 Why do paying-in books and cheque books have counterfoils?

4 If you receive a monthly salary, why is it useful to have a budget account? How does such an account work?

5 There must be three parties to a cheque and there could be five. Name these parties.

6 What do the magnetic figures on the bottom of a cheque mean?

7 Explain what each of the following mean: (a) 'refer to drawer'; (b) stale cheque; (c) 'stopped' cheque.

8 What is the effect of crossing a cheque? What is the difference between a general crossing and a special crossing?

9 What is the difference between a cheque crossed 'Account payee only' and one crossed 'Not negotiable'?

10 How can cash be drawn on a cheque which has been crossed?

11 How does paying an account by bank Giro save time and money?

12 Explain the difference between a standing order (or banker's order) and a direct debit.

13 What are the advantages of paying and receiving money in the form of cheques instead of in cash?

14 What is the difference between a branch clearing and a head-office clearing?

15 What is the function of the Clearing House and how does it work?

16 Obtain a paying-in slip from a bank and complete it as though you were paying in the following cash: six £5 notes; two hundred £1 notes; £80.50 in silver, including twenty 50p pieces; £1.75 in bronze coins. You also pay in the following cheques: £70.21 from *AB* Ltd; £35 from J. Smith; £201 from *XYZ* Ltd; £35.02 from Black Stores.

17 Make out a cheque with a crossing with no words in it. Make it payable to A. J. Simpson for the sum of £24.22. Show on the cheque how Simpson could pass it on to L. Williams. (1) How could you prove you had paid Simpson? (2) What difference would it have made if '& Co' had appeared in the crossing? (3) If Simpson passed on the cheque because he had no bank account, how *could* you have helped him?

CHAPTER 17

BANK CREDIT

Although banks charge fees for most of the services they provide, the major part of a bank's profits comes from lending money. There are various ways in which a bank can provide credit for its customers. First, it can provide a lump sum of money in the form of a *loan*. Second, it can allow a customer to draw cheques when he has insufficient money in his account to meet them. This is done by allowing him an *overdraft*. Finally, it can make it possible for a customer to buy things without paying cash for them. This is done by the use of *credit cards*.

17.1 BANK LOANS

The purpose of a bank loan is to provide the borrower with a lump sum of money. For example, a shopkeeper may wish to buy a refrigerator unit for £500, and instead of getting it on hire purchase he may decide to borrow from his bank and pay cash for it.

To do this he will make a formal application to the bank, and this might well be followed by an interview with the bank manager. The manager has the responsibility of deciding who it is safe to lend to. He will therefore ask the customer why it is essential to have the unit. The reply will probably be that the purchase would allow the shopkeeper to have a larger stock and thus make more profits. The manager will then probably ask to look at the customer's trading accounts to see if the business can make enough extra profit to repay the loan. He will also look at the customer's bank account to see if it has been conducted in a satisfactory manner.

The bank may ask for *collateral security*: that is, something given by the customer additional to his promise to repay. This could be deeds of any property the customer owns, a life-assurance policy, company shares, etc. Alternatively, someone of good financial standing may guarantee to repay the loan if the customer fails to do so. If no security can be offered and the bank manager has faith in the customer, he *may* agree to lend without security.

If the loan is granted, the customer's current account would be credited with the amount lent. He could then draw a cheque to pay for his purchase without overdrawing on his account. At the same time a loan account would be debited with the amount of the loan and the interest to be charged. The customer would be required to repay the loan by regular instalments, and as these are received they would be credited to the loan account.

17.2 PERSONAL LOANS

Banks will also lend to customers who are not in business. This is to enable people to pay cash for personal purchases such as a car or furniture, to meet education expenses, to pay for a holiday, etc. The applicant must have a regular income, and proof of this must be provided. The bank will also have to be sure that the customer will be able to afford the repayments, so enquiries will be made about his financial commitments.

The loan must be repaid by monthly instalments over an agreed period of 6 to 36 months. It is usual for the borrower to complete a standing order, transferring the instalments from his current account to his loan account.

17.3 OVERDRAFTS

A person may require financial help for short periods only. This will be because either his income or his expenses (or both) fluctuate a lot. For example, a salesman may have a fixed salary which he receives each month, and every three months he may receive the commission he has earned. Accordingly, for two consecutive months he will be short of cash and every third month he will have a surplus of cash. A shopkeeper in a seasonal trade will buy a lot of goods at a time when he does not sell many and in his busy period he will be receiving far more cash than he is spending.

In both cases, therefore, there will be times when there is a shortage of cash and times when there is plenty of cash. Over the year the person is solvent, but he needs cash at certain periods. He does not need a *loan*. What he requires is the right to draw cheques for things he has to pay for when he has no money at the bank. In return he promises to repay when his income is high.

This is done by providing an *overdraft*. This is an agreement to allow him to draw cheques, when necessary, which will put his account into debit. The amount up to which he may overdraw will be agreed. He will be charged interest on the *amount* overdrawn for *every day* it is overdrawn.

This amount could change almost daily. He will therefore endeavour to keep his debit balance as low as possible and to turn it into credit as soon as he can. This can be explained by referring to the bank statement shown in Figure 17.1.

It will be seen that Thomas started with a balance of £150 in hand. He then drew cheque numbered 259301 for £100, reducing his balance to £50. His next cheque for £80 resulted in him being overdrawn (shown as OD) by £30. A further cheque increased his overdraft to £130. He then paid in £50, reducing his debt to £80. His final payment put him into credit again. He therefore has to pay interest on £30 for two days; on £130 for three days; and on £80 for five days.

Fig 17.1 *statement of a current account where an overdraft has been agreed*

Statement of Account with
THE CENTRAL BANK LIMITED
High Road Blankton

Mr A. Thomas
15 Mill Road
Blankton

Account No.: 0775392

DATE 19..	PARTICULARS	PAYMENTS	RECEIPTS	BALANCES
5 Feb	opening balance			150.00
7 Feb	259301	100.00		50.00
10 Feb	259302	80.00		30.00 OD
12 Feb	259303	100.00		130.00 OD
15 Feb	Sundries		50.00	80.00 OD
20 Feb	Sundries		100.00	20.00

17.4 TO BORROW BY LOAN OR OVERDRAFT?

The rates of interest charged for loans are lower than those charged on overdrafts. This is because a bank knows how much it is lending in the case of a loan, whereas the amount which will be owing on an overdraft is unknown. A loan is not necessarily cheaper than an overdraft, however. The shopkeeper who borrowed £500 to buy a refrigerator must pay interest on that amount even if he does not spend it all. Also, the interest would be debited at the beginning on £500; six months later, interest would be charged on whatever is owing then. Therefore, he continues to pay interest on whatever is owing at six-monthly intervals, irrespective of what he had repaid during that time. This relates to 'the true rate of interest' (see Section 23.3). Thomas, however, pays only for *what* he owes for *the number of days* he owes it.

The choice between having a loan and an overdraft thus depends on how long the borrower expects to be in debt and for how much. Thomas was in debt for only a short period and the most he owed was £130. Accordingly, he would have been unwise to have a bank loan for £130.

Loans are for those who require capital sums; *overdrafts* are for those who expect to borrow varying amounts for short periods.

17.5 CREDIT CARDS

A person holding a credit card from a bank can buy goods without paying cash for them. A credit card has to be applied for, and when it is issued the bank will set the credit limit on it. This is the amount up to which a cardholder may owe the bank.

Goods and services can be purchased where the particular type of card is accepted. Most large shops, almost every hotel and airline and many garages display signs saying they will accept specified types of credit cards.

To buy something on credit the card must be shown to the seller. The buyer then signs a special form showing the cost of the purchase and receives a copy of it. The seller sends the form to the bank, which then pays the bill at a discount. (The seller therefore does not receive the full cash price but he benefits because of increased sales.) Every month the cardholder receives a statement from his bank, detailing the amounts the bank has paid and the sums received from the cardholder. The customer may settle all his debt every month. If he does this within 25 days, no charge is made. Alternatively, the repayment may be spread over a period, provided that at least 5 per cent of the account is repaid each month. In that case, interest is charged on the amount owing each month.

Figure 17.2 shows a credit card issued by Midland Bank.

17.6 THE LENDING POLICY OF BANKS

As we have seen, money standing to the credit of bank accounts belong to the customers who place them there. It does not belong to the bank. A bank *uses* some of that money, however, and even lends it to other people.

If a Mr Thomas has £1000 in his bank account, he can draw that money any time he wants to do so. The bank knows, however, that on average only a small proportion of the bank's funds belonging to depositors will be drawn in cash at any time. Therefore, it is not necessary for the bank to have £1000 in cash always available in case Mr Thomas wants it

Fig 17.2 *bank credit card*

suddenly. Consequently, it is safe for the bank to lend some of that money to someone else.

A certain amount *must* be kept in cash, of course. The Bank of England specifies that a bank must keep in cash an amount which is at least equal to 12½ per cent of its liabilities to depositors. This is known as the *minimum reserve ratio*. The bank therefore needs to set aside only £125 in cash against the possibility of Thomas demanding cash. The remaining £875 can be lent.

It may appear dangerous for a bank to keep only such a small amount of cash to meet possible demands for repayment. In fact, from the earliest days of banking it was recognised that only a small proportion of money left by depositors would be demanded at any one time. The banks rapidly became powerful because they acted on this principle.

Of course, the system can work only if there is confidence in the banks. In the early days of banking in America banks were often quite small, each town having its own bank. If customers lost faith in a bank – perhaps because of rumours about losses on its investments – there would be a 'run' on the bank. In a panic all the customers would attempt to draw out all of their money at the same time – and the bank, of course, would be unable to pay them.

Banks today are safer because they are so large and because they are strictly controlled by the government. They are also safer because of the following practices:

(a) Every bank must keep the minimum reserve ratio in its account at the Bank of England. This money can be withdrawn on demand by the banks.
(b) Some loans are made which are repayable at very short notice. Many loans are made in the financial market for only 24 hours. There is therefore a constant inflow of cash.
(c) All loans are issued on the condition that they can be 'called in' before the agreed time. If necessary, or if so ordered by the government, earlier repayment can be demanded.
(d) Most investments are made in 'liquid' securities: that is, those that can be sold quickly.
(e) Banks encourage people to leave money in deposit accounts by paying interest on them.
(f) Borrowers are chosen carefully. Money is not advanced for risky ventures. A businessman must show he can use the loan profitably. A private borrower must have a steady income.
(g) Security is required for most business loans.
(h) Rates are increased when borrowing has to be discouraged and reduced when the bank is anxious to lend.

17.7 INTEREST ON LOANS

Each bank sets it own *base rate*, which is usually about 2 per cent above the Minimum Lending Rate (see Chapter 18). The rate charged for any particular loan will be a figure above the base rate. A borrower who offers good security will pay less than one who is not so 'safe'.

EXERCISES

1 If a trader requires credit, when should he ask for a loan and when should he ask for an overdraft?
2 Compare bank loans with overdrafts as regards the methods of charging interest.
3 Give examples of *collateral security* for a loan.
4 What accounting entries does a bank make when it gives a loan?
5 Explain what a *personal loan* is.
6 Mr A. Wilkins has been in business as an outfitter for three years. He now has the opportunity of buying cheaply a consignment of suits made by a manufacturer who has become bankrupt. What enquiries should a

bank manager make if Wilkins asks for a loan of £1000 to buy the clothes?

7   In the circumstances given in the above question, what would determine the rate of interest Wilkins would be charged if he were granted the loan?

8   If you make personal purchases by using a bank credit card, how is a record of your buying made by the bank? What charge is made for allowing you to use the credit card?

9   Explain how the banking system makes the use of cash largely unnecessary.

10   Define the 'minimum reserve ratio' and explain its effect on bank lending.

11   What does a bank do to ensure it can meet any sudden and unexpected demand for cash by its customers?

CHAPTER 18

THE MONEY MARKET

The 'money market' is a term which is somewhat loosely applied to a number of financial institutions within the total banking system. As we saw in the two previous chapters, ordinary traders and private individuals do a lot of business through their banks, but the banking system extends beyond the High Street banks. In this chapter we will study institutions which gives specialist services concerned with circulating money and providing credit.

In the next chapter we will consider the 'capital market', which has some connection with the subject of this chapter. It is about institutions which bring together those who have money to invest and those who require capital for business.

In general, those in the money market deal in *short-term* financing and those in the capital market are concerned with *long-term* financing.

18.1 THE SCOPE OF THE MONEY MARKET

This market is concerned with the buying and selling of money in the form of credit. It therefore operates largely on *promises* - promises to pay interest, to repay loans, to provide cash, etc. Every transaction requires a price to be paid in the form of interest. All those in the market are aiming to pay rates which are lower than those they are receiving. These rates vary according to the different degrees of risk - and they are changing constantly. Everyone is therefore speculating on what will happen in the future. Can they keep their promises? Can others keep their promises to them? How will interest rates change? And so on. What one part of the market does has an effect on all the others.

Unless there was some control, things would get completely out of hand. Most of the control is by the Bank of England, which is at the centre of the market. It acts for the government and has the power to dictate to the market members.

We will therefore first look at what particular sections of the market do and then discuss the part played by the Bank of England.

18:2 DISCOUNT HOUSES

The 'discount market' consists of 11 Discount Houses which are members of the London Discount Market Association. The functions of a Discount House may first be broadly described as follows:

(a) To borrow, mainly from banks.
(b) To provide the government with money by buying Treasury Bills.
(c) To lend money by discounting Bills of Exchange.

Discount Houses borrow and lend for short periods. Like commercial banks, they lend out money which they owe to other people in the expectation they will have enough available to meet demands on them. They make money by 'juggling' with the many different rates of interest. In making their profits they provide essential services to the government and the business community, as is explained below.

18.3 BORROWING BY DISCOUNT HOUSES

In the previous chapter we saw that banks usually have money lent out at very short notice – sometimes even overnight. A bank will have surplus funds when the money coming in exceeds that which is going out. If that money is simply left in the bank it will be wasted because no interest is being earned on it. Because of the huge amounts involved, it is profitable for a bank to invest its surplus, even if only for two or three days. These amounts are lent to Discount Houses, and because they can be quickly taken back again they are regarded as being part of a bank's minimum reserve ratio. The money which must be paid back on demand is known as *call money* and that which can be repaid in a few days is called *short-notice money*.

A comparatively small amount of money is deposited with the Discount Houses by commercial firms.

18.4 BUYING TREASURY BILLS

As Discount Houses borrow money, they must put it to profitable use. One method is to 'tender' for Treasury Bills.

In order to raise money the government offers Treasury Bills every week to anyone wishing to buy them. Each Bill has a 'nominal' value of £10 000 and it contains a promise to pay that sum to whoever presents it to the government in three months' time. The Bills are bought at a discount: that is, below the nominal price. Most of the Bills are bought by the Discount Houses who tender for them: that is, they compete with one another so that the government gets the best price. If, therefore, a Bill is bought for £9 700, the government is lent that sum and has to pay back £10 000 three months hence. The difference is, of course, the interest on a three-month loan.

A House may hold a bill until it 'matures' in three months' time, or it may sell it to a bank within a few days or weeks.

18.5 DISCOUNTING BILLS OF EXCHANGE

Bills of Exchange are mainly used in international trade, and have been discussed in some detail in Chapter 10. However, because the discounting of Bills of Exchange is the traditional function of Discount Houses, we must first understand how these documents are used.

A Bill of Exchange is a promise to pay at a future date for goods which are bought today. The process can be explained with the assistance of Figure 18.1.

In January a company in London sells goods valued at £5000 to a company in Rome. The Rome company wants to pay for the goods in three months time but the London company requires payment now. Rome Ltd 'accepts' (that is, agrees to) a promise, drawn up by London Ltd, to pay £5000 the following April. It does this by signing a Bill of Exchange and giving it to London Ltd. The London company immediately sells the Bill to a Discount House, which pays £4 800 for it. In other words, the Bill is 'discounted'.

London Ltd therefore gets immediate payment, though it has to pay £200 for the privilege. Rome Ltd has the three months' credit it asked for and hopes that it will make enough profit in time to settle on the due date.

In April the Discount House will present the Bill to Rome Ltd and demand payment of £5000.

18.6 MERCHANT BANKS

Strictly speaking, merchant banks are the members of the Accepting Houses Committee, but the term is also used for other organisations. A merchant bank is always a very large financial institution and usually one with a long history. They include such famous companies as Rothschilds, Hambros, Samuel Montague and Morgan Grenfell. Their activities include the following:

(a) *Accepting Bills of Exchange.* Traditionally, merchant banks are *Acceptance Houses.* In the example given above of discounting a Bill

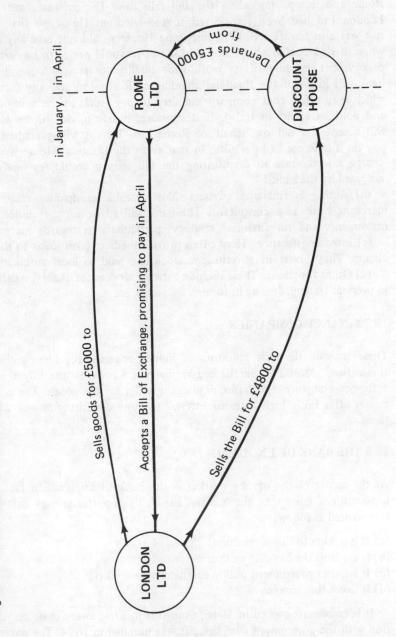

Fig 18.1 *discounting a Bill of Exchange*

of Exchange it will be seen that the Discount House runs the risk of Rome Ltd not paying when the Bill falls due. The promise made to London Ltd had been transferred to the Discount House, so that the risk was also transferred. Obviously, the House would not take any Bill where it had doubts about the debtor but it would prefer to be *certain* of payment. Because of its world-wide intelligence service a merchant bank will know of the financial standing of Rome Ltd and any factors which may affect that company's ability to pay (such as the economic and political affairs in Italy). If it considers it safe to do so, the *bank* will accept the Bill on behalf of Rome Ltd. Thus it will guarantee to pay on it if Rome Ltd defaults. In that event the Discount House would charge a lower rate in discounting the Bill than it would for one not accepted by the bank.

(b) Acting as financial advisers. Most sizeable companies retain a merchant bank as a consultant. The bank will advise on the choice of investments and on financial strategy, particularly as regards mergers.

(c) Providing finance. They often provide medium-term loans to their clients. They invest in government stock and lend to local authorities.

(d) Other functions. These include banking services for clients, assisting in overseas trading, dealing in foreign exchange, etc.

18.7 FINANCE COMPANIES

These provide the vast amounts of money required for hire-purchase transactions. Most hire-purchase agreements are between the buyer and a finance company, the latter paying the seller for the goods. The companies offer fairly high rates of interest to those depositing money with them.

18.8 THE BANK OF ENGLAND

At the centre of the money market is the Bank of England. In fact, it is sometimes known as the 'central bank'. Its importance may first be summarised as follows:

(a) It is banker to the government.
(b) It controls the banking system.
(c) It imposes government policy on the money market.
(d) It issues the currency.

It became state-owned in 1946, though it had had a very close association with the government ever since it was founded in 1694. The government department directly related to the Bank of England is the Treasury.

18.9 THE BANK OF ENGLAND RETURN

Every week the Bank publishes a 'return' in the form of a balance-sheet (as shown in Figure 18.2). This shows the Bank divided into two departments, but this is now mainly only of historical interest. The figures were intended to show the extent to which notes in circulation were backed by gold held by the Bank. The promise written on a bank note was at one time a promise to exchange it for gold on demand. The amount of notes which was not supported by gold reserves was known as the 'fiduciary issue': that is, it was issued 'on trust'. Today all the note issue is fiduciary issue.

The 'capital' belongs to the Bank. It will be seen that the total liabilities in the Banking Department far exceed the amount of notes. The Bank of England is like any other bank in that it could not meet the demand if all of its customers wanted to withdraw at the same time.

18.10 THE GOVERNMENT'S BANK

The Bank of England acts as banker to the government. It maintains accounts for the government and these are shown in the Return under 'Public Deposits'. The money received from taxation is paid into the Exchequer Account, and it is from this account that payments of current expenditure are made. The National Loans Fund records the government's borrowing and lending. Other accounts are for major government departments.

The amount in Public Deposits is small in comparison with what the government spends. This is because the aim is to avoid having 'idle money' in the account. Like any other bank, the Bank of England keeps no more money than is absolutely necessary, because unless money is invested it earns nothing. If the government is short of funds, it issues Treasury Bills or sells some stock. If it has a surplus, it buys back Treasury Bills. Buying back Bills has the effect of reducing the *National Debt*, which is the amount owed to lenders.

18.11 THE BANKERS' BANK

The bank holds the accounts of all the commercial banks, the Discount Houses, the Accepting Houses and some overseas banks. Banks must maintain part of their minimum reserve ratio in the form of cash at the Bank and, as shown below, this gives the Bank some control over lending by the banks.

Banks use their accounts at the Bank of England in the same ways that individuals use their bank accounts, except that the Bank of England

Fig 18.2 *Bank of England Return*

BANK RETURN

	Wednesday Jan. 16, 1980
BANKING DEPARTMENT	
LIABILITIES	£
Capital	14,553.000
Public Deposits	25,566,846
Special Deposits	27,935,000
Bankers' Deposits	622,361,519
Reserves & Other Accounts	686,427,756
	1,376,844,121
ASSETS	
Government Securities	720,637,324
Advances & Other Accounts	441,005,590
Premises, Equipment & Other Secs.	198,817,956
Notes	16,167,889
Coin	215,362
	1,376,844,121
ISSUE DEPARTMENT	
LIABILITIES	£
Notes Issued	9,650,000,000
in Circulation	9,633,832,111
in Banking Department	16,167,889
ASSETS	
Government Debt	11,015,100
Other Government Securities	8,004,442,810
Other Securities	1,634,542,090
	9,650,000,000

does not allow overdrafts. It is through the banks' accounts that debts between them are settled, by means of the Clearing House (as explained in Chapter 16).

18. 12 THE BANK AND GOVERNMENT POLICY

The government is responsible for the economic health of the country. It has to decide on measures which it considers to be necessary for the well-being of the people. Because it controls the Bank of England it can order the Bank to take certain steps which, because the money market is centred on the Bank, will have certain economic results. This can be done by using the following three methods:

(a) Altering the Minimum Lending Rate. As we have seen, the Discount Houses borrow from the banks money which they have to repay immediately if called upon to do so. Because of this short notice they pay a low rate of interest. Some of the money borrowed they lend *at longer periods,* which (of course) provides them with a higher rate of interest. It sometimes happens that the banks suddenly find themselves short of cash. If they demand their cash from the Discount Houses, the latter may not have it immediately available. Because they *must* let the banks have cash, all they can do is to borrow it from the Bank of England. They are then said to be 'forced into the Bank'. Because the Bank provides this 'long stop' it is said to be *the lender of last resort.*

The rate of interest the Discount Houses will have to pay the Bank of England will involve them in a loss. The figure is known as the *Minimum Lending Rate (MLR).* It is defined as *the rate at which the Bank will discount first-class Bills of Exchange.* To reduce the amount of this possible loss the Houses keep their rates to customers near MLR. It follows, therefore, that a rise in MLR will mean a rise in other rates.

When the Treasury announces a change in the Minimum Lending Rate (which is always done on a Thursday) it does so in order to have an effect on the economy. If it considers that people are buying too much, it can reduce the demand for goods and services by making borrowing more expensive. It knows that if MLR goes up the banks will put up the rates they charge. This will also reduce business development because some businesses will decide not to borrow in order to pay the cost of expansion as it would be too expensive.

Rates to depositors would also rise, so that people would be encouraged to leave their money with the bank. Again, this would reduce demand.

A change in MLR alters *all* rates of interest which are not fixed. A rise will mean more will be charged on hire-purchase transactions, hiring agreements, mortgages, etc. If banks *pay* a higher rate, then increased rates will be paid for deposits with building societies, savings banks, etc.

(b) Demanding Special Deposits. The banks can be instructed to put a proportion of their cash at the Bank of England on Special Deposit. That amount is then 'frozen', so that, until it is released by the Treasury, it cannot form part of the banks' available resources. This has a severe effect on the banks' ability to lend. Again, the intention is to reduce demand by the public.

(c) Open-market operations. Another method of reducing bank lending is to encourage investors to take money out of their bank accounts. To do this the Bank will sell government securities to the public through the Stock Exchange. The buyers will pay for these with cheques drawn on their bank accounts. If the aim is to *increase* bank lending, the Bank will *buy* securities by giving cheques to the sellers.

18.13 THE NOTE ISSUE

The Bank of England has a monopoly for the issue of notes and coin. For the majority of transaction cash is not used, because payments are increasingly made by various forms of transfer. In fact, we are fast becoming a 'cashless society' Nevertheless, notes and coins are still required in large quantities. At times of high spending (such as holidays) more cash than usual is required. The Bank of England issues notes and coins to the commercial banks as they require them. The Bank also replaces worn notes and coins with new ones.

18.14 OTHER BANK OF ENGLAND FUNCTIONS

(a) Maintaining registers of holders of government securities and paying interest on them.
(b) Engaging in international monetary negotiations.
(c) Holding reserves of gold and foreign currency.
(d) Maintaining a few private accounts.

18.15 OTHER CENTRAL BANKS

In some respects the Bank of England is unique, because in many other countries the central banks operate in other ways. The common factor is that any central bank is the 'government's bank', but in exercising financial control governments use their banks in different ways. In many countries the only method is by directives to other financial institutions. Many central banks (unlike the Bank of England) are involved in direct promotion of financial institutions in the private sector.

EXERCISES

1 Explain how a Discount House makes profits by buying Treasury Bills.

2 Money accepted by a Discount House from a bank may be 'call money' or 'short-notice money'. Explain the difference between the two terms. Why do banks lend money on these conditions?

3 Explain how the discounting of a Bill of Exchange benefits (a) the debtor, (b) the creditor, and (c) the Discount House.

4 What is the function of an Accepting House?

5 If a company had a merchant bank as its adviser, what services could it expect to receive?

6 Explain what a finance company does.

7 Explain the following items in a Bank of England Return: (a) Capital; (b) public deposits; (c) bankers' deposits.

8 What are the amounts deposited by banks with the Bank of England used for?

9 Why is the Bank of England said to be 'the lender of last resort?

10 Define the *Minimum Lending Rate.*

11 If MLR is raised, how is it likely to affect you personally?

12 If banks are required to place money on Special Deposit, how does that reduce the amount they can lend?

13 Explain the effect on bank lending if the Bank of England carries out open-market operations.

14 In what ways does the Bank of England differ from commercial banks?

15 A £1 note is signed by the Chief Cashier of the Bank of England and carries the following words: 'I promise to pay the bearer on demand the sum of one pound.' What does this really mean?

THE CAPITAL MARKET

Every business needs capital. Before setting up a business there must be a pool of money to buy the physical things which will be required and to pay the bills until the business is earning income. If a business wishes to expand at a later date, it will require more money. It may be able to provide that money itself by not paying out some of its profits, but in most cases it must go outside to get the money. The capital market provides the channels by which money is collected and made available to those who want it for use in business. In this chapter we will also see the part played by the Stock Exchange.

19.1 THE USERS AND THE PROVIDERS OF CAPITAL

Earlier in the book we saw that there were occasions when Zebedee's firm required more money. On the first occasion he took in a partner who provided the necessary cash. When he traded as a company, however, money was obtained from people who did not want to work in the business. Such people are known as 'investors' and at the end of chapter 3 we saw why people are willing to invest by buying shares in companies.

There are, therefore, two groups of people involved:

(a) **The users of capital**. These are people who require money in their businesses in order to make profits. If they have to ask others to provide it, they must promise to give them part of the profits which it is hoped will be made. Alternatively, they may promise to pay interest, whether they make profits or not.

(b) **The providers of capital**. These are people who have cash to spare. Cash which a person does not spend is known as that person's *savings*. If you have more money than you require, you would be foolish to keep it in a box. It would do no good there, so you would be wise to 'put it to work'. In other words, you would give it to someone who *does* need it and who will pay you for the use of it. (The banks do the same to avoid having 'idle money', as we saw in the previous chapter.)

We therefore have one group of people who *require* capital and who have the ability to make profits if they can get it, and we also have another group of people who have *spare* cash but who do not have the opportunity to put it into a business of their own. If the two groups could be brought together, both would benefit. The users of capital would have the money they want; the suppliers of capital would not be left with money which earned nothing. *The capital market exists to bring the two groups together.*

19.2 INDIRECT INVESTMENT

If you have £100 to spare, it would not be sufficient to help a business which wanted more capital. On the other hand, you want your £100 to earn something. How, then, can you join forces with the users of capital for your mutual benefit? The solution is to not invest *directly* with the users. We saw that many people bought shares in Zebedee Electronics when it issued its invitation to the public. In practice, however, very few people own shares *personally*. Most shareholders are organisations which use *other people's money* to buy shares. Much of the money used by these organisations is provided by 'small' people.

Although your £100 is too small to be of use to the company requiring more capital, if you and several thousand other people with £100 each put those small sums together there *would* be enough. What is required, therefore, is some organisation which is prepared to accept those small amounts, put them together and then invest the large sum. Such bodies are known as 'institutional investors'.

19.3 INSTITUTIONAL INVESTORS

These are concerns which use other people's money, often supplied in small amounts, to invest in large quantities. Much of their resources are the savings of individuals. It can be said that, whether he knows it or not, *every person who saves is an indirect investor in securities.* To show how institutional investors 'channel' savings to those who require capital, the functions of the more important of them are now listed:

(a) Assurance companies.
If you pay regular premiums on an assurance policy your intention would be to receive a lump sum when you retired or for your dependents to have it if you died earlier. In fact, you (and thousands of others) are giving money to the assurance company for it to invest in shares and property.

The company makes profits from these investments and passes some of them to you. This is why an assurance policy will pay you *more* than you pay by way of premiums. In effect, the company invests for you. The same principle applies in respect of payments made to a *pension fund*, which is usually administered by an assurance company.

Assurance companies handle larger funds than any other institutional investor.

(b) Trade unions

These organisations deal with very large sums of money which come from 'dues' paid by members. The profits on the investments are used to meet the expenses of the union, so that, indirectly, the members benefit.

(c) Charities

These also invest large amounts, the income from which is used for the benefit of the organisations.

(d) Unit trusts

These institutions are for those who *intend* their money to go into securities. Small investors buy 'units', each unit representing a part of the trust's total funds. The trust managers buy securities with the money. (Before selling units the managers state what sort of securities they intend to buy.) As the trust receives dividends and interest from its investments, they are distributed to the unit-holders as cash or they are used to buy more units for them.

(e) Investment trusts

These operate on the same principle as unit trusts, except that the investor is a *shareholder* of the investment company. This means that, as in any other company, the directors will decide what dividends to pay, whereas a unit trust must distribute *all* its profits.

19.4 HOW INSTITUTIONS BENEFIT SMALL SAVERS AND LARGE COMPANIES

The institutions benefit both those who require capital and those who save. If they did not exist, there would be no method whereby all the small surpluses held by people could be 'harnessed'. If people had nowhere to put small sums, the total of those sums, amounting to many millions of pounds a year, would be wasted. Industry would come to a halt if these sums were not collected and made available to it.

Figure 19.1 shows how the small savings of many thousands of people are brought together and channelled to companies as large sums. As the

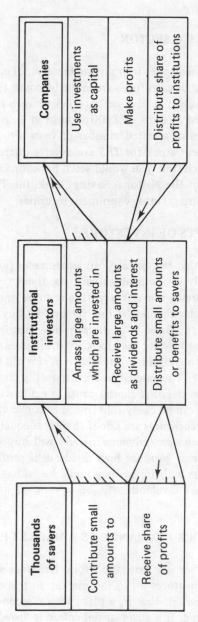

Fig 19.1 *channelling small savings to industry*

companies make profits, they pay part of them to the institutions, which in turn pass them to the small savers. Thus both savers and industry benefit.

19.5 THE PUBLIC SECTOR

Not all investment goes into private business, of course. We have seen how the government obtains funds from the Discount Houses, for example. The banks largely invest in government stock (known as 'gilt-edged securities'). These are issued in units of £100, bought at a discount and redeemed 'at par' at the end of a stated number of years. For example, you may buy some government stock for £85 and receive interest on it for 15 years, at the end of which time you would sell it back for £100.

The funds of the National Savings Bank, the Trustee Savings Bank and the National Giro go into government securities.

19.6 THE TYPES OF INVESTORS

We have seen that if you take out an assurance policy (or pay trade-union dues), you rely on company dividends, though you are not directly an investor in shares – nor was it your aim to be one. We have also seen that you can be a shareholder 'at one remove' by buying units or investment-company shares. Those who *directly* buy securities can be divided into types, according to what they look for in an investment:

(a) *Those who require safety above all else* will buy government or local authority stock. The rate of interest is usually comparatively low, but it is fixed and guaranteed. A capital profit is made when government stock is paid off and it can be easily sold to someone else at any time.

Company debentures are safe if there is adequate security.

(b) *Those who are prepared to risk* will buy ordinary shares in companies. These may produce high dividends if profits are large, and in that case their value will rise so they could be sold at a profit. Against this is the danger that dividends will be low or nil if the company does not prosper.

19.7 THE STOCK EXCHANGE AS A MARKET-PLACE

In Chapter 3 we saw how the Stock Exchange will assist in introducing shares and debentures on to the market. In this chapter we will consider its role as a *market*: that is, a place where 'second-hand' securities can be bought and sold. If a share or debenture is 'listed', its holder can have it sold on the Exchange to the highest bidder. This is a great advantage because if a holder wishes to obtain cash for his shares or debentures, he *cannot* sell them back to the company; if his share is not listed, or he has lent money other than on a debenture, there is no available market on which it can be sold. *The existence of the Stock Exchange therefore encourages investors to enter the capital market.*

The Stock Exchange provides the best example of what economists call a 'perfect market', and this for the following reasons:

(a) *All* the buyers and sellers meet in the same place.

(b) Competition between the buyers and between the sellers ensures the best price is obtained. This is made more effective because of the system of 'bargaining' (see Section 19.11).

(c) Companies are compelled to disclose more information than is demanded by law. The result is that people buying and selling shares are given facts they would not otherwise have. The Exchange will 'discipline' companies which try to deceive the market.

(d) Share prices are published every day, so that everyone knows what a share is worth at the end of each day.

(e) The members are bound by a strict code of conduct, so that a member of the public will always be treated fairly. If anyone loses money because a member has become insolvent, he will be compensated by the Stock Exchange.

19.8 THE MEMBERS OF THE STOCK EXCHANGE

The number of members is fixed, so that a person cannot become a member until there is a vacancy. Prospective members have to be nominated and must prove they have substantial financial reserves. Members have to be re-elected each year. They are divided into the following types:

(a) Stockbrokers

No one who is not a member may go on to the 'floor' of the Exchange to buy or sell shares. To deal in shares he must employ a *broker*. A broker will buy or sell shares within the price limit set by the investor. For doing this he is paid a commission according to a scale set by the Stock Exchange. A stockbroker is therefore an *agent*.

(b) Stockjobbers

These are the 'wholesalers' who deal only with the 'retailers' – the brokers. An investor may not deal directly with a jobber. Jobbers aim to make profits by dealing with brokers and other jobbers at one price and dealing with other members at a different price. They therefore buy and sell only for themselves and *not* as agents. Each jobber specialises in a section of the market, such as 'industrials', 'metals', etc.

19.9 HOW SHARES CHANGE HANDS ON THE STOCK EXCHANGE

Buying and selling shares on the Exchange is done by methods which do not operate elsewhere. Brokers and jobbers have separate roles to play because a person may not be a broker *and* a jobber. After an agreement has been made on the Stock Exchange which changes the ownership of shares, the company must be informed so that it may register the new holder. To illustrate the way in which a person wishing to buy shares obtains them from someone wishing to sell, we can trace through the transaction illustrated in Figure 19.2. We start by a Mr Purchase wanting to buy 500 £1 shares in Zebedee Electronics Ltd and a Mr Seller wishing to sell that number of Zebedee shares.

19.10 INSTRUCTING THE BROKERS

Each of the parties will know the approximate price of the shares because the price at the end of the previous day's trading will be published in the newspapers. Mr Purchase tells his broker, Mr Sharp, to pay no more than 500p for each share (share prices are always quoted in pence). Mr Seller tells his broker, Mr Blunt, that he will not sell below 480p each.

The responsibility of each broker is to get the best possible price for his client.

19.11 MAKING A 'BARGAIN'

Each broker will go to that part of the Exchange where there are jobbers who deal in Zebedee shares. Sharp will ask each jobber 'what price Zebedee?' *He will not tell the jobber if he is a buyer or a seller.* Each jobber will then give two prices. If one jobber says '490-493', he means he will buy from the broker at 490p or sell to him for 493p. Sharp will ask the same question of each jobber so that he will know which is offering him the best price. Assuming Jobber Blue gave such figures, and his selling price is the lowest, Sharp will disclose he is a buyer. He will therefore state that he will buy at 493p.

Broker Blunt will be making similar approaches. He finds that Jobber Green is offering the highest price and he sells to him at 485p.

The difference between the two prices quoted by each jobber is known as his 'turn'.

These agreements to buy and sell are known as 'bargains'. No contracts are signed because each member knows the other will honour the verbal agreement. This is why the Stock Exchange motto is 'My word is my bond.'

When Jobber Blue agreed to sell he probably had no Zebedee shares.

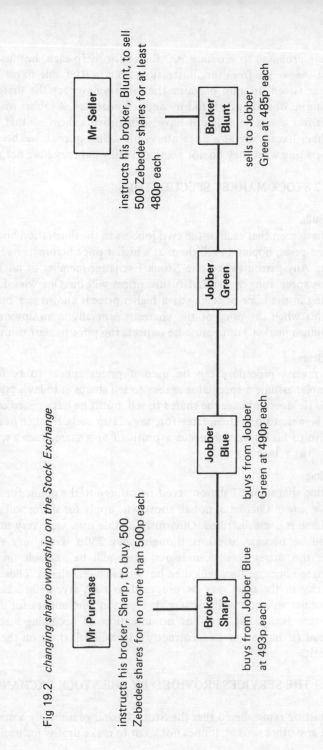

Fig 19.2 *changing share ownership on the Stock Exchange*

Mr Seller

instructs his broker, Blunt, to sell 500 Zebedee shares for at least 480p each

Broker Blunt

sells to Jobber Green at 485p each

Jobber Green

Jobber Blue

buys from Jobber Green at 490p each

Broker Sharp

buys from Jobber Blue at 493p each

Mr Purchase

instructs his broker, Sharp, to buy 500 Zebedee shares for no more than 500p each

Having promised to produce 500 shares for 493p each, he must then find some. As we see from the illustration, he was later able to get them from Jobber Green. In most bargains the jobbers never see the shares they are dealing in. What they do is to buy and sell *promises*. A jobber who promises to deliver shares he does not have *must* provide them, so that sometimes a jobber has to buy at a price above his selling price. It has been said that jobbers buy what they do not want and sell what they have not got!

19.12 STOCK-MARKET SPECULATORS

(a) Bulls

We have seen that each of the two jobbers in the illustration bought shares at one price, hoping to sell them at a higher price before he had to pay for them. Any person (whether a Stock Exchange member or not) who does this is speculating as to what future prices will be. One who does this by buying in the hope of selling at a higher price is known as a 'bull'. He will do this when the price of the shares is generally in an upward direction (a 'bullish market') or because he expects the price to *start* rising.

(b) Bears

The reverse procedure can be used if prices appear to be *falling*. For example, assume a speculator agrees to sell shares at today's price of 215p each. He does not have the shares to sell, but if he has guessed correctly he will be able to buy them later for, say, 210p each. He then has the shares to give to his buyer and makes a profit of 5p a share. Such a speculator is known as a 'bear'.

(c) Stags

Assume that some £1 shares were first offered to the public for 250p each. As we saw in Chapter 3, not all those who apply for shares will get them if the issue is oversubscribed. Obviously, if this issue were very successful, it would be because investors thought that 250p was a very good price. After the shares have been issued they will be available on the Stock Exchange because they will then be 'second-hand' shares. Those who were unlucky in the issue may be prepared to pay, say, 260p a share to any subscriber willing to sell. A 'stag' is a person who applies for shares when they are issued but who has no intention of becoming a shareholder. Instead (if he has guessed correctly), he will sell them on the market at a profit.

19.13 THE SERVICES PROVIDED BY THE STOCK EXCHANGE

It must be remembered that the Stock Exchange is merely a market-place. Like any other market, it does not exist to make profits for itself.

It provides a place for traders to meet and establishes systems for doing business. The Stock Exchange is unique, however, in that it provides services which go to the very root of the economy:

(a) *It helps industry to raise capital.* By approving companies which want to be listed it makes it possible for them to issue shares and debentures to the public. Investors are reluctant to buy securities unless there is a well-organised market where they can be sold.

(b) *It facilitates the exchange of securities.* Shareholders who want to 'cash in' their shares can sell them to those who wish to buy them. (This does not benefit companies, of course; it merely changes their shareholders. If a shareholder sells at a profit, the company has only what the first holder paid the company for the shares.)

(The above two points are illustrated in Figure 19.3.)

(c) *It protects shareholders.* (This was explained in Section 19.7.)

(d) *Small savers benefit.* Because there are outlets for the large funds of the institutional investors, the benefits of the investments flow back to assurance policy-holders, pensioners, trade-union members, etc.

(e) *It provides market facilities for the government.* The government can use the Stock Exchange to issue its securities.

(f) *It improves the moral standards of business.* The Stock Exchange imposes regulations on directors and companies so that they do not act unfairly towards investors. It also imposes standards of conduct as between companies.

EXERCISES

1 What is meant when it is said that institutional investors 'channel' savings into industry?
2 Name any institutional investor you have money with and explain how you share in the profits made by that investor.
3 In what respects are unit trusts and investment companies similar, and how do they differ?
4 How is income earned by holding government stock?
5 In what ways does the Stock Exchange resemble a fish market?
6 Why is the Stock Exchange said to be almost the 'perfect market?
7 Explain the differences between a stockbroker and a stockjobber. How do they earn their living?
8 Explain the different ways in which bulls, bears and stags aim to make profit.
9 How does a shareholder benefit if his shares are 'listed'?

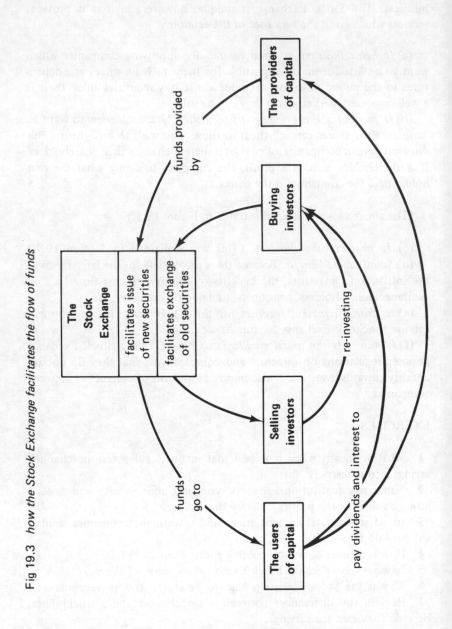

Fig 19.3 *how the Stock Exchange facilitates the flow of funds*

BUSINESS FINANCE

This chapter is about *using* capital in a business. If capital is borrowed, it must be put to work so as to produce sufficient income to pay the interest on the loan and leave enough over to provide a profit. If capital is in the form of shares, enough profit must be made to give the shareholders a satisfactory dividend. The major aim of any business, therefore, is to employ its capital in such a way as to provide the most profit. However, this must not be achieved at the expense of safety. In its efforts to make profits a company can 'over-reach' itself so that everything ends in disaster.

20.1 THE BALANCE-SHEET

Every year a business will draw up a statement to see how it stands financially. This statement consists of two lists and is known as a *balance-sheet*. One list will include all the things the business *owns*. These are its *assets*. The other list will show what it *owes* and these are its *liabilities*.

Every item has to be valued. One item in the assets list will be the amount of cash the business has on its premises and another will be the amount standing to the credit of its bank account. These items can, of course, be valued exactly but others can only be given an approximate valuation. The aim is to show what an item would be worth if it were converted into cash, but this is obviously difficult to achieve. For example, if a company bought a machine for £5000 two years ago, it is unlikely to be worth that now. It would be 'second hand' if it were sold, and even if it were not sold it would have had two years' wear. To get a figure for the balance-sheet an assumption is made that the machine has fallen in value by a certain amount each year. These reductions in value are called *depreciation* and are calculated as follows.

Assume the owners expect the machine mentioned above to last for 10 years and that it could then be sold for £200 as scrap. This means it will fall in value by £4800 over a period of 10 years. On average, therefore, it will depreciate at the rate of £480 a year. On the balance-sheet showing the position when the machine was two years old it would appear as follows:

Machine (at cost)	5000
less depreciation	960
	£4040

Other assets include 'debtors'. This item is the total amount owed by customers to the company. The company may consider that some of its debtors will not pay, so to be realistic it deducts those amounts it is doubtful about receiving. Again, the intention is to show, so far as is possible, the true figure in cash terms.

(Today, most balance-sheets are in a vertical form: that is, the net assets – total assets less trade liabilities – are listed above the capital. To make it easier to understand, however, we will look at them in the traditional form: that is, with the liabilities on the left and the assets on the right.)

20.2 THE OPENING CAPITAL

Capital is wealth which has been set aside (i.e. saved) in order to produce more wealth. When Mark Zebedee first went into business he had £10 000 which he had saved. As this was the amount he put into the business, it can be said that the business had an opening capital of £10 000.

Zebedee had calculated that he would have to spend some of that money before he could start trading. He was also wise enough to realise that he must keep much of the capital in the form of cash because he would have to pay a lot of bills before the business brought in money. There would be his suppliers to pay and such items as rent, electricity, insurance, etc., to deal with.

Having bought the things he needs to start with, Zebedee could draw up a balance-sheet showing the position as it was on the first day. This would be his *opening* balance-sheet. We will assume he spent as follows:

(a) £800 on furniture and fittings – these would include work-benches, office furniture, etc.
(b) £900 on equipment: that is, machines and apparatus.
(c) £1000 on raw materials and components – this would be the amount he had paid to suppliers for the things he will require in production.

All these items were paid for in cash because it is unlikely that people would be willing to give credit to someone who has not even *started* trading.

His opening balance-sheet would be as shown in part (a) of Figure 20.1. It will be seen that although the amount of capital is the same it has changed in form. Instead of it all being in cash it now includes other items.

Capital is shown as a liability because *it is the amount the business owes Zebedee.*

20.3 HOW TRADING ALTERS THE CAPITAL

In his first year Zebedee will be making his products and selling them. At the end of the year he will again count his assets and liabilities and draw up a balance-sheet. That statement will be entirely different from the one he started with. To show why it altered we must look at what he did during the year. The following account will indicate why the balance-sheet shown in part (b) of Figure 20.1 is very much different from his opening one:

(a) He purchased no more furniture or equipment but the depreciated values have been calculated.

Fig 20.1 *balance-sheets*

(a) Opening balance-sheet

Liabilities	(£)	Assets	(£)
Capital	10 000	Furniture and fittings	800
		Equipment	900
		Raw materials	1 000
		Cash at bank	7 300
	£10 000		£10 000

(b) Subsequent balance-sheet

Liabilities		(£)	Fixed assets	(£)	(£)	(£)
	(£)					
Capital at start	10 000		Furniture and fittings (at cost)	800		
add profit	2 200		less depreciation	80	720	
	12 200		Equipment (at cost)	900		
less drawings	1 500	10 700	less depreciation	90	810	1 530
Trade creditors		2 000				
Electricity		85	Current assets			
			Raw materials		1 200	
			Finished goods		5 000	
			Debtors		400	
			Cash at bank		4 635	
			Cash in hand		20	11 255
		£12 785				£12 785

(b) He was buying raw materials and components during the year. He was also making them into goods which he sold. The balance-sheet shows the value of the unused materials and his stock of unsold finished goods.

(c) He has been receiving payments from his customers but at the end of the year they owe him £400.

(d) His cash (including £20 'loose change') has been considerably reduced.

(e) He owes £2000 for materials.

(f) He has an outstanding bill for electricity.

It will be seen that the balance-sheet shows only the *totals* of various items as they were on the day of the balance-sheet. The *events* during the year which caused the balances to change (such as purchases and sales, money spent and received) would be recorded daily in his account books.

We can now look at how a year's trading has affected his capital. During the year his sales (*including those he has not been paid for yet*) exceeded his costs (*including those he still owes*) by £2200. This is his *profit*. The business therefore owes him more than it did a year ago. However, during the year he draw out £1500 for his personal expenses. In other words, he had been taking some of the profits to live on before he knew how much they would be. At the date of the balance-sheet, therefore, the capital amounts to £10 700.

Adding up the assets indicates they are worth £12 785. Although these legally belong to the business, they have not been fully paid for, however. The business is *really* worth £12 785 less the £2085 which is owed: that is, £10 700. This figure is known as the *net worth* of the business. It is the amount owed to the owner, or its *capital*.

20.4 FIXED ASSETS AND FIXED CAPITAL

Fixed assets are those which are fairly permanent and which are continuously contributing to profits. The furniture and equipment in Zebedee's business are essential, but in helping to make profits they are not *used up*. Once bought, a machine will go on making goods for years and will always remain the original machine.

The total of the fixed assets make up the *fixed capital*.

20.5 CURRENT ASSETS AND WORKING CAPITAL

Current assets are those which are continuously changing and being used up in the course of trading. Zebedee's materials and finished goods are constantly being drawn on and added to; the amount of the debtors and the cash will change every day. The current assets represent ready cash and items which are in the process of being turned into cash. They provide the income to meet liabilities which have to be paid fairly soon. These are known as *current liabilities.*

Working capital (otherwise known as *circulating capital*, because it is continuously moving) is the amount of surplus funds which is available to pay liabilities due on demand or at short notice. It is therefore the difference between current assets and current liabilities. Zebedee's working capital, therefore, is £11 255 *less* £2085; that is, £9170.

(Any *long-term* liabilities are not included because immediate cash does not have to be available to pay them.)

20.6 THE WORKING-CAPITAL RATIO

It is dangerous for a business to be low on working capital because it is from this source that current liabilities have to be paid. The relationship between current assets and current liabilities is known as the *working-capital ratio.* It is generally accepted that the ratio should be at least 2:1: that is, current assets should amount to twice current liabilities. A business can be making good profits, but if its ratio is so low that it is unable to meet its current liabilities it will collapse.

20.7 LIQUID CAPITAL

This has some relevance to the working-capital ratio. It is that amount which is in the form of cash or which can be converted into cash almost immediately. Zebedee can count only his cash as his liquid capital, but it is quite adequate to meet his liabilities.

20.8 CAPITAL OWNED AND FUNDS USED

The capital *owned* in Zebedee's business amounts to £10 700, but this is not the same as the funds it is *using*. If Zebedee had borrowed £1000, he would be using that sum as well as his own money. He owes £2085, which means he is *using* that amount although it does not belong to him. After all, if he paid his debts his capital in the form of cash would be reduced. On the other hand, he is *owed* £400, so the amount of his own capital he can use is reduced by that amount. Therefore, the funds which are being *used* can be calculated as follows:

Provided by Zebedee	10 700
Provided by creditors	2 085
	12 785
Used by debtors	400
	£12 385

20.9 THE YIELD ON FUNDS

A businessman will always relate what he gets *out* of his business in the form of profits to what he has put *into* it. This is expressed as a percentage and is known as the *yield on funds*. If, after working hard for a year, a businessman finds that his funds have yielded him 10 per cent on his capital and that it is unlikely to increase, he may wonder if it is worth the worry to remain in business. If he can get more than 10 per cent on an investment, he would do better to close his business and live on interest.

Sometimes the yield will rise if some of the capital is borrowed. When Zebedee made a profit of £2200 his yield was 22 per cent of his capital. Assume, however, he had increased his capital by 50 per cent by borrowing £5000 at 12 per cent and this resulted in a 50 per cent increase in profits to £3300. His yield would then be as follows:

Business profit	3300
less loan interest	600
Personal profit	£2700

$$\frac{2700 \times 100}{10\,000} = 27 \text{ per cent}$$

20.10 BORROWING CAPITAL

The above example shows how borrowing can benefit the owner. This happens only when the rate of profit is more than the rate of interest, however. If the profit were only £1500, the yield to Zebedee would be 9 per cent, whereas if he had provided the extra money himself it would have been 10 per cent.

Other considerations relevant to borrowing part of the capital include the following:

(a) *The more that is borrowed, the less that is likely to be lost by the owners.* If a company needed more capital, it might issue more shares to the present members. If the company failed, the shareholders would lose an increased amount of money. If the extra money were borrowed, however, and the company failed, the members would only lose their first investment.

(b) *Interest on loans must be paid.* If a company is going through a bad period but prospects are good, it can sometimes keep going by paying no dividends on its shares. If it has a loan, however, it may not survive to the better days because if the lenders are not paid their interest the company will be wound up.

(c) *Loans have to be paid back*, so that annual amounts may have to be set aside out of profits. This will reduce the dividend.

(d) *Lenders may interfere with management.* Large lenders to companies often insist on having directors on the board so that they can prevent the company from doing anything they disapprove of.

(e) Usually, *security has to be given*, so that the charged asset is 're-stricted'. If a company gives a mortgage on property it owns, it cannot sell it and it may be limited in how it uses the property.

(f) *Interest on loans is 'tax allowable'*: that is, tax will be levied on the profit remaining *after* the interest has been paid. If a company makes a profit of £120 000 and tax is at 40 per cent, it will pay £48 000 in tax. If it has to pay interest of £20 000, however, it will be taxed on £100 000: that is, it will pay £40 000. Consequently, borrowing has reduced the tax by £8000. In effect, therefore, the loan has cost £12 000 and not £20 000.

20.11 OBTAINING FUNDS FOR EXPANSION

If a business is prospering, it may decide to expand. This will require more funds, the available sources for which will be amongst the following (the first two have already been discussed in relation to Zebedee's business):

(a) By taking in partners.
(b) By admitting shareholders to a private company; by issuing shares as a public company.
(c) By a company issuing debentures (see section 3.10).
(d) By borrowing from a bank or some other financial institution.
(e) By 'ploughing back' some of the profits.
(f) By getting extended credit from suppliers.
(g) By obtaining assets on hire purchase (such as office furniture).
(h) By hiring assets instead of buying them (such as company vehicles).

It will be seen that the last three do not result in an inflow of cash. Instead, they result in the business *laying out less cash*. More will have to be paid out each year in the form of reduced discounts from suppliers and charges for hiring and hire purchasing, but this may be cheaper than borrowing. Also, the disadvantages of borrowing which have already been discussed would not apply.

20.12 APPRAISING A BALANCE-SHEET

If a person is invited to lend money to a business or give it credit, he will study the balance-sheet to get some indication of the stability of the company. A prospective investor in a business would do the same. The balance-sheet will provide only certain information because the rate of profitability over a period of years must be looked for elsewhere in the company's books. The following information can, however, be ascertained from a balance-sheet:

(a) **The liquidity of funds**. There must be adequate current assets to meet current liabilities. There must be sufficient cash to meet immediate demands.

(b) **The form of the capital**. If the business has borrowed heavily, a large proportion of the trading profits will be taken in paying interest. A fall in profits will increase the burden. Enquiries should be made as to when loans are due to be repaid and what provision has been made to do so.

(c) **The creditors and debtors**. If the business has a lot of creditors, it may indicate it has difficulty in paying its bills. If there are a lot of debtors, this may mean the business has been giving credit unwisely and that some of the debts will never be paid.

(d) **The value of the assets**. Are the assets really worth the figures given? If, for example, a machine has a depreciated valuation of £10 000, would it really fetch that sum if it were sold?

20.13 PROFIT

The profit on a particular transaction is the difference between what is paid for an article and what is received for it when it is sold. In its simplest form profit could be calculated as being the difference between the cash held at the beginning of a period and that held at the end. If a man spends £20 on buying apples and then sells them from a stall, he may have £25 at the end of the day. The increase in cash amounting to £5 would be his profit.

Such a simple method cannot apply to a business because

(a) some goods may be bought and sold on credit;
(b) the owner may have drawn out some of his capital or put some more in;
(c) some money would have been paid out which did not relate to *trading*.

Suppose that at the beginning of a period a trader had capital consisting of cash amounting to £1000. He then bought goods for £500 for which he paid in cash and he obtained a further amount costing £200 on credit. He then sold the goods for £1200, of which £1000 was paid in cash. He received a bill for electricity amounting to £50 which he paid. A bill for £20 for insurance he did not pay. He withdrew £100 for his personal use.

Figure 20.2 shows that his cash balance increased by £350 but that his profit was £430. The profit he made on the goods is the difference between their cost (*whether or not he paid for them all*) and what he sold them for (*including money he did not receive*). The profit therefore takes account of what he is owed (an asset to him) and what he owes (a liability).

The difference between the cost of purchases and what they are sold for is called *gross profit*.

His expenses amounted to £70, of which he paid only £50. These are items which have no direct relevance to *trading*: they have to be paid irrespective of the amount of buying and selling he does. They have to be deducted from the gross profit and what is left over belongs to him. That amount is the *net profit*.

Fig 20.2   *cash balance and profit*

CASH

	(£)	(£)
Opening balance		1000
add sales		1000
		2000
less goods	500	
electricity	50	
drawn	100	650
Closing balance		1350

Increase in cash £350

PROFIT

Sales		1200
less purchases		700
Gross profit		500
less expenses		
electricity	50	
insurance	20	70
Net profit		430

212

He withdrew £100 from the business but this has no effect on its profitability.

There is therefore no direct relationship between changes in cash balance and profit.

20.14 TURNOVER

The value of sales made is the *gross turnover*. In the example shown in Figure 20.2 it amounted to £1200. *Net turnover* is the amount of gross turnover less goods which have been returned. Net turnover therefore means the amount of *effective* sales.

20.15 PROFIT PERCENTAGE

To say that in the above example the gross profit was £500 and the net profit was £430 does not really indicate the profitability of the firm. It does not show if *good* profits were made because it does not say what the profit figures are related to. If a man does a *lot* of business and at the end finds he has made a net profit of £430, it would not have been worth his while. On the other hand, if his sales had amounted to only £600, he would have made a very handsome profit.

The *gross profit percentage* relates the gross profit to the turnover by using the following formula:

$$\frac{\text{Gross profit} \times 100}{\text{Turnover}}$$

The figure for the example would therefore be

$$\frac{500 \times 100}{1200} = 41.67 \text{ per cent}$$

This is the profit made on trading, but out of it must be paid the 'overheads'. This would leave the *net profit percentage*, which in the example would be

$$\frac{430 \times 100}{1200} = 35.83 \text{ per cent}$$

20.16 THE RATE OF TURNOVER

A firm expects to make a profit on every sale. It therefore avoids, so far as is possible, having goods in store awaiting sale. It is expensive to keep goods in stock because of storage costs. Also, some goods may deteriorate, while others may become unfashionable if left unsold for too long.

Suppose that two shops, dealing in the same type of goods, each buys at the rate of £12 000 per annum. Shop A spends £6000 in January and a further £6000 when it restocks in July. Shop B buys goods every month. The second shop not only reduces storage costs and the risk of deterioration but, also, it spends only £1000 at a time. It sells the goods in a month so that it is again able to spend £1000 for the next consignment. Shop A has to find £6000 each time it buys and has to wait six months to recover what it has spent.

Stock is 'turned over' when it has been sold and replaced by new stock. The number of times this is done in a year is known as the *rate of turnover* (which is sometimes referred to as the *rate of stock turn*).

To calculate the rate of turnover the basic formula is as follows:

$$\frac{\text{The cost price of goods sold}}{\text{The average stock at cost price}}$$

The amount of sales is, of course, shown in the accounts at the *selling* price, so that figure has to be converted to give the *cost* price of sales in the formula. This can be done if the gross profit percentage is known. For example, if sales were £18 000 and gross profit were $33\frac{1}{3}$ per cent of sales, the profit would be £6000. Therefore, the cost price of the goods sold would be £12 000.

The average stock can be calculated by adding together the amounts held each time the stock was counted and dividing by the number of times the stock was counted. If stock were counted only once a year, then the closing stock is added to the opening stock and divided by two.

The following is an example of calculating the rate of turnover:

Stock held: 1 Jan £20 000; 1 April £22 000; 1 July £21 000; 1 Oct £24 000; 31 Dec £23 000
Sales for the year: £300 000
Gross profit: 25 per cent of sales

*   *   *

Average stock $\dfrac{110\,000}{5}$ = £22 000

Sales at selling price	300 000
Gross profit	75 000
Cost of sales	£225 000

$$\text{Rate of turnover} = \frac{\text{Cost of sales}}{\text{Average stock}} \quad \frac{225\,000}{22\,000} = 10.22 \text{ times}$$

This indicates that on average stock has been sold 10.22 times during the year. On average, each item has spent a little over a month in the business. Whether or not this is a satisfactory rate depends upon the type of business. Food, of course, would have to be turned over far faster than this, but the rate would be higher than that which applies to most shops selling non-perishable goods.

If the rate of turnover can be increased without reducing prices, profits will rise. To increase sales it may be necessary to cut prices, however. Although a smaller profit would be made on each sale, the over-all profit will rise if total sales increase enough. This is why supermarkets adopt the policy of 'small profits, quick returns'.

20.17 STUDYING TRENDS

A businessman will be concerned not only about his figures for the present year but also with how they compare with previous years:

(a) *If the gross profit percentage is falling*, it may be due to one of the following. (i) Stock is being wasted or stolen. Overstocking may result in too many goods being destroyed because they have deteriorated. There may be waste in making up goods (for example, carelessness in cutting meat into joints). There may be too many breakages. Stock may be pilfered by the staff or 'shoplifters'. (ii) Poor buying has resulted in some goods not being demanded by customers. (iii) The cost of goods has risen without any increase to customers.

(b) *If the net profit percentage is falling but the gross percentage is not*, it means that the overheads have become more costly. There may have been some lack of control – perhaps electricity is being wasted, for example. Staffing may have increased more than is justified. If overheads generally have become more expensive, selling prices may not have been raised sufficiently to compensate.

(c) *If the yield on funds is falling*, the owner is getting a reduced return on his investment. This could be due to a fall in profits generally, of course, but it may be caused by an increase in the interest paid on loans. If rates in general are rising, this tends to reduce profits if the trader is using borrowed capital. Even if profits remain the same, the trader is comparatively worse off when rates are rising. Thus a trader earning profits of 20 per cent on his capital would not be unhappy if interest rates generally were 10 per cent, but he would be concerned if interest rates were to rise to 17 per cent.

20.18 BUSINESS COSTS

A manufacturing business will incur two types of costs. To show this we can take as an example a company which makes tin cans. If it doubles its output of cans, it will use twice as much tin, of course. Accordingly, the amount spent on tin will double. Perhaps more people will be employed, and although the cost of wages will not double it will certainly increase. Such costs are known as *variable costs* because they vary when output alters.

Other costs *will not* alter, no matter how much the rate of production changes. If the company makes 1000 cans a week or 10 000 cans a week, the amount spent on office lighting and heating, insurance, staff salaries, etc., will change very little, if at all. These are known as *fixed costs* because they do not change as output alters.

It follows that the fixed costs will be the same, irrespective of the amount produced. The total costs of producing 1000 cans will include fixed costs. The total cost of producing 10 000 cans will include the *same amount* of fixed costs. The more that is produced, the smaller the proportion of the cost of each unit which is taken up by fixed costs.

20.19 THE BREAK-EVEN POINT

Figure 20.3 shows that a company's fixed costs amount to £10 000. The variable costs amount to £1 a unit. Therefore, to produce 10 000 units costs £20 000; that is, £2 a unit. If, however, 30 000 units are produced, it will cost £40 000, because the fixed costs are spread across a larger output. At the higher figure, therefore, each unit will cost £1.33 to produce. If output amounts to 40 000 units, the unit cost falls to £1.25.

The goods are sold for £1.50 a unit. Thus the price is unchanged no matter how many are sold, but the cost reduces as production increases. The chart shows that if 20 000 units are produced, there will be no profit and no loss. This is known as the *break-even point*. Below that production level losses will be made; above that figure there will be an increasing profit rate.

20.20 BUDGETARY CONTROL

This is a system used in every sizeable business whereby *targets are set*. These may be for output (to produce a certain number of units), for costs (to keep expenses down to certain levels), for sales, for profits, etc. If the performance does not meet the target, the difference is known as the *deviation*.

Budget areas are fixed, each with its own target. Budgets for particular

Fig 20.3 *break-even chart*

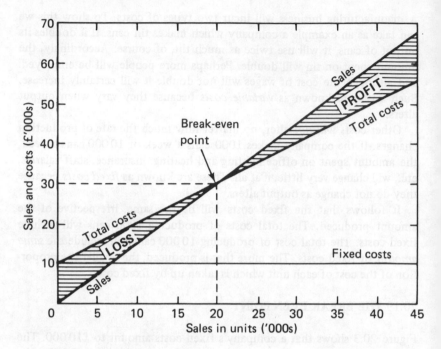

areas are called *subsidiary budgets* and they are co-ordinated into a *master budget*.

The system therefore makes it possible to set an over-all target, such as the amount of sales, and for this to be subdivided into targets for geographical areas or products. Everyone has something to aim for, and management will plan on the assumption that the targets will be achieved. Where there are deviations management can identify the causes and either remove the causes or, where that is impossible, adjust the target.

20.21 THE DISTRIBUTION OF PROFIT

Figure 20.4 shows the order in which profits are distributed. It also illustrates the following principles:

(a) Loan interest is paid before the profit figure is extracted. Part of the capital is provided by lenders but their reward is not a distribution of profits.

(b) Tax is paid before any other allocation from profit is made. It is assessed on the amount of profits *after* payment of interest.

(c) Part of the remainder is placed to reserve, which *increases* the capital.

Fig 20.4 *distribution of a company's profits*

Income and expenditure   **Capital**

Sales   *less*   costs and expenses
       loan interest ——————— paid to ———→ lenders
    Profit

Distributed as
   tax ————————————→ passed to Inland Revenue
   dividends ——————————— paid to ——————→ shareholders
   surplus ——————————— placed to ——————→ reserve

EXERCISES

1 When a business opened it had raw materials which were purchased for £10 000. These were later turned into goods for sale, and they were then sold for £14 000, of which £2000 is still owing. Show how these events altered the *form* and the *amount* of the capital.

2 The following items appear in a balance-sheet, and in respect of each one state whether it is a *current asset*, a *fixed asset*, a *current liability* or a *long-term liability*: (a) trade debtors; (b) investments; (c) loan secured by a mortgage; (d) delivery van; (e) subscription owing to a trade association.

3 The working-capital ratio of a certain company is said to be 1:1. What does this mean? What conclusions can be drawn if 1 per cent of that company's assets is in the form of cash?

4 A company has issued shares with a nominal value of £50 000. It has borrowed £10 000 from a bank and owes £5000 to trade creditors. Amounts owing to the company total £25 000. What is the *capital owned* and the *funds used*?

5 A business has a capital of £50 000, contributed solely by the owner. In the past year profits amounted to £10 000. (a) What yield did the owner get on his funds? (b) What would his yield have been if he had borrowed a fifth of the capital at 15 per cent? (c) Explain why the two yields differ.

6 What effect does taxation have on the cost of loans?

7 Explain the different consequences of raising additional capital by the following methods: (a) issuing more ordinary shares; (b) ploughing back profits; (c) borrowing from a bank.

8 A man has capital of £1000 in cash. He buys goods for £1100, paying

£800 in cash. He sells the goods (except for one consignment which had cost £100) for £1500. He receives £900 in cash on these sales. (a) How much profit or loss did he make? (b) Show his present balance-sheet.

9 Distinguish between *capital, turnover* and *profit*. A retailer turns over his stock four times a year. His selling price is obtained by increasing the cost price by 40 per cent. Selling expenses amount to 15 per cent of turnover. If the turnover for the year was £20 000, find (a) the amount of net profit, and (b) the average value of stock carried at cost price.

10 Explain why there would be differences in the rate of turnover, the gross profit and the amount of working capital in a retail grocery store and a shop selling television sets.

11 The turnover of a firm during a year was £56 000. This gave a gross profit of 25 per cent of selling price. Expenses amounted to £11 000 and the average stock held throughout the year was £5250 at cost price. Find (a) the net profit, and (b) the rate of stock turn.

12 The sales of a company amounted to £700 000. Its gross profit was £140 000. Overheads totalled £35 000. Calculate the *gross* profit percentage and the *net* profit percentage.

13 Refer to Figure 20.2 and draw up a balance-sheet to show the position at the end of the trading period.

14 Refer to Figure 20.3. What is (a) the gross profit, and (b) the net profit, when sales amount to 30 000 units?

CHAPTER 21

PERSONAL FINANCE

In many respects *every* person is in business. We all have to relate what we spend to what we earn, so that, consciously or not, we 'budget'. As private individuals we are also like businessmen in that we have to choose carefully our methods of saving. Similarly, we have to take steps to insure ourselves against various forms of risk.

In this chapter, therefore, our concern will be with the handling of personal financial affairs.

21.1 THE IMPORTANCE OF BUDGETING

'Budgeting' means planning what you pay out in relation to what comes in. Unless this is done you may spend unwisely so that you have less left over than you would otherwise have. A far more dangerous stage is reached if you commit yourself to spend more than you have available. Mr Micawber in *David Copperfield* said 'Annual income twenty pounds, annual expenditure nineteen nineteen six, result happiness. Annual income twenty pounds, annual expenditure twenty pounds ought and six, result misery.' The figures are out of date but the principle is as true today as it was when Dickens wrote those words. In fact, the danger of insolvency is greater today because living on credit has become an accepted way of life for many people. The need to budget carefully is therefore more important than it ever was.

Most people can predict fairly accurately what their income will be. Usually, almost all of it will be in the form of wages, with a certain amount coming from savings invested. Against this can be set an estimate of what has to be spent. This is less easy to calculate, but it can be divided as follows:

(a) *Compulsory deductions* are made for income tax, national insurance and any other deductions your employer may make (such as contributions to a pension fund). These amounts are fairly predictable.

(b) *Essential payments* must be made for food, clothing, rent, etc. Although these items must be paid for, the amounts spent can sometimes be reduced by buying economically (as is explained in the next chapter). On the other hand, prices may rise while income remains unaltered.

(c) *Optional spending* relates to those things which are bought with whatever is left over after paying for essentials. This does not necessarily mean they are 'luxuries'. If you regard meat as being an essential, you have the choice between buying the best quality and buying an inferior one. At one level of quality it may be regarded as being a luxury.

Part of the optional spending may be in the form of savings. This involves an extended kind of budgeting in that it means spending *now* for something required in the *future*. The reverse of this is also part of budgeting, because if you buy something on credit you are committing *future* income for something you receive *now*. The difference is that if you buy on credit your payments become *essential* payments; therefore, they have an earlier claim on income than savings have.

21.2 THE MOTIVES FOR SAVING

In making a choice between the different methods of saving you must first ask yourself some questions about why you intend to save:

(a) What do you want to save *for*? If you intend to save in order to buy something, you will need to be able to draw out the money when you require it. However, in some forms of saving the money cannot be withdrawn until a certain time has elapsed. So a distinction needs to be made between saving for a purchase (money to be available *when* you need it) and saving for no particular purpose (to be available at any time).

(b) You must also ask what it is you want from your savings. Do you want a regular income, or do you want to make a capital gain by withdrawing or selling on a certain date?

(c) Do you intend to save regularly or at such times you can afford to, or have you a lump sum to put away?

21.3 THE CHOICE OF SAVINGS METHODS

Keeping in mind the above motives, the following must be considered in choosing a form of saving:

(a) The rate of interest
The amount of interest varies between one safe form of savings and another, usually because of the differences in convenience to the saver.

Money put into a savings account which you can draw on as you wish earns a lower rate than money which can be drawn only on notice. It is lower still than on money which cannot be drawn at all until a specified time.

Interest on some savings is taxable and on others it is 'tax-free'. If you pay income tax, you will get less than 10 per cent on savings which pay interest of 10 per cent which is taxable. It is therefore important to compare what you *actually* get between one form of savings and another.

Some interest rates are fixed and some are variable at the discretion of the body concerned. The interest paid by building societies, Trustee Savings banks, commercial banks, etc., can be altered, usually following a change in Minimum Lending Rate. Money in National Savings give fixed rates of interest. If interest rates generally are rising, those receiving fixed rates will be worse off, of course, but the reverse will apply when interest rates are falling.

(b) Safety

Most forms of savings used by individuals are very safe. Those which are not offered by the government (which are 'as safe as the Bank of England') are available from organisations which are strictly controlled by law. Money deposited with banks, insurance companies and the larger building societies can be regarded as being safe. A person who puts money into company securities, however (either by buying shares or trust units), is really an *investor* and is aware of the risks involved.

(c) Ease of withdrawal

Care must be taken not to 'lock away' money which may be required at any time. A building society will give a good rate of interest if you deposit a lump sum on the understanding you will keep it there for, say, four years. Under no circumstances would you be able to withdraw it before then. A person with a sizeable sum could put into such an account money he was *sure* he would not require to draw on, while another sum could be placed in a more accessible account.

21.4 FORMS OF SAVINGS

(a) Banks

The services offered to savers were discussed in Chapter 16. The aim of a saver should be to keep in a current account the minimum amount which will not attract bank charges and to leave the rest in a deposit account to earn interest. When necessary, sums may be quickly moved from one account to the other.

(b) Trustee Savings banks

These offer savings accounts for small investors. Amounts may be easily paid in and drawn out, using branches throughout the country.

(c) Building societies

These offer a variety of facilities. Any amounts may be put into 'deposit', 'savings' or 'share' accounts and fairly large sums can be drawn on demand. 'Bonds' offer higher rates of interest but they cannot be drawn on until the end of the agreed term. The interest on building society savings is 'tax paid': that is, the building society pays the tax. Not more than £30 000 may be invested in any one society.

(d) Post Office savings

National Savings Bank accounts. Any amount up to £10 000 may be placed in an ordinary account and up to £50 may be withdrawn on demand. The first £70 of interest is not taxable. A higher rate is paid on investment accounts but it is taxable. Up to £50 000 may be deposited on such accounts and withdrawals require one month's notice.

National Savings Certificates provide a capital gain after being held for a stated length of time. Little profit is made if they are withdrawn before then. The gain is tax-free.

Premium Bonds are issued in £1 units. They offer no interest but each unit is entered in a monthly lottery. These provide the chance of winning prizes, some of which amount to several thousand pounds. The amount invested can be withdrawn at short notice.

National Giro Bank. Interest is paid on deposit accounts. These can be used in conjunction with National Giro services (see Section 21.8).

21.5 MAKING PROVISION FOR THE FUTURE

There are various methods for setting money aside to provide for the future. They are therefore forms of assurance based on savings:

(a) Endowment assurance

Besides guaranteeing a lump-sum payment in the event of death before a specified date, this can be a profitable method of saving. Regular premiums are paid on the understanding that on a stated date the assured will receive a specified sum or a pension. If a 'with-profits' policy is taken out, a proportion of the assurance company's profits are added to this amount. As previously explained, this type of policy will provide the assured with more than he has paid in.

(b) Annuities

These require payment of a lump sum to an assurance company, in return for which a guaranteed annual amount will be paid after a specified date, usually until death. The possibility of a 'profit' is, of course, unpredictable because it depends upon how long the annuitant lives to draw the income. There is no income if the annuitant dies before the date the income is due to commence.

(c) National Insurance

Every employed person and every self-employed person must pay National Insurance contributions. These provide benefits under the National Health Service in the form of medical and hospital treatment. Wage-earners also qualify for unemployment pay when they are out of work and sick pay when they are not earning because of illness or accident.

21.6 TAXES

A person pays taxes in two forms:

(a) Income tax and capital gains tax are levied on what a person *receives*. The rate of income tax increases as a person's income rises; capital gains are taxed at a fixed rate.

(b) Other taxes are paid on what a person *spends*. Many items have value-added tax in the price and there is excise duty payable on such purchases as petrol, alcoholic drinks and tobacco.

Consequently, a wealthy person pays a proportionately higher amount of tax on income than a poorer person does. However, both pay the *same* rate when they buy something which carries a tax in its price and also on capital gains. There is little a person can do to influence the amount of income tax and capital gains tax he pays, but the extent of his spending and the sort of things he buys will affect the amount of other taxes he pays.

(The various taxes have been explained more fully in Chapter 12.)

21.7 BUYING A HOME

Most people who buy their own homes do so by obtaining a mortgage from a building society.

A person buying property by means of a mortgage becomes the *owner* of the property at the outset. To that extent, therefore, it is like any other method of buying on credit. However, the owner cannot sell his own property before the mortgage is paid off because to do so he would have to hand the 'title deeds' to his buyer. The title deeds are legal evidence of the existence of the property, and when a mortgage is granted the lender keeps the deeds until the loan is repaid.

The 'mortgage' is a promise to repay a loan. It also states that if the terms of the loan are not kept, the lender can sell the property. If a lender does have to do this, he takes from the proceeds of the sale only what is owing to him and pays the balance to the borrower. This is because, of course, the lender is selling something which belongs to the borrower.

A person applying for a mortgage must have a regular income. The building society will advance only part of the purchase price and that amount will depend upon the size of the applicant's income.

The effective cost of a building society mortgage is reduced because the interest is allowable against income tax. *The cost of buying a home with the aid of a building society mortgage* therefore includes:

(a) the deposit;
(b) the total of the repayments *less* tax allowance on the interest;
(c) local authority rates;
(d) insurance (every property must be insured for an amount decided by the building society); and
(e) maintenance of the property.

When comparing these costs with that of renting, it must be remembered that they do result in an asset being acquired. Paying rent provides no 'return' and is an everlasting cost.

21.8 METHODS OF MAKING PERSONAL PAYMENTS

(a) Through the banking system
The uses of cheques, bank Giro, standing orders and direct debits have been discussed in Chapter 16.

(b) In cash
'Legal tender' is that amount of cash which a creditor must accept in payment of a debt. Notes are legal tender for any amount. One cannot be difficult and demand that a creditor accepts a pile of coins, however. Bronze coins can be offered for only up to a total of 20p; 50p coins are legal tender up to a total of £10; other cupro-nickel coins are acceptable up to a total of £5.

(c) Transfers through the Post Office
Postal orders are issued for amounts ranging from 5p to £10. Paying by using postal orders is not a convenient method because a Post Office has to be visited in order to purchase one. A postal order can be crossed, but if this is done one must be sure the payee has a bank account to pay it

into. Uncrossed postal orders can be cashed only at Post Offices. Because of the 'poundage' payable on every order, they are expensive when compared with cheques.

Urgent payments can be made by the use of *Telegraph Money Orders*. These can be issued for amounts up to £100. The dispatching office sends an authority for payment to be made by the office nearest the payee. Cash can be sent by *registered post* (see Section 15.2).

The *National Giro* system is operated through the Post Office. For *one account-holder to pay another* a transfer form must be completed. This form is sent to the Giro centre by the payer (using envelopes which require no stamps) and the amount is transferred to the payee's account. Giro cheque accounts are also available, so that *Girobank cheques* (see Figure 21.1) can be sent to those *without* Giro accounts. Up to £50 can be drawn in cash from a cheque account at either of two named Post Offices. No charges are made on Giro accounts in credit. Regular payments can be made by standing orders and direct debits.

Non-account holders can pay account-holders by using 'inpayment' forms obtainable from Post Offices and for which a standard fee is payable (see Figure 21.2).

(National Giro must not be confused with the bank giro system – see Chapter 16.)

21.9 PERSONAL INSURANCE

An individual (and a home-owner in particular) should insure himself against risks so that he will have some compensation in the event of an untoward incident. The main forms of personal insurance are as follows:

(a) Home-buildings insurance

This provides cover against loss caused by fire and many other possible events. The amount a house should be insured for is what it would cost to rebuild it today if it were totally destroyed. This figure would probably be higher than the amount paid when the house was purchased. The amount of cover should also include the cost of fees to surveyors, solicitors, etc.

(b) Home-contents insurance

This insures against loss of, or damage to, the contents of a house. Again, cover should be taken for the replacement values. If you bought an ornament for £20 five years ago, it may cost £50 to replace it today. On the other hand, you could not claim it had a 'sentimental value' of £100! (Figure 8.2 in Chapter 8 gives an example of the terms in a home-contents insurance policy.)

Fig 21.1 *Girobank cheque*

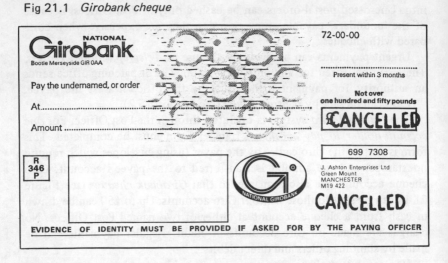

Fig 21.2 *National Giro inpayment form*

(c) Other forms of personal insurance

These include: *personal accident insurance*, providing payment on death or injury caused by an accident; *travel insurance*, to cover medical expenses in case of illness or accident while abroad; *motor insurance*, for damage to motor-vehicles; *life assurance*, to provide a lump sum and/or an income for dependants upon the death of the assured.

All insurance premiums are based on the probability of the risk occurring. (This is explained more fully in Chapter 8.) Initially a premium is calculated on information provided by the person wanting the insurance. An example of the questions to be answered in a 'proposal form' is given in Figure 21.3.

Fig 21.3 *a life-assurance proposal form*

PROPOSAL FOR LIFE ASSURANCE	
Please give a definite answer to each question ; ticks or dashes are insufficient.	
Full name of the person whose life is to be assured *Please use BLOCK Capitals.* If any change has taken place in the name it should be stated.	
Residence .... *Please use BLOCK Capitals*	
Whether married or single	
Present profession or occupation .... *Please give full particulars* Is any change likely to take place? .... If so, what?	
Place and date of birth .... Certificate of birth, if not already furnished, should be forwarded with this proposal, in order that the policy may be issued with "Age admitted."	
Amount of assurance desired ...	£...............................
Class of policy required?	....Without Participation in Profits
Term or number of premiums payable	....
Are you likely to engage in any Military, Naval or Air Force service?	
(a) To what extent are you likely to engage in aviation as a fare-paying passenger of a recognised air line?	*(a)*
(b) In what other forms of aviation or aeronautics are you likely to engage?	*(b)*
Do you engage or intend to engage in motor racing or testing?	
Have you ever resided abroad? ... If so, where and for how long? .... Have you any intention or prospect of going abroad? .... If so, where?	

I the life to be assured, declare that the statements are true and I agree that such statements shall be the basis of the proposed contract of assurance.

Witness..

Signature of the
person whose life ....
is to be assured

Address..   *Date*...................................

EXERCISES

1 The amount of a person's income is usually fairly predictable, but how a person spends his income varies between one individual and another. Explain the importance of budgeting in relating expenditure to income.

2 What special considerations apply if a person has included a number of credit repayments in his budget?

3 Assume you have a fairly large amount of money you wish to save. You decide to put some of it in a building society savings account which would allow you to draw up to £250 on demand. The rest you intend to put into building society bonds. These pay a much higher rate of interest than the savings account, but you would not be able to draw out the capital during the next five years. How would you decide what proportion to put into each account?

4 Two people each earn exactly the same amount in a year. Explain why there is a difference in the amount of taxes each pays, directly and indirectly.

5 How does the 'profit' received by savers differ between (a) National Savings Bank accounts, (b) National Savings Certificates, and (c) Premium Bonds?

6 Explain the advantages of taking out an endowment 'with-profits' assurance policy.

7 To what extent is it a 'gamble' to buy an annuity?

8 Compare your position as a buyer of a house through a building society with that of buying a refrigerator on a credit sales agreement.

9 How is buying a house a form of saving?

10 If you owe someone £50 and you decide to pay him all in coins, why does the law say he may refuse to accept them?

11 To what extent is paying someone by sending him a postal order an unsatisfactory method?

12 (a) If you had a National Giro account, how would you pay (i) another Giro account-holder, (ii) someone who does not have a Giro account? (b) How would you pay a Giro account-holder if you yourself had no Giro account?

13 Two years ago you bought a house for £20 000. How would you decide the amount to insure it for?

CHAPTER 22

PERSONAL ASPECTS
OF BUYING

Everyone is a buyer. We all buy goods, such as food, domestic articles, newspapers and books, etc. In most cases one has a choice in buying goods. It is therefore possible to compare prices between, for example, different brands of tea, different makes of shoes, and so on. Often, however, when comparing prices one is not comparing 'like with like'. Thus one brand of tea may be cheaper than another merely because it is of an inferior quality. To make a true comparison, therefore, one must allow for differences in the products.

In some instances, however, one has *no* choice. This would be the case where the price is fixed by law (as applies to milk, for example). One can rarely make a choice about public services. If you have to travel to another town by train, the fare will be fixed. (You may have a choice if cheaper fares are charged at certain times of the day, but this would be no help if you did not want to travel at those times.)

To buy efficiently demands some thought and planning. However, even the most expert buyer could be given an unfair deal unless there were safeguards to prevent that happening. Therefore, in this chapter we will not only consider the principles of sound buying but also how the law and various bodies protect the consumer.

22.1 WISE BUYING

Some people are 'good shoppers' - others are not. Before buying anything the following questions need to be answered:

(a) Do you need it?
This question is not always so nonsensical as it may seem. Obviously, you must buy food, but do you need to buy this particular item? You may already have a sufficient stock of it at home, or something very much like it. The question is, however, usually applicable to 'luxuries'

and 'near-luxuries'. If you go out to buy such an article, then, obviously, you have already decided you want it. On the other hand, you may buy something which you had no intention of getting when you left home. This is known as *impulse buying* – buying something on the impulse of the moment. You may see something which attracts you, but after you have bought it you realise it was not such a 'good buy'. This applies even if the article is particularly cheap. A 'bargain' is not a bargain if you do not really want it.

(b) Can you afford it?
Good buying depends upon *good budgeting*; that is, relating what you spend on non-essentials to the money you have left after buying essentials (such as food and rent) and any saving for other essentials (such as clothes and furniture).

If you cannot afford to pay cash for your purchase, you may decide to buy on credit. This gives you a whole lot of other questions to answer and these we will consider in the next chapter.

(c) Is it the best time to buy?
Essentials must, of course, be bought now, but for other goods there may be a better time to buy. If a shop is shortly going to have a 'sale', you may be lucky enough to get the article cheaper than it now is. If you know the price is going to go up, it may be sensible to buy now something which you do not need immediately. If you have a home freezer, it is obviously wise to buy fruit when there is a glut because it will then be very cheap.

(d) Which is the cheapest?
If you can buy goods of the same quality at different prices, it pays to 'shop around' by comparing those prices. In Chapter 5 we saw that some stores sell their 'own brands' cheaper than the proprietary brands. Sometimes a store will advertise 'loss leaders'. These are selected goods offered at particularly low prices merely to encourage people to come into the shop. Standard goods can often be bought at discount stores at prices very much lower than those charged in other types of shops.

(e) Do you need the best?
Many goods are sold in different grades of quality. Unless you must have the best quality, it is wasteful to pay its higher price. Some grades of coffee are very expensive, but unless you are a connoisseur of coffee why buy the best? The same can be said of wine. If you are buying a carpet for a room which is rarely used, it is pointless to pay a high price for a carpet which is made to withstand a lot of wear. A buyer should start

by deciding what he *wants* and then study the prices of goods which satisfy those requirements. A person living alone should not buy a washing-machine which can take a heavy load of washing and which has a lot of 'gadgets' he or she does not need.

(f) How much should you buy?

Goods bought in large packs are cheaper by weight than those bought in smaller packs. However, if you use one normal-size packet of breakfast cereal in a fortnight, would you be wise to buy a 'Jumbo' pack which will last six weeks? Each meal will cost you less if you buy the big packet, but have you room to store it; will the contents deteriorate before the end of six weeks; can you carry it home if you have made a number of other large purchases? The person who has a home freezer benefits, of course, because he can buy large quantities of foods (such as meat and fish) which he or she can keep fresh. 'Home freezer centres' specialise in supplying food to such people.

22.2 HOW SHOPPING HAS CHANGED

Earlier in the book we saw that shopping methods have changed in recent years. In many instances this has benefitted shoppers, but it also entails problems:

(a) Self-service is now the generally accepted practice in the grocery trade. It has meant, however, that grocers no longer provide delivery services, so that the non-car-owner is at a disadvantage. Other disadvantages are those of large-scale retailing, which were discussed in Chapter 5.

(b) Many goods are pre-packed, giving the advantages of convenience and improved hygiene. This means, however, that often the goods cannot be examined before purchase. Frequently, the cost of the packing increases the price.

(c) 'Convenience foods' have become more popular. These are purchases which can be immediately converted into edible products, such as 'instant' custard and cake mixes. Often, however, the contents are not of the highest quality, some tend to lack flavour and the price is usually high.

(d) More clothes are made of synthetic fibres. Generally, these provide benefits, but they often require special treatment in washing, drying and ironing.

(e) As regards domestic appliances, the emphasis is on reducing human effort. Washing is no longer a drudgery because of washing-machines; the kitchen chores of cutting, grinding, whisking, blending, etc., are made much easier by the many appliances on the market. It is obvious, however, that the more complicated such pieces of equipment are the more likely they are to go wrong.

22.3 BUYING 'BRAND NAMES'

Most goods are sold under 'brand names'. These are registered trade marks, so that not only does the same name appear on all the goods of one make but the *style* of the name is always the same. A study of Figure 22.1 will show that not only is the name 'Coca Cola' known all over the world but also that it is always written in the same form; and all the products of Heinz and Findus are packed in containers on which the lettering and its surrounding never vary.

Branding provides the following advantages:

(a) *The make is immediately identifiable.* Because shoppers are so familiar with the design, they can readily see and recognise it on the shop shelves.

(b) *Advertising makes the brand widely known.* Frequent publicising of the 'image' (particularly in television 'commercials') make it a 'household name'.

(c) *Shoppers know exactly what they are buying.* The standard of

Fig 22.1 *examples of branding*

the contents do not vary, so. that baked beans of a certain brand tastes the same as any other beans of the same brand.

(d) *Branding increases sales.* Because of the above advantages, branded goods have large scales. This leads to a reduction in their prices.

Branding relates to goods other than groceries, of course. Almost any product sold on a large scale does so under a recognisable 'label'. This applies to cars and washing-machines as well as to toothpastes and cigarettes.

22.2 SALES PROMOTIONS

Manufacturers and retailers frequently adopt schemes to promote sales: that is, to increase them. Whether or not these benefit consumers is sometimes doubtful. If a scheme increases sales it may result in a reduction of prices, but the inference is somewhat remote. For example, it is very doubtful if *competitions* benefit the consumer. These usually require a competition form to be sent to the manufacturer accompanied by, say, six packet tops of the product. Apart from the lucky winners, the only person to gain would probably be the producer. *Coupons* are sometimes given with products. These can be exchanged for 'free' gifts, or they may entitle the holders to reductions on future purchases. Generally, however, the advantages to consumers are small.

Trading stamps were for some years an important part of retailing. They are issued to customers in amounts proportionate to the sum they spend in the shop. They can then be exchanged for goods provided by the trading stamp company or they may be cashed. Some say that as the retailer has to buy the stamps this increases his prices. The reply to this is that because more people shop where stamps are given those retailers can afford to reduce their prices. Many large retailers never issued trading stamps, however, and yet continued to prosper. Eventually, most supermarkets followed, so that now only a comparatively few retailers issue stamps.

The influence of *advertising* has been discussed in Chapter 14.

22.5 CONSUMER PROTECTION

Although there is much the consumer can do to buy wisely, he is nevertheless very much in the hands of those he buys from. We have seen that there are some safeguards against exploitation by advertisers, but the consumer needs far more protection than that. (When a person buys on credit he needs even more protection. This important aspect is discussed in the next chapter.)

In recent years there has been a considerable increase in measures to protect the consumer. Before considering them in detail they can first be broadly summarised as follows:

(a) *By passing Acts of Parliament.*
(b) *By providing consumer-advice services.*
(c) *By industries subscribing to codes of practice.*
(d) *By indicating standards through labelling.*

22.6 WHY CONSUMERS NEED PROTECTION

Manufacturers and retailers exist in order to make profits, and if left alone they could do so by acting unfairly to consumers. The following are some of the practices they could adopt:

(a) They may agree not to compete against one another so as to keep prices exceptionally high.
(b) They may quote prices in such a way that buyers would not realise they were paying more than is reasonable. For example, to say that something is 'Ten pounds off the recommended retail price' would be deceptive if the manufacturer, by agreement with the retailer, deliberately inflated his 'recommended' price.
(c) The product may be adulterated with inferior ingredients.
(d) The ingredients may be harmful or the article may be dangerous to use.
(e) The quantity of the commodity may not be stated, so that price comparison is impossible.
(f) The seller may refuse to repair or replace a faulty product.
(g) The buyer may be deceived by dishonest advertising.
(h) A person buying on credit may unknowingly agree to terms which are harsh.

22.7 THE OFFICE OF FAIR TRADING

This office, established under the *Fair Trading Act 1973*, protects the consumer in the following ways:

(a) It collects information about selling practices and, where necessary, proposes new legislation to prevent abuses by sellers.
(b) It prosecutes traders who break the law.
(c) Under the *Consumer Credit Act 1974* (see Chapter 23) it licences traders who deal in credit.
(d) It encourages traders to adopt codes of practice.
(e) It publishes information for consumers.

22.8 OBLIGATIONS AND RIGHTS ON A SALE OF GOODS

Once you have purchased something the seller takes on obligations to you. These are set out in the *Sale of Goods Act 1979*. They are as follows:

(a) *The goods must be of a 'merchantable quality'.* This means they must work properly. If you buy a television set and it does not give a satisfactory picture, or if a tea set you have bought includes a cracked plate, you acquire rights of compensation.

(b) *The goods must be 'fit for their purpose'.* Anything you buy should do what it is supposed to do. A teapot which does not pour properly obviously does not function as it should. If you *ask* for an article which will do a specified job, it must do just that. If you tell a shopkeeper you want a drill for making holes in concrete and he supplies one which will only penetrate wood, he has not sold you something for the purpose you stated.

(c) *The goods must be as described.* If the pack described a blanket as being blue and when you unpacked it you found it was pink, the seller has failed in his obligation to you. The same would apply if a saleswoman sold you a dress which she said was all wool and you found it was a mixture of wool and nylon.

The *buyer's rights* in any of those circumstances are any one of the following:

(a) He can reject the goods and ask for compensation. The full price must be refunded *only* if the goods have hardly been used and the buyer *acts at once*. In other cases he may get partial compensation. If the buyer has suffered because of a defect (for example, a carpet may be damaged if a washing-machine overflows), compensation may be claimed.

(b) He may ask for the article to be replaced or repaired.

(c) He may be given a credit note to buy something else. (A buyer cannot be compelled to accept a credit note.)

None of these rights can be taken away from a buyer, even if he signs a document which appears to do so. Any undertaking or guarantee given by the seller is *additional* to the buyer's legal rights.

A retailer cannot tell a buyer to return the goods to the manufacturer 'because it is *his* responsibility'. If goods are faulty, the responsibility rests with the *retailer*.

These rights do not belong to the buyer if:

(a) he should have seen the goods were faulty when he bought them;

(b) the seller did not *say* the goods would be suitable for the purpose; or

(c) he bought them from someone 'not in the normal course of business' – for example, if he bought them from a private seller and not a shopkeeper.

The *Supply of Goods and Services Act 1982* extends the above protection to *services*. For example, if a plumber provides the taps he is fitting he has the same obligations as has a seller of taps.

22.9 PROTECTION FOR INACCURATE DESCRIPTION OF A PURCHASE

The *Trade Descriptions Act 1968* relates to goods and services. If a trader inaccurately describes any good or service he is providing, he can be fined or imprisoned. This can refer to what the goods will do, what they are made of, where they are made, and so on.

22.10 PROTECTION CONCERNING PRICES

The *Trade Descriptions Act 1968* also makes it illegal to describe prices falsely. For example, if a trader crosses out £2.70 on a price ticket and shows the new price as £2.20, he must, if he is not to commit an offence, have sold such articles for £2.70 for at least 28 consecutive days in the last six months. If this is not the case, he must make it clear, by (for example) marking the ticket as 'Price last week £2.70. Today's price £2.20.'

It is also illegal to show price comparisons which are vague. '3p off' is deceitful because it does not say off *what*. 'Up to 20 per cent off' is vague because it *could* mean 1 per cent off only. The same applies to 'save up to £20'; '£10 below normal shop prices'; and so on.

Shop 'sales' attract many customers, some of whom think that because an item is in a 'sale' it must be a bargain. The honest purpose of having sales is to enable shops to get rid of stock which they have had difficulty in selling. Some shops, however, had *bought* goods especially to put into 'sales', thereby giving the impression they were genuine reductions. Any such goods must now be clearly marked as 'special purchases'.

The Prices Act 1974 introduced 'unit pricing'. This requires that on some articles the price must be indicated by weight. For example, packs of bacon rashers will not be of all the same weight. Each pack must show not only its price but the price per pound.

22.11 OTHER LEGISLATION TO PROTECT CONSUMERS

(a) Weights and Measures Act 1963
The increased use of pre-packed food has meant that it is now comparatively rare for a customer to see his purchases weighed when he buys

them. In a supermarket, meat, fish, cheese, etc., are, in the main, already wrapped and priced. This Act makes it necessary for many items to have the quantity indicated on the pack. Increasingly, the quantity is given in metric, the packs being clearly marked 'Metric pack', as shown in Figure 5.2 of Chapter 5.

(b) Food and Drugs Act 1955
Under this Act it is an offence to sell unfit food or to mislead people about its nature, substance or quality. It is also an offence to state falsely the nutritional value of the food. The label must list the ingredients and their proportion of the whole (for example, the amount of meat in sausages and of the colouring in sauces). The name and address to be used for making a complaint must be given. The Act also lays down standards of hygiene at the manufacturing and retailing stages.

(c) Consumer Protection Act 1961
Under this Act regulations may be made about any type of goods to prevent or reduce the risk of death or injury. For example, there are regulations about the wiring of electrical equipment, the material in soft toys and the paint on solid toys, the design of baby cots, etc.

(d) Unsolicited Goods and Services Act 1971
In the past some suppliers sent to people goods (such as Christmas cards) they had not asked for. With the goods were statements that if the goods were not returned within a stated period they must be paid for. This was made illegal under this Act. If you receive goods you have not ordered and do not wish to buy, you can send them back within six months. Alternatively, after six months you can keep them. They then become your property, so that you could even sell them if you so wished. At any time during the six months you may ask the supplier to collect them from you and if he does not do so within 30 days you may keep the goods.

(e) Consumer Credit Act 1974
This relates to buying on credit and hirepurchase transactions. Because this is a very important aspect of trading, it is dealt with separately in the next chapter.

22.12 CONSUMER-ADVICE SERVICES

Various bodies provide help and advice to consumers:

(a) Local authorities
Consumer Protection Departments investigate complaints about untrue advertising and misleading descriptions of goods and services. They enforce

the law concerning the composition and labelling of food and for breaches of the *Consumer Protection Act.* Health Departments enforce regulations concerning the storage and handling of food. Some local authorities operate Consumer Advice Centres.

(b) Citizens' Advice Bureaux

These give free advice on a wide range of matters, including those relevant to consumer protection.

(c) Nationalised industries

Each of these has a Consumer Consultative Council which will investigate complaints and give advice.

(d) The Consumers' Association

This is a private organisation which tests, compares and reports on goods and services. This information is made available to some 700 000 subscribers to *Which?* and its associated magazines. Scientific tests are made on products, and manufacturers take very seriously any criticism of their products which is published. Products are compared as to performance, quality and cost, the result being to identify the 'best buys'.

22.13 CODES OF PRACTICE

Various trade associations have drawn up codes of practice which their members are expected to comply with. It is a self-disciplining system whereby an association voluntarily sets standards for its members. It will investigate complaints from the public concerning the service provided by any of its members and will take action against any member who breaks the code. Earlier in the book there was given an example of the code which operates in the advertising industry. There are many other such organisations operating codes of practice, such as the Association of British Travel Agents, the Motor Agents' Association and the Association of British Launderers and Cleaners. Members display the symbol of their Association as an indication to consumers of their acceptance of prescribed standards of service.

22.14 STANDARDS LABELS

There are a number of institutions which allow manufacturers to display a symbol on their products to show that the goods are of a standard set by the institution. Before giving permission to show the symbol the institution tests the product. It is therefore an advantage to a manufacture if an institution will give its 'seal of approval', because consumers will then buy the product with confidence.

The British Standards Institution awards the well-known Kitemark for products which meet its standards of quality. It will also award the Safety Mark for goods which comply with BSI standards of safety. These goods include gas cooking appliances, gas fires and lighting fittings. Other institutions which award labels include the Design Council, British Gas and the Home Laundering Consultative Council. These are all shown in Figure 22.2.

Fig 22.2 *standards labels: Kitemark; Safety Mark; Design Council; British Gas; Home Laundering Consultative Council*

EXERCISE

1 Define 'impulse buying' and give two examples.

2 If you think the price of sugar will rise steeply in the near future, should you buy large quantities of it now?

3 Describe how you would 'shop around' if you intended to buy (a) a side of bacon, (b) a refrigerator, (c) a second-hand car.

4 It is not always worth buying the highest-quality product. Give an example of when it *would* be economic to get the top quality.

5 State the advantages and disadvantages to consumers of (a) pre-packed foods, and (b) convenience foods.

6 For some years more and more married women have gone out to work. How has this changed shopping habits?

7 How does product branding benefit consumers and suppliers?

8 Give examples of sales promoting, and in each case state if you. think the consumer benefits from it.

9 Assume you bought an electric iron and found it did not work properly because its face was not smooth. What rights (if any) would you have against the shopkeeper from whom you bought it and the manufacturer who made it in the first place?

10 Under what circumstances would you *not* have these rights?

11 You tell a shopkeeper you require some glue to mend a piece of china. The shopkeeper offers you 'Grippit, the all-round fixative', saying 'This is a new product. You could try it and see if its does the job.' Half

an hour after applying the glue the china object falls apart again. Can you demand a refund of your money?

12 Give three examples of offences under the *Trade Descriptions Acts 1968.*

13 Define (a) *unit pricing,* (b) *loss leader,* (c) *unsolicited goods.*

14 Explain the activities of the Consumers' Association.

15 Comment on the following price descriptions: (a) 'Reduced by 10 per cent'; (b) 'Last week's price 10p a pound; today's price 8p a pound'; (c) 'Save 10 per cent by buying a Jumbo pack'; (d) 'Down 4p for one week only'.

16 Explain the statement that 'Codes of practice are forms of self-disciplining.'

17 If you intended to buy a gas fire, how could you ensure you bought one which was of good quality, safe and reasonably priced?

CHAPTER 23

BUYING ON CREDIT

To obtain goods on credit means to 'buy now, pay later'. The system is also known as 'deferred payment'.

Businesses largely operate on credit. For example, a grocer hopes to sell most of his goods before he has to pay for them. An *individual*, however, may use credit for only a few of the things he buys for his personal use, or he may even *never* buy on credit. On the other hand, most *services* can only be obtained on credit. Thus bills for electricity and telephone charges are paid after the services have been received. Some credit buying is therefore inevitable.

Broadly, there are three ways of paying for goods after you have acquired them:

(a) In a *credit sale* you become the owner of the goods immediately and you pay for them later.

(b) In a *hire-puchase transaction* you do not become the owner until you have finished paying the instalments.

(c) Money can be *borrowed* to buy goods with. This is *not* credit buying because you give the seller cash which you have borrowed from someone else, probably a bank. Alternatively, bank credit cards are used so that you owe the cost of the goods to your bank. These methods have been discussed in Chapter 17.

23.1 WHEN IT IS SENSIBLE TO BUY ON CREDIT

(a) From time to time a person may buy something which costs a lot of money. It is now generally accepted that a television set is not a luxury. Almost every family has one, but they are expensive to buy. A person could of course save up to buy a set, but until he had enough saved he would not be able to watch television. As he has to put money aside every week, why not do it while enjoying television?

(b) Buying on credit may save money. Suppose you spend £4 a week on bus fares to get to work. You may decide to buy a bicycle for £80 (including interest), paying for it by weekly instalments of £4. For 20 weeks it would cost you no more to go to work than it did before, and after that your travelling would cost nothing (apart from maintenance). Also, you would own something of value.

(c) If the price of an article is rising, it may be worth while buying it before you can afford to pay cash for it. Suppose you are saving up to buy a motor-cycle. The price may be going up faster than your rate of saving. It would then be better to buy it now on credit before the cost gets out of your reach.

(d) People can enjoy a higher standard of living because they can buy 'luxuries' they could not otherwise afford. Also, they can buy better-quality items. If you can only spare enough cash to buy a cheap suite of furniture, it may soon wear out; credit would allow you to make a 'better buy'.

23.2 WHEN CREDIT BUYING IS UNWISE

(a) When you buy on credit you are committing your future. You are undertaking to set aside part of your *future* income for something you are buying *now*. If you make too many promises, you may find you are paying out more than you can afford. Even if you have enough income *now* to meet the instalments, you may not have it in the future. You may become unemployed or be ill; other expenses (such as food and rent) may rise, leaving you with a smaller surplus.

(b) People can be encouraged to buy beyond their true needs. There is the temptation to buy things which are not really necessary or which are of an unnecessarily high standard.

23.3 THE COST OF CREDIT

Almost invariably, credit has to be paid for in the form of interest. Often the rate is high, particularly for hire purchase. The cost of something bought on credit is therefore the cash price plus the interest. What you are *really* paying in interest, however, is not always what it first appears to be:

(a) The true rate of interest
Assume you buy something with a cash price of £100. You are told that the interest charged will be 9½ per cent and that you will repay the total of £109.50 by 12 monthly instalments. What you may not realise is that each time you pay an instalment you reduce the capital

(a) The true rate of interest

Assume you buy something with a cash price of £100. You are told that the interest charged will be 9½ per cent and that you will repay the total of £109.50 by 12 monthly instalments. What you may not realise is that each time you pay an instalment you reduce the capital sum owing, so that each month you owe less and less of the £100. The monthly interest is always based on *£100*, however. In fact, what is known as 'the true rate of interest' amounts in this case to about 18½ per cent!

(b) Comparing interest with the benefit received

Although interest must be paid, the benefit obtained from having the article may more than compensate. As we have seen, buying a bicycle (and paying the interest) shows a gain on travelling by bus.

(c) The effective cost of credit

If you have capital in realisable investments you could, of course, use some of it to pay cash for an asset instead of getting it on credit. In that case the benefit of paying no interest on your purchase would have to be offset against the loss of interest received on your investments. On the other hand the effective rate of interest paid for credit could be said to be reduced by the amount continued to be received from the undisturbed capital.

(d) The market value of the good

It must be remembered that the market value of most things falls immediately the purchase is made. If you buy a car for £4000 cash, you will not be able to sell it for that figure because the car will then be second-hand. If the credit interest amounted to, say, £800, the 'loss' would be even greater, of course.

23.4 FORMS OF CONSUMER CREDIT

In the past most large retailers were reluctant to give credit. Today, they *encourage* credit buying. The result has been that the older methods are less frequently used and new methods have been introduced. These are discussed in the following sections.

It is important to remember that in any form of consumer credit *except hire purchase*, the goods belong *immediately* to the buyer. If the buyer does not pay, the seller cannot recover the goods *because they are not his*. All he can do is to sue the buyer for the amount owing.

23.5 MONTHLY ACCOUNTS

This system is only available to a few customers. They are people of good financial standing who buy substantial amounts from a shop. The method is used by 'high-class' stores (such as Harrods) who allow their customers to pay their bills monthly. No interest was charged in the past but usually a charge is now made for late settlement. This method is disappearing rapidly.

23.6 BUDGET ACCOUNTS

These require regular payments, in return for which the customer may buy goods valued at, say, 24 times the monthly payment. Thus monthly payments of £5 entitle the customer to credit up to £120. As the debt is reduced, the credit can be 'topped up' to £120, if necessary. The system is therefore sometimes known as *revolving credit*. Interest is charged on the balance outstanding each month. This method is used particularly by some chains of tailors.

23.7 IN-STORE CREDIT CARDS

These are a development of the budget-account system and is being used increasingly by large stores. Approved customers are given credit cards for use in the store. They agree to pay a minimum of £5 a month and can then spend up to 12 (or, in some stores, up to 24 or 30) times the monthly payment. When making a purchase all the customer has to do is to show his card. Interest is charged on the amount owing each month.

23.8 TRADING CHECKS

These are issued in various denominations from agents who call on customers and who also collect the repayments. The checks can be used for making purchases from those shops which will accept them. The repayments are usually spread over a 20-week period and a service charge is made. The retailer 'sells' the checks back to the check company at a discount. The system is largely restricted to the clothing trade.

23.9 CREDIT SALE AGREEMENTS

These are agreements to buy goods by paying instalments and which are *not* hire-purchase agreements.

23.10 HIRE PURCHASE

The difference between a hire-purchase agreement and the methods listed above is indicated by its name. Under a hire-purchase agreement you

(a) agree to *hire* the article for a set period, after which you have
(b) the option to *purchase* it.

Assume you want something which has a cash price of £100 and that under a hire-purchase agreement you have to pay 60 weekly instalments of £2 each (the interest being £20). The legal position would be that for 59 weeks you would *hire* the article at a weekly rent of £2. During that time, therefore, the article would not be yours. You would then have the 'option' of *buying* the article for £2.

23.11 CONSUMER CREDIT ACT 1974

This Act has far-reaching consequences. It became necessary because many people had signed agreements without fully realising what they were doing, particularly when they were 'talked into' doing so by unscrupulous salesmen. The Act protects consumers by making the following provisions:

(a) The red-warning sign
If you sign a hire-purchase agreement (for up to £2000), or a credit sales agreement (of over £30 and up to £2000), *away from trade premises*, it will have on it a warning, printed in red, to read it carefully. In a hire-purchase agreement the warning is as follows:

This document contains the terms of a hire-purchase agreement. Sign it only if you want to be legally bound by them.

Signature of hirer. . . . .
The goods will not become your property until you have made all the payments. You must not sell them before then.

Unless a person sees and reads this warning he may unknowingly be signing a *loan* contract and he would not then get the protection of the Act.

(b) The 'cooling-off' period

If a person signs a credit agreement *in his home,* he must be given a copy of it then and a second copy must be sent to him by post. *He has the right to cancel the agreement in writing if he does so before the end of the third day after receiving the second copy.* This is known as 'the cooling-off period'. If the customer does cancel the agreement, any deposit he has paid must be returned.

(The above two provisions do not apply to contracts signed at the premises of the trader or a finance company because all such firms are subject to control under the Act. The intention is to protect people who are called on by salesmen and those who buy through the post.)

(c) Recovery by the owner

If a hire-purchase instalment is overdue, the owner must send the hirer a letter giving him at least a further seven days in which to pay.

Once one-third of the total cost has been paid the owner can recover the goods *only by going to Court.* The Court may decide to fix terms for the hirer to discharge the debt instead of allowing the owner to repossess. (There is, of course, no right of recovery in a credit sale agreement.)

(d) Termination by the hirer

A hirer may terminate the agreement at any time by returning the goods. He must, however, pay half the total cost, unless the Court decides otherwise. If he has already paid more than half, he must pay any overdue instalments. The hirer may also have to pay for any damage sustained by the goods.

23.12 CREDIT BUYING AND COMMERCE

Buying on credit is now so widespread that it has a very important bearing on commerce:

(a) Manufacturers and retailers encourage it because it increases spending. This benefits consumers, because if there is a strong demand for an article it can usually be mass produced. Due to the availability of credit facilities a large number of people can afford to buy, for example, dishwashers. Because of the consequent large demand for dishwashers they can be mass produced. This, and the competition between manufacturers to meet the demand, results in their prices being much lower than they would otherwise be.

(b) In-store credit cards are sponsored by retailers because they encourage cardholders to do more of their shopping in the store. If a person could buy an article in store A as well as in store B, he is more likely to buy it in store A if he has a credit card for that shop. The interest charged on such cards is much lower than for other forms of credit. The stores have, in fact, to finance this form of trading from their own resources, but they consider it is worth it to retain their customers.

(c) Most hire-purchase contracts are made with a *finance company* rather than the seller. The company in effect buys the article for the consumer and collects the instalments from him. Such businesses are very profitable and handle enormous sums of money. As a consequence, investment is encouraged.

(d) Commerce is so much influenced by the amount of credit buying that, where necessary, the government will intervene. If the economy is suffering because too much is being borrowed, the government may place restrictions on the amount of credit which may be given. Alternatively, the government may *encourage* credit buying in order to boost the demand for products.

EXERCISES

1 What is the basic difference between hire purchase and any other method of buying on credit?

2 Give examples of when it is a form of economy to buy on credit.

3 Why should one 'budget' when considering entering into a credit transaction?

4 What is meant by 'the true rate of interest'?

5 Why do you think the monthly-account system is disappearing?

6 What is the difference between budget accounts and in-store credit cards?

7 Why are credit cards offered by retailers?

8 Define a *credit sales agreement*.

9 Why should you never sign a credit document without first reading it thoroughly? How does the law attempt to ensure consumers *do* read credit documents?

10 Explain the 'cooling-off period' in credit transactions and why it is provided for by law.

11 A salesman visits you at your home and you promise to buy a washing-machine from him. The following day you go to his office and sign the agreement. Have you the right to cancel the agreement afterwards?

12 Assume you are buying a car under a hire-purchase agreement. You find you can no longer afford the instalments. Can you return the car to the motor agent you bought it from?

13 Under what circumstances can the owner repossess an article held by a hirer?

14 In what ways do (a) manufacturers, (b) retailers and (c) consumers benefit from the credit system of buying?

15 A young married couple are considering the purchase of a television set, the cash price of which is £208. If they buy it on hire purchase, they must give a deposit of £70 and repay the balance by 78 weekly instalments of £2.20 each or 104 weekly instalments of £1.80 each. They have savings of £280 in a building society. Neither of them knows much about hire purchase. What advice would you give them?

INDEX